Tactical Performar

Tactical Performance explores creative protest in unique depth, looking at the possibilities for direct action and theatrical confrontation with some of the most powerful institutions in the world. It effectively combines theory and practice, illustrating the basic principles of artful activism in an absorbing, accessible manner.

L.M. Bogad draws on his own experience as a writer, performer, and strategist working with groups such as the Yes Men, the Clown Army, Reclaim the Streets, and La Pocha Nostra, to share the most effective nonviolent tactics and theatrics.

An inspiring practical and theoretical guide, *Tactical Performance* is essential reading for anyone interested in creative pranksterism, subvertisement, cultural sabotage, and the global justice movement.

L.M. Bogad is Associate Professor of political performance at the University of California at Davis. He is the author of *Electoral Guerrilla Theatre: Radical ridicule and social movements*, the plays *Haymarket, Tahrir, COINTELSHOW: A patriot act*, and *Economusic: Keeping score*. He is the founding director of the Center for Tactical Performance.

Tactical Performance

The theory and practice of serious play

L.M. Bogad

LONDON AND NEW YORK

First published 2016
by Routledge
2 Park Square, Milton Park, Abingdon, Oxon OX14 4RN

and by Routledge
711 Third Avenue, New York, NY 10017

Routledge is an imprint of the Taylor & Francis Group, an informa business

British Library Cataloguing-in-Publication Data
A catalogue record for this book is available from the British Library

Library of Congress Cataloguing-in-Publication Data
Bogad, L. M.
Tactical performance / L.M. Bogad.
pages cm
Includes bibliographical references and index.
1. Theater—Political aspects. 2. Radical theater. 3. Protest movements.
4. Social movements. 5. Political participation. I. Title.
PN2051.B64 2016
792.02'2—dc23 2015030556

ISBN: 978-1-138-91783-5 (hbk)
ISBN: 978-1-138-91784-2 (pbk)
ISBN: 978-1-315-68879-4 (ebk)

Typeset in Bembo
by Keystroke, Station Road, Codsall, Wolverhampton

Printed and bound in Great Britain by
TJ International Ltd, Padstow, Cornwall

TO CONSPIRE means to "breathe together,"
huddling close, sharing the intimacies of breath
and desire, respiration and aspiration.
TO CONFIDE is to share faith, to trust in
a terribly treacherous environment.

Let us conspire and confide together.

Contents

Illustrations

Acknowledgements

Many thanks to Carnegie Mellon University's Center for the Arts In Society, both for the "Arts and Controversy" Fellowship, during which I began writing this book, and for a stint as a Distinguished Visiting Lecturer in Political Performance during the G20 Summit in Pittsburgh. The "Humanities and Political Conflict" Fellowship at Arizona State University's Institute for Humanities Research also provided me with invaluable space and time, and collegial conversation and debate. The University of Iowa's Obermann Center for Advanced Studies' "Art and Cultural Politics of Carnival" Fellowship, perfectly timed immediately after the Clown Army's peak at the G8 in Scotland, enabled me to sort out and analyze some of the wonderful madness in which I had just participated. Three artist residencies at Blue Mountain Center, and two at Mesa Refuge, were enormously helpful.

I'm also grateful for the opportunity to deliver keynotes and lead workshops in Tactical Performance at venues where I was challenged with the tough questions and praxis that I needed to revise and develop these ideas: in Cairo during the first phase of the Egyptian Revolution at Fayoum Art Center, Townhouse Art Center, and American University of Cairo; at the University of Tampere and the Baltic Circle International Theatre Festival in Helsinki; in Riga for the "Dirty Deal" Theatre and BaND; at the University of Trondheim; with the "Deconstruction–Creative Resistance" crew in Reykjavik just before the financial collapse and popular uprising there; at the International Headquarters of the ever-defiant and brilliant Erroristas in Buenos Aires; for the Enmedio Collective in Barcelona and for the Assemblea de Drets Socials de l'Eixample on the grounds of the old military barracks they had occupied; for Columbia and New York Universities' "Theatrum Mundi/Global Street" symposium; with Nato Thompson at Kadist in San Francisco; for the Two Degrees Festival in

London; at the University of Amsterdam, and the Free University of Berlin; and at the Hemispheric Institute for Performance and Politics' *Encuentros* in São Paulo and Montreal. Earlier versions of some of the materials in chapters 1, 2, 3, 4, 5 and 7 appeared in: *A Boal Companion*; *Social Identities: Journal for the Study of Race, Nation and Culture*; *TDR: The Drama Review*; *Place and Performance*; *Contemporary Theatre Review*; and *Theatre Survey*.

Thanks to friends, colleagues, and comrades. For donating photographs: the superlative Fred Askew, a true hero of the movement, Andrew Boyd, Mona Caron, muralist for the multiverse, Matthew Dutton, Oriana Eliçabe, Ben Kieswetter, and Lisa Merrill. Many friends read individual chapters and shared with me precious outside perspectives: thank you to Max Alper, Shane Boyle, Andrew Buchman, Marco Ceglie, Joe Delappe, Joe Dumit, Andrea Gibbons, Noah Guynn, Phil Howard, Leslie Kaufmann, Dennis O'Brien, Praba Pilar, Lea Redmond, Ben Shepard, and Doug Sofer.

Thank you to Peter B. Collins and his radio program, and C.S. Soong of KPFA's "Against the Grain," for asking me the hard questions live on the air.

And, as ever, thanks to the B4B/RTS/CIRCA collectives, my parents Walter and Suzanne, Gail Evra, Jason Montero, James Wengler, John Jordan, and Chuck "Yeo" Reinhardt (1943–2013).

Introduction

A red carpet on the picket line

Tactical performance

> Never in American history had a group seized the streets, the squares, the sacrosanct business thoroughfares and the marbled halls of government to protest and proclaim the unendurability of their oppression. Had room-size machines turned human, burst from the plants that housed them and stalked the land in revolt, the nation could not have been more amazed.
>
> —Martin Luther King (1964: p. 16)

Nashville, 1960: A whites-only lunch counter in a department store. A group of African–Americans, dressed formally, sits at the counter. They are quiet, polite, and when refused service, they sit calmly, read books, and wait patiently. They behave as if the change they want to see in the world has already been enacted, as if they have equal rights. A racist mob forms behind the sitting group, and begins to taunt, jeer, and finally to attack them. The white police arrive . . . and arrest the victims of the violence, not the mob. This sociodrama creates not a palliative Aristotelian catharsis, but a canny kind of *critical catharsis.* An alarmed national and global audience responds with outrage to this spectacle of cruelty and injustice, and a reluctant federal government is pressured to intervene.

Edinburgh, 2005: An army of clowns faces a squad of riot police. They play with the police absurdly and imaginatively, dusting their armored boots and offering them tickles with their feather dusters. A clown kisses a riot shield. This is an *irresistible image*: even one's ideological opponents are compelled to reproduce it even though it undermines their narrative. The image circulates around the world and provides a different, dissonant, and dissident view of the global justice movement, which had been widely criminalized in the public sphere.

Berkeley, 2011: A strike and walkout has been called at the U.C. campus to protest tuition raises and budget cuts. At the picket line at the main gate to the campus lies a long red carpet. The carpet is manned by "businessmen" who are begging people to cross the picket line so they can break the strike, lower wages, and fire people. A playful device becomes a space of public shaming: unlike the usual outcome in these circumstances, nobody crosses the picket line. Soon the carpet becomes a joyful space for the picketers, joking and improvising on and around it. Soon, my red carpet is in demand for picket lines throughout the Bay Area. (In fact, an unknown person has it: whoever you are, if you are reading this, could you please return it, or at least promise to keep using it on picket lines?)

These are examples of *tactical performance*, or the use of performance techniques, tactics, and aesthetics in social-movement campaigns. These examples don't look much like each other on the surface. Each involves different stakes and dangers, and different matrices of risk considering the relative privilege of the protagonists. There are also differences in tone. Some actions are performed in the key of human dignity; others sound off in the key of clown. But they are all examples of savvy artist–activists using their craft as a force multiplier in confrontations with the state, corporations, and other rivals or opponents. Tactical performance can function as a crowbar that provides leverage and pressure for social progress. Of course, in the case of mistakes and miscalculations, that crowbar can break or rebound, causing painful self-inflicted wounds.

These performances are creative responses to restriction. Public space in Western democracies is increasingly privatized and regulated. Conventional protest has been hemmed in with remote, cage-like "free speech zones," harassed with preemptive arrest, surveillance, and infiltration, and hampered by the weight of its own cliché. Faced with these challenges, activists use performance to communicate desires and grievances convincingly, to build momentum for their movements, and to discourage (or increase the political price of) violence from authorities.

Social amnesia versus praxis

Imagine a chess game between a veteran player, who has memorized many gambits and extended strategies, and a narcoleptic amnesiac. When it is his turn, the amnesiac, earnest and hardworking, confronts each move anew. In the spirit of improvisation and with a can-do attitude, the amnesiac scans the board. What is the situation now? What's the best move in the moment? Which pieces are threatened? Is there an opening for an attack? The amnesiac, who is quick-witted and observant, makes the best possible move given the immediate situation, then goes back to sleep.

The chess master, far from assuming the victory is a lock, notes down every move the amnesiac makes, cross-indexing it with a tome containing a long history of moves and countermoves. Thinking several moves ahead and noting the patterns in the amnesiac's choices for future reference, the chess master makes the best possible move given the entire situation, writes it in his ledger, and awakens the amnesiac for his next move.

The chess master represents the position of most states and corporations in this world of social conflict. These powers create institutions of learning and think tanks, which studiously construct an institutional memory. What strategy worked before? What mistakes have we made that we must never make again? Why did we lose that battle, and how can we be sure to win next time? What are the behaviors, habits, weaknesses, and strengths of our opponents? Certainly, states often make the mistake of "fighting the last war" instead of the current one, and the powerful often fall victim to hubris. Nevertheless, corporations and states usually have a well-developed, intergenerational strategic memory.

Social movements all too often behave like the amnesiac chess player. Unlike the state and corporations, these tactical players have no well-paid employees with pensions whose sole job it is to record and analyze history and strategy. Far too often, despite their boldness, talent, energy, and commitment, they reinvent the wheel instead of improving on it; repeat old mistakes instead of learning from them; and repeat predictable moves. All of these phenomena can lead to rout where victory was possible. Sociohistorical memory and institutional memory are as crucial to collective action as individual memory is to a game of chess.

This metaphor is loose. Social conflict is not chess. It is far messier; more complex, fluid, and confusing. The game is never over and there is never a final victor. The rules and boundaries of the board are ever-shifting. There are not even two sides. Sometimes in popular education, the Marxian dialectic is simplified into a process between two prime conflicting forces—thesis and antithesis. However in any historical moment, confrontations may illustrate a trialectic, quadrilectic, or quintilectic dynamic as multiple contradictory forces battle, and latent or inert forces are activated and join the fray from unexpected corners. Also, movements do have their own memory systems: folklore, stories, archives, evolving repertoires of resistance, training centers, and historians.

Nevertheless, let the chess metaphor stand for a moment. This book is one small attempt, among many others, to add to the budding counter-institutional memory of social movements in their ongoing tactical interaction with elephantine opponents. It tries to offer some tentative, non-dogmatic, and ever-evolving principles of best practice for tactical performance.

This book is written from a desire to achieve victories, big and small. Whether it's a national campaign to overturn an established policy and law; or spontaneous dissent that spreads by poetic osmosis on an almost molecular level, a sort of *dissensmosis*; we *mean* it. We want to win. And performance can be an important ingredient for victory.

Project description and theory

This study draws from my own experiences in fieldwork and creative practice. Its limitations in scope and depth follow the limitations of my own praxis as an artist and activist—mostly in the US and Europe. This is a non-exhaustive, regional effort, with the intention of adding to the body of knowledge already accumulated, and to make connections between different groups and efforts. There has been a recent pedagogical turn amongst my larger tribe of colleagues and collaborators—from the Yes Men to The Other 98% to the Laboratory of Insurrectionary Imagination to La Pocha Nostra. Perhaps we are just getting older and want to sit back and bore other people with our stories. Or maybe we feel we have made enough embarrassing mistakes and it's time to share those stories so others can avoid ours, and make new and better mistakes in the years to come. Regardless, workshop-giving entities such as the Center for Artistic Activism, Movement Generation, The Center for Story-Based Strategy, and the Yes Lab, as well as recent books such as *Beautiful Trouble* (Boyd & Mitchell, 2012a), *An Action a Day* (Hudema, 2004), and *Re:Imagining Change* (Canning & Reinsborough, 2010) are all attempts to consolidate and disseminate our generation's thoughts about artful activism and organizing. This volume is an attempt to add a performer's perspective to this ongoing conversation about best practice, and theories of cultural intervention and creative disruption, in support of or as part of social movements. It is also an exploration of the fraught relationship between movements and artists, and issues of solidarity, coalition, and self-critical praxis.

This is not a book of overarching strategy or global insights. I am writing about artist–activist efforts from a participant–observer's perspective, and must mark my bias and position as such. Sometimes I recount brainstorming conversations between colleagues and myself, or give examples of whimsical or strange artistic actions that were tried, or considered and rejected, to give an idea of the creative process. I have worked as a writer, strategist, and performer with most of the groups I talk about in this book, though certainly not all. These groups are tactical players rather than strategic powers, in De Certeau's sense of the term (1984). They do not make the rules of the game, but can deliberately misinterpret or subvert them. They scavenge, filch, and repurpose the dominant players' words and tropes for cultural sabotage, subvertisement, and social-movement organizing. They operate with the understanding that symbolism and ritual are a tangible aspect of power and not just window dressing (Kertzer, 1988). Though rarely operating under such harsh domination as the artful and wise peasants and imperial subjects that J.C. Scott studies, they seek new contexts for the wiles and subtle "weapons of the weak" (1985). Their goal is to add new tactics to the repertoire of contention, and to revamp old tools so they don't get rusty with disuse, or dull with overuse. They contribute performance chops to the art of moral protest, the building of subaltern counterpublics (Fraser, 1997), and the sustained collective contention that defines social-movement activism.

Some key exemplars of tactical performance

This book focuses on examples from the twenty-first century, but the following is a partial contemporary genealogy of tactical performance. The five examples below obviously vary in scope, emphasis, goals, and agendas. Yet I have included them because they all engage in serious play. They operate as guerrillas in the cultural terrain in which they live, achieving surprise through a combination of transgression and prefiguration. "Serious play" is a familiar term from ethnography, referring to play and ritual that help to resolve societal conflict; here I am repurposing the term for an activist context, referring to ludic or playful actions that agitate in support of a social movement.

The American civil rights movement

> One witness [of a sit-in] later told a reporter it was like a scene from a science fiction movie, where a stunned city is laid siege by aliens or giant grasshoppers . . . White Nashville was just not ready for this. It had never had to deal with black people this way. These waves of well-dressed, well-behaved young black men and women were something no one had seen before . . . this was

> about education, pricking consciences . . . if some of these white onlookers went back to their own homes . . . and began talking about this in heartfelt terms . . . then we had achieved one of our main objectives.
>
> (Lewis, 1999: p. 96)

Tactical performers can draw inspiration and strategy from the US civil rights movement, which showed the potential of using disciplined mass performance for progressive social change. The civil rights movement has been studied through economic, legal, religious, and many other lenses, but it was also an exercise in strategic, disciplined performance for a remote audience. Organizers at the time theorized their actions as "sociodrama" and cannily cast leading "characters" based on their suitability for symbolic parts.

In a 1960 interview on the US news show *Meet The Press*, Dr Martin Luther King, Jr. reveals both the bias of the interviewer and his own strategic outlook. Lawrence Spivak asked King why the movement engaged in disruptive and illegal direct actions such as sit-ins, instead of just sticking to boycotts of segregated businesses and other legal measures:

> SPIVAK: But wouldn't you be on stronger grounds, though, if you refused to buy at those stores and if you called upon the white people of the country to follow you because of both your moral and your legal right not to buy?
>
> KING: I think, Mr. Spivak, sometimes it is necessary to *dramatize* an issue because many people are not aware of what's happening. And I think the sit-ins serve to *dramatize* the indignities and the injustices which Negro people are facing all over the nation. And I think another reason why they are necessary, and they are vitally important at this point, is the fact that they give an eternal refutation to the idea that the Negro is satisfied with segregation. If you didn't have the sit-ins, you wouldn't have this *dramatic*, and not only this *dramatic* but this mass demonstration of the dissatisfaction of the Negro with the whole system of segregation.
>
> (*Meet the Press*, 1960; my italics)

Spivak argued that a boycott would be a better strategy because it breaks no law—people can buy whatever they want with their own money.[1] King, whose movement had successfully used boycotts in the past, countered that sit-ins were technically against the law, but that a *dramatization* of the conflict and issues was necessary, and that the morally fuelled transgression of unjust laws was one important way to achieve this.

The civil rights movement operating in the Deep South was outnumbered and outgunned. The violent state and paramilitary white supremacist organizations such as the Ku Klux Klan ruled the landscape with terror. How could the movement win? One important element of their overall strategy was to use performance as a political crowbar, or force multiplier, for the movement. They used what they called *sociodrama* as the lever to topple a racist regime made predictable by its own arrogance.[2] Sociodramas were confrontations designed to attack the unjust power structure directly and dramatically, triggering a hostile response that would expose the structure's cruelty on the global stage.

"Creative suffering" or "redemptive suffering" was another key element of the movement's self-theorization. Several key organizers had gone to India to train with organizers of the Gandhian movement there, and were influenced heavily by Gandhi's concepts of *satyagraha* or "insistence on truth," an insistence that was enacted physically through disruptive nonviolent action.[3] African–Americans were suffering violence and depredation on a daily basis in America; the movement posited that, with creativity, this suffering could be channeled, focused, and dramatized into a form that could change the political landscape. This suffering was a constant aspect of life in racist America; the idea was to enact a productive exchange for that suffering through superior organization, higher spirituality, and intelligent stagecraft at a specific point of articulation of power (such as a racially segregated lunch counter). The suffering triggered by the actions of the civil rights movement might be redemptive spiritually on a personal level for participants; it was also intended to be redemptive collectively as it broke down the worst aspects of the Jim Crow system. The civil rights movement used diverse tactics such as lawsuits, boycotts, marches, concerts, freedom rides, and mock elections to dramatize the disenfranchisement of black people. I will focus on the sit-in.

Imagine a typical sit-in confrontation as following a three-act dramatic structure. Act One: a group of African–Americans, wearing suits and dresses, some carrying books, and joined sometimes by white allies, sit at a segregated lunch counter, quietly requesting service and thus breaking the racist law. They are told to leave and perhaps insulted, but they quietly sit, some reading. Act Two: a racist white mob accumulates in response to this "outrage." The mob becomes increasingly aggressive to the activists. They jeer and taunt the group with racist slurs, blow cigarette smoke in their faces, pour hot coffee on them, and burn them with their cigarettes. The activists endure the abuse without retaliating

Figure I.1 Civil rights sit-in by John Salter, Joan Trumpauer, and Anne Moody at Woolworth's lunch counter. A crowd of people pours sugar, ketchup, and mustard on them in protest. Courtesy of Library of Congress. Photo by Fred Blackwell. Sourced under fair use.

or retreating. The mob grows increasingly violent and begins to punch the sitting people, even dragging them to the ground and kicking them. Act Three: the white police finally arrive on the scene of the crime. They part the crowd and arrest, not the violent white racists, but the brutalized peaceful activists. *Fin.*

Such sociodramas, played out in cities across the South, hoped to generate empathy for the activists and their cause. These actions used stage logic, blocking, identification, and an unsettling hybrid of critical alienation and emotional identification. Any director of traditional theatre will tell you that when you *block* (meaning to aesthetically and communicatively arrange the position and movement of bodies on stage) one character attacking another from above and behind, an audience will almost always identify with the one being attacked. We all understand at our core the vulnerability of being attacked from above and behind even if it has never happened to us; this is a deployment of theatrical biomechanics that generates empathy. Our mirror-neuron network is activated and we can feel the nerve-shadow of the menace and pain suffered by the victim.

And when multiple characters attack that victim in a cowardly fashion, identification with the victim is even stronger. The victim is quietly reading a book when attacked? Has not physically provoked the attack? Does not strike or even curse or shout back when attacked? Our empathy is joined by sympathy. Hardcore sadists and racists may not be moved to identify with the activist victim, and will have their own countervailing response to it, but they are not the target audience of this performance. The respective violence and nonviolence of the aggressors and the victims create an *identification*, or emotional investment in the fate of the victim. This identification is the goal of classic Aristotelian theatre—but instead of identifying with an actor on stage playing a character, the remote viewing audience identifies with the dramatized plight of an actual person, playing themselves, in a dramatized social conflict arranged for maximum effect, with their oppressors provoked into playing visibly despicable roles. The mass media amplified these sociodramas for a national and global audience.

These Aristotelian elements of the sociodrama are powerful in their own right. But in Aristotelian theatre, identification is intended to lead to catharsis as the protagonist meets a tragic fate—an excitation of pity and fear that shakes up the audience emotionally, provides a release with the story's resolution, and yields an individual moral lesson: beware the flaw within yourself that struck down this admirable but tragic hero, whose pride (for example) was their downfall. However, for an activist sociodrama, Aristotelian identification needs to lead not to catharsis, but to something more troubling and lasting that aggravates and agitates the viewer long after the confrontation is over. The twist in the plot that arrests catharsis is the police arrest itself. When the agents of the state arrive, and arrest the wrong people—when they arrest the nonviolent victims with whom we have identified, and not the cruel and cowardly attackers—there is no catharsis. There is no satisfying resolution that provides a moral lesson and closure. The injustice, the "unearned suffering," that occurs is intensified in a surprising way, and is allowed to stand. This is a twist ending of the worst sort. It combines Aristotelian identification with Brechtian *Verfremdungseffekt*—or *distantiation effect*, making the familiar strange and discomfiting, so that we see it anew and are unsettled and amazed. The oppression of African-Americans on a daily basis had been going on for so long in the US that white privilege became the natural state of affairs; hence, these sociodramas made it strange, disturbing, agitating, and, for some, unacceptable.

The takeaway thesis of viewing this spectacle: the fault was not in our stars, nor in ourselves, but in our system. The only way to find moral resolution was to contribute personally in some way to the social struggle, to exercise real agency to join the social movement, and to seek catharsis through direct, personal action in the world: to get "onstage" and into the conflict to try to change the story. I refer to this hybrid form, which combines the emotional power of Aristotelian identification with the agitating and radicalizing potency of Brechtian *Verfremdungseffekt* as *critical catharsis*; a catharsis that only finds release through political participation.[4]

Aristotle, Brecht, and Boal

Aristotle wrote his *Poetics* ([335 BCE] 1997) in response to his mentor Plato's anti-theatrical bias. In Plato's *Republic* ([*c.* 380 BCE] 1992), there would be no place for theatre as it was merely an imitation of reality and thus deceptive and a step even further away from the Ideal. Aristotle tried to advocate for the theatre as a crucial moral corrective in a republic. His formula for how to use identification with a protagonist to bring an audience to catharsis and the learning of an important personal (not collectively and socially subversive) moral lesson has great lasting influence on theatre and film to this day. Aristotle was very prescriptive about all elements of tragedic plays; all elements (set, script, and costumes) had to be designed to create, in the end, the most powerful catharsis for the audience. He even ranked, in numerical order, what kinds of plot twists were the best, and the best qualities of a protagonist's character for maximum cathartic impact (superior moral fiber, but with a tragic flaw that brings success but then tragic downfall; he also felt that only noble-born males were worthy protagonists).

Over 2,000 years later, Brecht denounced Aristotelian identification and Stanislavskian "emotional realism" as a populace-numbing hypnotic that functioned in a way similar to the "narcotics trade." He laid out a system of "nonaristotelian" theatre that would resist the emotional manipulation of identification in favor of the unsettling *Verfremdungseffekt*, popularly translated as "alienation effect" but more accurately as "distantiation effect." Brecht also prescribed acting, directing, and staging techniques, and the ideal types of protagonists, all devoted to the purpose of activating the socially critical faculties of the audience through surprising or shocking distantiation. The goal was to expose social and systemic injustices that had been naturalized; to make the familiar strange and the strange familiar.

A generation after Brecht, Augusto Boal moved further into an "anti-Aristotelian" theatre, reacting against the great architect of identification and catharsis, to the point that he devotes a great deal of his seminal *Theatre of the Oppressed* (1979) to a critical analysis of Aristotle's *Poetics*. Boal denounced Aristotle's system as coercive and oppressive and called for a theatrical system that provided a dialogical imaginative structure in which spect-actors could safely rehearse for reality, or experiment with ideas for sociopolitical action to break actual oppressions in their own lives. A discussion of the use of Boal's methods in action planning follows in Chapter 1.

All the elements of performance were considered by this movement. Message discipline, costume choices, songs, and the physical movements and bearing of marchers and sit-in activists were coordinated in great detail. Activists rehearsed "offstage," including keeping calm in the face of brutality, to prepare for nonviolent, public, "onstage" action, which dramatized the cruelty of Jim Crow laws, and the dignity and humanity of the protestors for a television audience. The pressure that these public spectacles generated paved the way for federal intervention; the movement experienced setbacks in moments when their performance discipline broke down.[5]

There are many examples of the movement carefully "casting" citizens to serve as symbolic figures for high-profile actions, but perhaps the best and most well-known is that of Claudette Colvin versus Rosa Parks. Claudette Colvin was a young African–American woman who, on 2 March 1955, refused to give up her seat on a bus to a white person in Montgomery Alabama, and could have become the symbolic figure for the legal bus boycott that the civil rights movement planned to stage in Montgomery. Colvin did indeed participate in the victorious US Supreme Court case to desegregate the bus system, but the movement chose not to publicize her case on the national stage; she was a teenager and had become pregnant while unmarried, which were controversial personal details in the historical context. Instead, the movement chose Rosa Parks to be the public protagonist in the struggle for bus desegregation; she was a trained and capable activist, and as a married, "respectable" woman in the conventional definition of the times, the movement felt she would serve better as a symbol of the movement for the national audience. Nine months after Colvin took her individual, spontaneous action, Parks took the same action—planned and backed by the movement. She refused to give up her seat, and it was her arrest and legal case that was publicized narratively as the provocation for the historic bus boycott. For those arguing that the movement should have embraced Colvin for her bravery, it is vital to remember the violent, oppressive, and highly pressurized conditions in which the civil rights movement was operating. The stakes were high and it was impossible for the movement to fight every cultural battle at the same time. Still, this was a difficult and controversial decision to make and shows the challenges of "casting characters" in a public campaign. It required discipline to accept these decisions and move forward as a movement, and of course there were divisions and arguments as a result.[6]

Casting was just one aspect of the overall interplay between *discipline* and *affect* in this movement's actions. Emotional affect was one of the goals of the public sociodramas—to encourage and galvanize the movement, to inspire those potential recruits still hesitant to join the movement, and to gain the support of those on the national and international stage who had until then been apathetic, uninformed, or neutral. However, to achieve this emotional affect and impact upon others required tight discipline over their own emotions behind the scenes. Before many of these actions—sit-ins, Freedom Rides, marches—those who wished to participate were required to sign a pledge of conduct agreed upon by movement organizers. An example from Nashville, entitled Nonviolent Discipline of the 1960 Nashville Student Sit-in Movement (Oppenheimer & Lakey, 1965: p. 81)[7]:

> **Don't strike back or curse if abused.**
> **Don't laugh out.**
> **Don't hold conversations with floor workers.**
> **Don't leave your seats until your leader has given you instruction to do so.**
> **Don't block entrances to the stores and the aisles.**
> **Show yourself courteous and friendly at all times.**
> **Sit straight and always face the counter.**
> **Report all serious incidents to your leader.**

Refer all information to your leader in a polite manner.
Remember love and nonviolence.
May God bless each of you. ”

These signed agreements between the activists and the organization were contracts for performative and emotional discipline—agreements on what one would wear (costume), how one would carry oneself (affect and bearing), what one could carry (props), and personal comportment, bearing, and the rules of engagement with opponents and passersby (script). These actions required tremendous coordination and discipline in detail.

They also required a radical form of rehearsal. If the goal was to break unjust laws, endure beatings nonviolently, and thus expose the cruelty of the system, the activists had to prepare, to train themselves out of human automatic-reflex, lizard-brain, fight-or-flight responses to deadly dangerous situations. So, in "backstage" settings like living rooms, church halls, and community centers, activists took turns playing themselves, and playing white racists. They would taunt, torment, and physically attack each other, in character. The ones playing themselves would practice staying nonviolent and enduring the abuse. As Congressman John Lewis, who at the time was one of the young leaders of the movement, describes:

> . . . We began acting out the kinds of situations we might be confronted with during an actual protest. [Leading organizer and trainer James] Lawson taught us specific tactics to protect our bodies during an attack. He showed us how to curl our bodies so that our internal organs would escape direct blows. He told us how important it was to try to maintain eye contact with our assailant even as the blows were raining down because that eye contact could be a viscerally disarming thing. He showed us how to help one another, how if one person is taking a beating, others could put their bodies in the way, diluting the force of the attack.
>
> We role-played, teaching ourselves how to respond to verbal and physical assaults. We staged little sociodramas, taking turns playing demonstrators and antagonists. Several of us would sit in a row of folding chairs, acting out a sit-in, while the others played waitresses or angry bystanders, calling us niggers, cursing in our faces, pushing and shoving us to the floor. Always, Jim Lawson would be there, hovering over the action, pushing, prodding, teaching, cajoling. It is not enough, he would say, simply to endure a beating. It was not enough to resist the urge to strike

> back at an assailant. "That urge can't *be* there," he would tell us. "You have to do more than just not hit back. You have to have no *desire* to hit back. You have to love that person who's hitting you. You're *going* to love him."
>
> . . . The numbers at our weekly workshops swelled. Dozens of students, black and white, joined us and began taking crash courses in nonviolent action. Blacks played white roles in our training sociodramas, and whites played black. It was strange—unsettling but effective, and very eye-opening as well—to see a black student pushing a white off a chair, screaming in his or her face, "Coon!" and "Ape!" and "Nigger!", or to see a white student shoving a black, yanking his or her hair, yelling "White trash!" and "Nigger lover!"
>
> (Lewis, 1999: p. 84 & 91)

This was radical rehearsal for radical action. The backstage rehearsals and training were then followed up with "dry runs" of the actions to get participants ready: they would walk to a whites-only lunch counter, ask to be served, and when refused, would simply leave. Just doing that action was emotionally challenging and a good preparation for the actual sit-ins to come, making the action more tangible and imaginable. John Lewis said that having rehearsed for the action made him much less afraid when he actually was being cruelly beaten by a mob of white supremacists during the initial Freedom Ride. "Our workshops had been like little laboratories in human behavior and response to nonviolent protest," Lewis wrote. "Now we were seeing real humans respond in almost exactly the ways Jim Lawson had taught us they would . . ." (Lewis, 1999: p. 99).

Lewis was prepared for the action; it was the people that were beating him who were not disciplined, who were not prepared, who had not rehearsed, who were responding automatically, and who were playing out their role perfectly in the sociodramatic script—as the despicable and malevolent antagonists. For New Gandhians like James Lawson, one of the most important trainers of nonviolent activists in the movement, this was more than just a tactic; it was a spiritual and religious state of being, internalizing the love for one's oppressors. Other more secular activists treat this kind of work solely as an effective tactic. There were also hybrid attitudes; MLK himself used to say behind the scenes "we're going to love the *hell* out of them." Even the most committed nonviolent leaders admitted that in extreme cases, self-defense was necessary.

Figure I.2 Civil rights activists rehearse for a sit-in at a segregated lunch counter. The activist playing himself endures having smoke blown in his face by other activists role-playing white racists harassing him. Photo by Howard Sochurek/The LIFE Picture Collection/Getty Images.

Figure I.3 From the same rehearsal for action. The activist practices maintaining composure, reading a book, while enduring the smoke being blown in his face. Note, on the chalkboard in the background, a map of the restaurant where the action will take place. Photo by Howard Sochurek/ The LIFE Picture Collection/Getty Images.

Whether spiritual or secular, there is an *anticipatory* aspect to this form of activism. The white power structure was more powerful, but had a vulnerable spot: their monopoly on force and legal power made them arrogant, and thus predictable. The sit-in activists *anticipated* the predictable (violent, hateful) response of the white citizenry and police, and *incorporated* that response into their own sociodrama. They designed and enacted a scene in which they would be seen as the protagonists and the racist power structure as the antagonists on the global stage. Their radical "backstage" rehearsals prepared them for a "front stage" confrontation on their own terms. As they endured beatings and filled the jails—often in coordinated waves of sit-ins, in which one group would be beaten and arrested, only to be immediately replaced by another wave of sit-inners, and so on—their everyday suffering under racist hegemony was converted into creative suffering that had progressive impact. As they filled the jails and refused to pay bail, on some occasions activists were released *without bail* in an example of successful *satyagraha*.[8] At the same time, homes and churches were bombed and black activists were assassinated by white terrorists as the struggle deepened.

Some opponents were more tactically savvy than others; Commissioner "Bull" Connor of Birmingham was a perfect opponent, predictably brutal. Others, such as Mayor Pritchett of Albany, actually took the time to read Dr King's writings, and defused some actions of the civil rights movement by spreading prisoners out through many different jails, or slowing activist momentum with promises of concessions that were never honored.

This spectacle of "creative suffering" and the cruelty of state-sponsored white supremacy and racism triggered an international response that was of great concern for America's image abroad at a critical time. The US was presenting itself as the bastion of the Free World against the Soviet Union, which terrorized its own citizens. It did not fit the script when the world watched American police and white racist mobs brutalizing peaceful African–American citizens and depriving them of their human and civil rights. Tennessee Governor Buford Ellington was not entirely wrong when he bitterly complained that "these sit-ins are instigated and planned by and staged for the convenience of the Columbia Broadcasting System" (Lewis, 1999: p. 105). This looked especially bad to the people of color in the so-called "Third World" whose Cold War allegiance the US was seeking. After being beaten by white racists and then arrested by police as those who had beaten him cheered, Lewis noted:

> . . . I felt no shame or disgrace. I didn't feel fear, either . . . I felt exhilarated . . . I felt high, almost giddy with joy . . . it was really happening, what I'd imagined for so long, the drama of good and evil playing itself out on the stage of the living, breathing world. It felt holy, and noble, and good.
>
> (1999: p. 100)

The civil rights movement took into account this global geopolitical strategic situation as much as they did the necessary micropersonal tactics when staging their sociodramas. It was this combination of savvy, strategy, and courage that made their actions so impactful. Both President Kennedy and later President Johnson, who were not eager to alienate the "Dixiecrats" in their own party, felt enough pressure generated by the movement to address partially their civil and human rights agenda despite the tremendous power and wealth arrayed on the other side of the struggle. As Randall Kennedy states:

> Although John F. Kennedy is widely perceived now as having been a friend of the civil rights movement, for much of his brief presidency he evinced little commitment to the crusade for racial justice. He sympathized with the dissidents, but he was also keenly attuned to the obstructive power of Southern Congressmen . . . Primarily concerned with managing the Cold War and reforming tax policy, Kennedy avoided taking positions that they would perceive as unambiguously hostile.
>
> Kennedy's stance changed drastically, however, after events in Birmingham forced his hand . . . captured by television crews and photojournalists, images of brutality traveled across the country and around the globe, prompting many observers to demand a presidential response . . . In explaining his decision to deploy the National Guard to enforce the court-ordered desegregation of the University of Alabama, Kennedy showed the ever-present influence of the Cold War on his thinking: "When Americans are sent to Vietnam or West Berlin, we do not ask for whites only . . ."
>
> (Kennedy, 2014)

Philippe Duhamel (2004), citing George Lakey, describes this kind of sociodrama as a "demonstration dilemma"; a public action that puts authorities in a situation where they have no good move to make. If they crush the protesters, they damage their standing in the court of world opinion, assuming authorities are vulnerable to the pressure of world opinion. However, if they do not respond, then actions that damage their authority or undermine the unjust status quo will be allowed to stand, in a way that inspires further and wider resistance.

It seems that the action must be transgressive for this latter fork of the decision dilemma to operate—it must break unjust rules. The sit-ins are a model example of the decision dilemma. For example, after a few rounds of these sit-ins, officials in some Southern cities realized they should change their own tactics, and not always crush the activists violently. This was an intelligent move, but it enabled the activists to take actions that prefigured the elimination of Jim Crow laws—and to show the world, through performative enactment, that no great social harm would be done, and the world would not end if, for example, public facilities were desegregated. The most potent actions seem to be *simultaneously transgressive and prefigurative*—breaking the unjust rules and performing a vision of a future, better world. They are a hybrid of direct action that directly impacts the unjust social problem, and indirect action that performs a value in a way that affects public opinion.

The civil rights movement, with its savvy sociodrama, creative suffering, courage, intelligence, and powerful strategic dramaturgy, continues to inspire generations of activists. However, nonviolent activism, like the structure of communications systems and the state itself, has changed over time. With cable news' constant hunger for compelling content, and the internet's connectivity, social movements now have broader access to global audiences. However, that audience is increasingly fragmented and overwhelmed by a flood of images and an intensification of the society of the spectacle.[9] Social movements must work diligently and intelligently to create irresistible images that will grip the imaginations of the population, to achieve direct or indirect impact on policy and possibility. Current social movements recognize the power of entertainment to draw audiences and they increasingly rely on satirical and ironic sensibilities. The Yippies, members of the Youth International Party of the late 1960s, illustrate this stylistic shift.

The Yippies

The Youth International Party made some of the most famous countercultural and outrageous "zaps" or creative disruptive actions of the late 1960s and early 1970s in the US. They dumped a suitcase of dollar bills on the New York Stock Exchange from the balcony above. The brokers, already adrenalized by the frenzy of the trading floor, jumped over each other to grab the money. The chaos shut down the exchange for the day, and made more visible the rapaciousness of the institution. The Yippies attempted to form a human chain around the Pentagon with the intention of levitating and exorcising it of its demons, with help from the poet Allen Ginsburg and other countercultural luminaries. They nominated Pigasus the Pig for President. Of course, they faced legal trouble, but they used their trials, such as the famous Chicago Eight case, as opportunities for courtroom antics: dressing in judicial robes and other costumes, and talking back to the judge. They were mostly white, long-haired, counterculture "freaks," and they looked very different from the activists of the civil rights movement.

But many of them, including *über*-Yippie Abbie Hoffman, had been young activists in the civil rights movement and had taken beatings and learned many lessons from those confrontations. They admired that movement's understanding of theatrics and the role of modern media in the struggle. They had a different position in society—they were more privileged racially and economically. They also had a different agenda. They did not seek assimilation or equality through an appeal to the conscience of the central bourgeois public sphere, but rather sought to nurture a total counterculture that would help to overthrow the established order. With many hits and misses along the way, they became masters of mass media manipulation to blow minds, open minds, and promote radical action and a rebellious youth culture across the nation.[10]

The Yippies learned the lessons of sociodrama from the civil rights movement, and adapted them to their radically different agenda, societal position, and anticipated audience and desired reception. Theirs was a deliberately polarizing rather than unifying logic, pitting generational sensibilities against each other. They designed actions for wider countercultural struggles designed to activate the imagination and prefigure a better reality, influenced by theorists such as Herbert Marcuse, Guy Debord and Marshall McLuhan. Much like the Dutch Kabouters (Bogad, 2016), they embraced absurdity, ludic action, and the ineffable, rather than reaching to the mainstream for support on specific policy changes.[11] In recognition of this commonality, they even signed a whimsical international treaty with the Kabouters' Orange Free State, co-signed by the Diggers. The Yippies, with few resources, made a tremendous noise in the public sphere and encouraged a counterculture to grow. However, ACT-UP, which came a decade later, had a more specific and urgent agenda based on specific policy changes.

ACT-UP

ACT-UP, or the AIDS Coalition to Unleash Power, have provided key innovations in creative confrontation from the 1980s until the present day (Shepard, 2009). They are a key example of a performance activist organization that has won tangible policy results, much like the civil rights movement. Their surface-level style and appearance are different from the civil rights movement, but they follow in the same tradition of creative suffering, and continuing the ongoing, modular, evolving set of principles for tactical performance. Motivated by the rage and grief of the AIDS crisis, ACT-UP drew on the graphic design and theatrical skills of its members to create powerful actions.

They succeeded in changing the positions of politicians, and the legal regulations on AIDS research and drug policy of both the state and major drug corporations, all through the use of civil disobedience alongside strong graphics and other visual elements of protest. In their demonstrations, they bravely faced police beatings and caught the eye of a national and global audience. They were willing to be transgressive in their actions with both savvy and relentless "zapping" and "bird-dogging"[12] of individual decision-makers. (An example of an effective ACT-UP action from 2004 is discussed in Chapter 4 of this book.)

As Critical Art Ensemble founding member Steve Kurtz said:

> ACT-UP was a clinic in terms of how to do the graphics. When we were starting out, it was the height of the AIDS crisis and ACT-UP *changed FDA policy*. The icons they put together to construct solidarity, with their video wing, and their graphics wing, Gran Fury . . . it really convinced us that over time if you get enough artists and people contributing to the culture, it creates this language of resistance. That's what brought us into it; that showed us that cultural politics really means something.
>
> (Kurtz, 2014)

And what did Kurtz's group do with that inspiration?

Critical Art Ensemble

Critical Art Ensemble (CAE) is a group of radical theorist–artists who bridge the gap between the art world and social movements adroitly, while engaging the public with a radical critique of biotechnology, militarization, neocolonialism, and hypercapitalism. CAE has proven masterful at coopting money and resources from art institutions and diverting them to work for social-justice campaigns.

CAE engages in a savvy and streetwise exchange with elite art institutions. Museums gain radical cultural cachet by commissioning CAE, showing how democratic and open-minded they are. On the other hand, CAE needs actual capital to fund their projects. This exchange of cultural capital for fiscal capital enables CAE to pay for their more ambitious projects.[13] In return, these commissions also give CAE continued social capital. For example, in 2002, CAE received an "obscene" (Kurtz's word) honorarium to give a presentation at an art institution in Adelaide in Australia. They promptly used this money to fund a direct action project with aboriginal activists in that town. Aboriginal groups in that city had long been calling for a dual naming of Victoria Square, so that the name of the British imperialist monarch would be paired with the indigenous people's name for that place, Tarndanyungga. The city council refused this change; so the activists took direct action. In collaboration with CAE, they dressed like city workers, and replaced half of the square's twenty signs with signs that said "Tarndanyungga." The city took the guerrilla signs down. However, after a few months, they agreed to grant the square dual names (Crowley, 2002).

CAE produces work that ambushes audiences with bizarre interactive and troubling displays in the lobbies of museums or in shopping malls; oil spills in public fountains; helicopter rides that lift participants "to hover at a height that allows them to visualize the economic separation of the top 1% from the bottom 99%"; and other mischievous projects (Critical Art Ensemble, 2015). They also publish theoretical tracts and books on issues such as electronic disturbance/resistance, surveillance, and military technology and propaganda. They place a high value on the element of surprise, and where possible they try to set up their installations with that in mind.

> If you want our work to work right, you need the audience to *discover* us, not come to see us. It works best when people are genuinely asking: What is this? Why is this going on? The institutions want the radical cachet of having us there, so they usually don't want us to just set up outside. We want to be in a liminal place—the lobby or the cafeteria. We just did it with the oil spill. Don't tell anyone CAE is coming. We called ourselves CAN AMERICAN ENERGY (the same initials as CAE). The fans will look for the crypto clues.
>
> (Kurtz, 2014)

On the day of the opening of the new Toulouse Museum of Contemporary Art in 1999, a huge and diverse crowd lined up for blocks to attend. CAE was there with their project Cult of the New Eve, a lobby installation in which they simulated a cult that worshipped genetic perfection and solicited genetic swab-samples from passersby, testing them for genetic adequacy, to the outrage of many.

> They put us in the lobby, which was great. The first thing people would see is Cult of the New Eve. By the way, just the week before France had made cults illegal! People had no idea what to make of it. Is it fake? Is it real? Is it art? Is it social movements? Is it politics? Why are we taking people's DNA? This is a great start. People really engaged with us, while drinking our genetically modified beer. On the second day the mayor is saying cults should not be in the theatre, and the curator is saying "This is satire, it's theatre, you philistine!"
>
> (Kurtz, 2014)

CAE provides artist–activists with a compelling example of how to engage and counter-coopt the art world, while collaborating with social movements and directly engaging the public with strange, surprising, and thought-provoking interventions.

The Zapatistas

As Jeff Conant has pointed out in his book *A Poetics of Resistance: The revolutionary public relations of the Zapatista insurgency* (2010), the Zapatistas are an inspiration for the global justice movement across the world. Their uprising in 1994 in Chiapas, Mexico, and their continuing defiant creation of an alternative society, demonstrates to mainstream Mexico, in words and deed, the possibility of a better world. It also inspired creative resistance to neoliberalism across the Global North, which had lagged behind the Global South in terms of such resistance for many reasons, including privilege. The Zapatistas combined practical community organizing, the building of effective counter-institutions, autonomous decision-making councils and economies, and the actual taking of territory with a revolutionary poetics. The latter included an "air force" made up of poems folded into paper airplanes and "flown" onto a military base, and Subcommandante Marcos' beautifully bizarre and mischievous communications, denouncing neoliberalism, often while engaging in Platonic dialogue with a heroic cockroach named

Durito. Although not a heavily armed movement in a literal sense, their global profile gave them a cultural power and capital that has enabled them to survive and continue to devise new radical strategies in the politically hostile context of neoliberal Mexico.

As Conant said in a recent interview:

> What is unique and so powerful about the EZLN is that they understood history as performance, and using the stage of history, they used the popular revolutionary myths of Mexico, and the deep symbolism of ancient indigenous myths—in their actions, uniforms, communiqués, the symbolic dates they took action, all were shot through with complex references to cultural dynamics. That's the foundation of their genius.[14]

The EZLN (Zapatista Army of National Liberation) evoked the memory of Emiliano Zapata, the untarnished martyr of the Mexican Revolution, who was also of indigenous descent, to represent its indigenous and revolutionary cause.

> Their impact on the Global North had less to do with imagination than bringing issues together. Their uprising on January 1, 1994—the day that NAFTA came into effect—was the first in response to NAFTA. This uprising successfully connected the wonky and seemingly obscure issues of corporate globalization with bread-and-butter issues.

More recently, Subcommandante Marcos declared himself to no longer exist, and he changed his name to that of a recently murdered comrade, a schoolteacher with the *nom de guerre* Galeano (after Eduardo Galeano). To honor this comrade, and to end his role as a spokesperson for the movement—the EZLN's horizontalist and collective profile was at odds with having a white Professor of Communications as a media-darling spokesperson—Marcos said at the funeral, "Marcos is Dead! Long Live Galeano!" From their radical uprising, to the naming of their base La Realidad or Reality, to this final declaration of Marcos's own obsolescence, every action of the EZLN resonates symbolically.

Even with these inspiring examples to follow, tactical performances often fall flat or backfire due to overblown rhetoric, ideological blind spots, or poorly conceived theatrics; noting these failures is as important as studying successes. By studying these and many other examples, we can posit a few tentative principles for further testing on the field of struggle.

Principles and practices of tactical performance

Figure I.4 Creative direct action can help to convert old tactics and tools into new ones. Image by L.M. Bogad.

What would winning look like?

In my tactical performance workshops, I ask participants to envision what winning would look like. I push them. I push them further. It can be difficult to imagine winning, but we must envision short-term and long-term goals before deciding on tactics. If we can define a win, whether poetic or policy-oriented, and think backwards from that vision, we can design a sociodrama with strong action logic and prefigurative power.[15]

Praxis makes perfect

Praxis is an active feedback system between theory and practice that allows each to improve the other. It is crucial. Artist–activists must learn from wins and losses without disengaging theory from practice. The "action faction," who dismiss any studious aspect as "academic," can make mistakes that would be easily avoided with a sense of history and reflection. Of course, "analysis paralysis" plagues those who expound on theory without testing and revising it in the world of conflict.

But Exxon does praxis too

States and corporations have finely honed institutional memories. They learn from mistakes and victories, and preserve that knowledge. As stated earlier, social movements sometimes have shorter memories. It is crucial to build up a counter-institutional memory of tactical innovation, to avoid becoming predictable and thus easily defeated or contained.

Pressure points on the body politic: symbols, rituals, and interventions

Community organizer Saul Alinsky in his *Rules for Radicals* (1989) advocates for a kind of *political jiu-jitsu*, with which activists can use their opponents' superior force and momentum against them. I would slightly adjust this idea, favoring instead a *political aikido* that focuses on the identification and manipulation of joints and pressure points on the body politic. We can apply performative acupressure upon these points—actual and symbolic sites that with minimal force and maximum creativity can unlock many possibilities, and free up calcified structures. Like acupressure, it can relieve old tensions while making possible new movement.

We can make a distinction between force, power, pressure, and violence. These are loaded terms with heavy legacies. When discussing violence, the systemic violence of the social structure must be acknowledged. The renunciation of physical violence does not mean the abdication of all impactful action—force that creates pressure, as opposed to violence. Gandhi spoke of "soul force" in his design of *satyagraha* actions that, while they generated great pressure for change, rigorously refused to cause bodily harm to the imperial oppressor. Power can be something to change, use, diffuse, or defuse. To some, violence includes property damage; to others it does not. A group must decide for itself its definitions and philosophies on the use of force, power, and violence. Nonviolent force can create great pressure in the right context. On the other hand, some violent action yields no actual pressure on social systems, which are designed to absorb, magnify, and retaliate.

As tactical players, it is crucial that we know our cultural terrain. We are not the strategic power. We cannot afford to ignore the contours of the territory we are navigating—where the pitfalls lie. Too often radicals exile themselves to the cultural margins where the air is cleaner but the foot traffic is sparse. Symbolically powerful nodes to intervene in, and potent rituals to subvert and repurpose, can be found where the people are, culturally and geographically.

Tactical performances should have well-constructed action logic (Boyd & Mitchell, 2012a). The action may be prefigurative—giving the world a view of a better future. It may also be transgressive—breaking formal or unwritten laws and rules of the land to draw focus on their unjust nature. Or playful, or solemn. Obviously it can include many of these elements, but these should be conscious choices with a calculated purpose and desired impact. What kind of site are you targeting? Is your intervention targeting: a point of production (a toxic plant)?; a point of destruction (an ancient old growth forest about to be cut down)?; or a point of consumption (a big-box store or mall)? Or is it intervening on a more mental and cultural level, a point of assumption—the ideological, invisible assumptions that the dominant culture has made about a certain issue. Of course, you may be targeting multiple such sites with the same action—usually the "point of assumption" is being targeted along with geographical sites; but the action should be designed with the site in mind (Boyd & Mitchell, 2012a).

This action logic is calculated for maximum storytelling impact as well as direct impact on the social problem in question. Civil rights sit-ins were all of these things at once: they provided a vision of a better world. They exposed the injustice in the legal system, the power structure and the dominant culture, and they had a direct impact on the unjust structures through targeted direct action. They also told a powerful story, which their opponents obligingly entered as antagonists. Another example is the Indians of All Tribes (IAT) occupation of Alcatraz Island from 11 November 1969 to 11 June 1971.

When IAT activists took over Alcatraz Island, their action had both practical and symbolic impact. It told a bitterly humorous story. Alcatraz was a very significant site, perhaps the most storied prison in the US. However, it had been abandoned for years, and its legal status and usage were being debated. IAT seized this opportunity.[16] When they landed and occupied the island, they invoked the classic colonialist "right of discovery" and issued a statement that both drew attention to the plight of Native Americans and called for a new use of the island to help to rectify that plight (see the box below). The statement is a masterful, bitterly humorous inversion of the history of white colonization of native land. It mocks the rationalization for white colonization, the specific phrasing of many broken treaties, and even evokes the infamous sale of Manhattan. However, it is not just a history lesson: its irony reflects the deplorable conditions of Native Americans, and calls for a "Bureau of Caucasian Affairs" to be established on the Island. This ironic goal was complemented by a more serious, but never-realized goal of converting Alcatraz into a Native American cultural center.

Native American statement on Alcatraz Island

We, the Native Americans, re-claim the land known as Alcatraz Island in the name of all American Indians by right of discovery. We wish to be fair and honorable in our dealings with the Caucasian inhabitants of this land, and hereby offer the following treaty: We will purchase said Alcatraz Island for 24 dollars in glass beads and red cloth, a precedent set by the white man's purchase of a similar island about 300 years ago. We know that $24 in trade goods for these sixteen acres is more than was paid when Manhattan Island was sold, but we know that land values have risen over the years. Our offer of $1.24 per acre is greater than the 47 cents per acre the white men are now paying the California Indians for their land. We will give to the inhabitants of this land a portion of that land for their own, to be held in trust by the American Indian Government for as long as the sun shall rise and the rivers go down to the sea—to be administered by the Bureau of Caucasian Affairs (BCA). We will further guide the inhabitants in the proper way of living. We will offer them our religion, our education, our life-ways, in order to help them achieve our level of civilization and thus raise them and all their white brothers up from their savage and unhappy state. We offer this treaty in good faith and wish to be fair and honorable in our dealings with all white men. We feel that this so-called Alcatraz Island is more than suitable as an Indian Reservation, as determined by the white man's own standards.

> By this we mean that this place resembles most Indian reservations, in that:
>
> 1 It is isolated from modern facilities, and without adequate means of transportation.
> 2 It has no fresh running water.
> 3 The sanitation facilities are inadequate.
> 4 There are no oil or mineral rights.
> 5 There is no industry and so unemployment is very great.
> 6 There are no healthcare facilities.
> 7 The soil is rocky and non-productive and the land does not support game.
> 8 There are no educational facilities.
> 9 The population has always been held as prisoners and kept dependent upon others.
>
> Further, it would be fitting and symbolic that ships from all over the world, entering the Golden Gate, would first see Indian land, and thus be reminded of the true history of this nation. This tiny island would be a symbol of the great lands once ruled by free and noble Indians.
>
> (Johnson, 1996: p. 53–55)

IAT worked with labor leaders, including longshoremen who ensured the delivery of supplies, sympathetic Hollywood stars, and community organizers from other sectors of society. After a long occupation and many mishaps, IAT was forced from the island by authorities, and did not achieve their ironic goal of setting up a Bureau of Caucasian Affairs to reflect the condescension and exploitation of the government's Bureau of Indian Affairs. Nevertheless, they struck a blow in the battle of the story—the story being the historical narrative of the ongoing depredation of Native Americans—providing an inspiring example for further resistance.[17]

The battle of the story versus the story of the battle

The theorist–activists at the Center for Story-Based Strategy[18] have aptly pointed out that we are trying to fight the battle of the story, but things can all-too-easily degenerate into the story of the battle. What does this mean? We are trying to tell a story with our creative actions (about the environmental hazards of fracking, for example) while our opponents are trying to tell a different story (about the economic advantages of natural gas extraction). These narratives do battle in asymmetric warfare. Activists are armed with savvy, artistry, and charm; and their opponents have cable news stations and newspapers in their pockets. Fair enough. However, when our actions degenerate into pitched battles with the police, the corporate media can all too easily ignore the battle of the story and focus on the story of the battle—the protesters who were beaten and arrested, or the windows that were broken. Unless your goal is to create a violent spectacle about the over-policing of political activity, or you have crafted a sociodrama in which the violent over-reaction of the state tells the story you wish to tell, these results may not match your intention. It is not the social movements' choice whether or not they will be attacked by the state. However, creative choices and contingency plans can help the movement focus on the battle of the story, regardless of what happens.

One good example of an action that relentlessly fought the battle of the story occurred in 1998 in Boston Harbor. A pair of conservative congressmen had devised a clever performance in favor of the Flat Tax. They declared that they would have a public event on the deck of the Boston Tea Party Museum, a replica of an eighteenth-century ship in Boston Harbor. They would ceremoniously dump the current tax code in a box into the harbor and make statements in favor of a simpler flat tax and federal sales tax.

This was a very clear performance concept with elegant symbolic design. All Americans know the tale of the Boston Tea Party: it is one of the US creation myths.[19] By dumping the tax code into that historically symbolic harbor, in one motion Dick Armey equated himself with the heroes who helped found the country, and the current US tax code with the oppressive levy that sparked a revolution. Good storytelling. Like the cultural modes of irony and satire, the techniques of tactical performance are transideological, and available to the moneyed and powerful as well as to social movements.

A great deal of media appeared for the event: leading congressmen can get that kind of attention, especially when they are doing something interesting. However, just as the congressmen were about to dump the tax code into the water, a little rubber raft paddled out from behind the ship and stopped right under them. In the raft a man and a woman held a baby doll and a sign saying "WORKING FAMILY

LIFE RAFT." Bobbing in the water right under the big tax code box, they shouted "No! Don't flatten us with your flat tax! Don't sink us with your sales tax!"

The congressmen and their aides were stunned, but then it got weirder. Among their clean cut, suit-and-tie wearing entourage, several members immediately started pointing rudely at the Working Family Life Raft and jeering "Yes! Sink them with the sales tax! Flatten them with the flat tax! Do it!"

What would you have done if you were Dick Armey? If you don't drop the box, your event is canceled by a couple of lefties in a life raft. If you do drop it, you're doing something that enters their matrix of symbolic meaning rather than yours.

Armey stayed in character as a true neoconservative, and he dropped the box on the raft. The Working Family Life Raft capsized to complete the metaphoric picture, and the occupants flailed around as if drowning, plastic baby included. This provided amazing pictures for the media

Figure I.5 The Working Family Life Raft paddles under the congressmen about to dump the tax code, as "TEA," off the Boston Tea Party Museum, just in time to radically alter the symbolic meaning of their performance. Photo by David L. Ryan/The Boston Globe via Getty Images.

and the event received regional and national attention on television and in newspapers.

The Working Family Life Raft intervention was the work of Andrew Boyd and United for a Fair Economy (UFE), a Boston-based group that specifically works on issues such as economic justice, working directly against policies like regressive flat taxes and sales taxes. Armey and company walked into this group's hometown, taking the opposite stand on their core issue, so they had to respond. UFE's action involved luck, but also strong action logic and principles. They used social camouflage to infiltrate the Republican entourage, which would be much harder to do in our current surveillance and security state. More importantly, they studied, understood, and respected the symbolic story the conservatives were telling. They devised an action that would enter that symbolic frame and completely shift its meaning to their ends. The Working Family Life Raft conveyed an image of vulnerability and hard work—they had to paddle themselves over the waves with great effort, they could only move slowly, and could be easily tipped over, evoking the plight of the working poor. As the Life Raft got into position, the congressmen were no longer Revolutionary-War patriots, freeing Americans from evil taxes. They became oppressors of the underprivileged, callously drowning them for their own political ends. Even the central prop, that big box representing the tax code, became the weapon with which libertarians and neoconservatives will submerge and immiserate the struggling poor.

UFE took advantage of the large media presence that the important congressmen had attracted. They created a charmingly nonviolent and clever action. That transgressive mischievousness—not shouting down the congressmen, nor insulting them, but being playfully "naughty"—created more *frisson* and interest in what they had done. They didn't hurt anyone; rather immersing themselves in cold water in a disarmingly poignant action while leaving their opponents high and dry. They created a visually strong set of recognizable images that were irresistible to the media: in fact, even conservative pundits such as Rush Limbaugh could not ignore the event. The intervention told a clear story in an amusing way, and stayed on topic.[20]

It should be about what it's about

We can tell a better story if it's about what it's about: if the action is clearly connected to the issue and tells a story that can excite, galvanize, and recruit support. A mass of protesters may block a major bridge and disrupt traffic in protest of their government's bombing of another country. Their intention is to stop "business as usual," show general defiance, and call attention to the problem. The only trouble with this approach is the two elements—a blocked bridge here and a bombed city there—may not read to the general public as connected. There may be resentment and confusion for those who can't get home from work without any positive tradeoff—an increase in pressure on the state, or support for the movement.

But when dockworkers refuse to unload munitions from a ship to protest a war policy, this action is more powerful because it tells a story. The Gandhian movement's famous Salt March was a massive act of civil disobedience that read clearly to the global public. It was about the British taxing salt and forbidding the colonized Indian public from harvesting salt from the ocean. Opponents, supporters, and neutral observers read it as such. Provoked by this clear action, at least they discussed the right questions. Civil rights sit-ins were also clearly about what they were about, and that was a major part of their power.

The irresistible image versus the hegemonologue

Social movements often face a formidable cultural phenomenon in the form of what I call the "hegemonologue"—the hegemonic monologue of common neoliberal ideology that drones on from big and little screens, with favorite themes being the criminalization or pathologization of dissent, and the inevitability of predatory and unrestricted global capitalism. However, sometimes through luck, pluck, and skill, artist–activists can create an irresistible image that interrupts this hegemonologue, even if only temporarily. An irresistible image is so compelling or beautifully troubling that even one's ideological opponents must reproduce it, even when it undermines their narrative in the battle of the story. A clown kisses a riot shield—and tabloids that have been criminalizing the global justice movement for years print the photo. These images on their own may not have tangible results, but they do help movements to gain momentum or to weaken the determination of their opponents.

Example: Performing the censored image—One Thousand Coffins

Under the Bush administration, the executive branch seized unprecedented power to limit the constitutional right to free assembly. Activist groups were regularly infiltrated, put under surveillance, and preemptively arrested. Audience members for government-planned events were carefully screened, and prepicked citizens or soldiers often rehearsed questions to give the impression of openness and spontaneity. To circumvent such restrictions, groups like Billionaires for Bush, Reclaim the Streets, and the Oil Enforcement Agency used humor. However, One Thousand Coffins relied on creative, but somber theatrics to convey its message.

One Thousand Coffins was formed in response to the US government's ban on the filming of the coffins of dead American soldiers arriving home from Iraq. This image ban was a strong move on the administration's part. Though constitutionally questionable, it showed their understanding of the symbolic power of those flag-covered coffins coming home from the war overseas. The ban was contested legally, and eventually was overturned by President Obama. However, artists Mike DeSeve and Jenna Hunt organized a team to assemble hundreds of flag-covered cardboard coffins, and to carry them in a mournful parade down the streets of New York City during the 2004 Republican National Convention. They performed the censored image for the world to see, and it may have had greater impact than if it had never been censored at all. This spectacle was reproduced on television and on front pages around the world; a creative coup both for the nonviolent anti-war movement and the anti-censorship cause.

One Thousand Coffins provides an example of the potential power of a simple well-crafted graphic. Because it had resonated so strongly, artist–organizers Jenna Hunt and John Clarence Lake continued the coffin project, choosing more aesthetically controllable and symbolically powerful sites for future actions. In the bustle of the protest march in New York City, precision and orderliness were lost, but the event remained a haunting display of the images forbidden by the Bush administration. Hunt and Lake worked with Iraq Veterans Against the War (IVAW), Veterans for Peace (VFP), Military Families Speak Out (MFSO), American Friends Service Committee, and the National Campaign for Non-Violent Resistance, to organize ritual processions and displays of the coffins on a Trail of Truth and Mourning from the Women's Memorial at Arlington National Cemetery to the Ellipse behind the White House on 2 October 2004, and at the Lincoln Memorial on 23 October 2004. These veterans' groups gave the project political legitimacy and insight, aesthetic expertise, and improvements on the original idea.

Hunt and Lake envisioned a respectful and orderly aesthetic. The coffins were painstakingly assembled and arrayed at precise intervals, at Arlington, the Ellipse, and around the Reflecting Pool for the Lincoln

Figure I.6 Protesters perform the censored image, carrying one thousand flag-covered coffins through the streets of New York City. Photo by Joe Raedle/Getty Images News/Getty Images.

Memorial event. These involved sixteen-hour, backbreaking days of hauling, assembling, and arranging, all done with the cooperation of military and civilian activists and other volunteers. Hunt was struggling with the symbolism of the coffins and flags, wanting to include acknowledgment of the Iraqi casualties. In dialogue with VFP, they agreed to reflect an estimate of the war's casualty ratio by assembling ten black-fabric covered coffins representing the Iraqi dead for every one American-flag covered coffin representing American casualties. Hunt emphasized that they worked in close dialogue with anti-war veterans' groups to create events intended not only to protest against the war, but also as a way of processing grief:

> They didn't have to be all about the pomp and circumstance of military ceremoniousness. That has its place and its beauty, but this was a different space and way. The coffins provided effigies that took on a symbolic life of their own. Parents of fallen soldiers put photos of their lost son or daughter on top of a coffin. There were yellow ribbons with the names of soldiers who had died, laid on top of the coffins or attached to a display. It was a painful but transformative ritual of mourning and loss. At the

> Lincoln Memorial, we read the names of the soldiers who had died, which took hours. We wanted to make it clear that peace activists are not against our soldiers. They are our sons, daughters, mothers, sons, wives, husbands. We're not just so-called, "no-good hippies" or however the Right depicts us.[21]

Indeed, most of the marchers were themselves soldiers, veterans, or war-bereaved families, wearing mourning clothes or uniforms. IVAW led the procession from Arlington to the Ellipse, with the coffins carried behind their banner. Members of IVAW, VFP, MFSO, and bereaved military mother Cindy Sheehan gave speeches at the Ellipse. With the use of the symbolically powerful props, uniforms, and national monuments for settings, these events showed instead of told, embodying the adage "peace is patriotic."

As a coda, Hunt and others brought the coffins and flags to the Counter-Inaugural protest on 20 January 2005. Like the 2004 Republican National Convention in New York City, this event was more chaotic and harder to control. Some of the flag-covered coffins were left in the street by marchers retreating before advancing police, and were run over by police cars. While Hunt and her colleagues were cleaning up, she noticed that many Republican partygoers were streaming down the street from one celebratory event to another. The One Thousand Coffins crew decided to fold the American flags according to military regulations and offer them to the cheery Bush supporters as they walked past. If anyone stopped to chat, they would amicably explain that each flag represented an American soldier lost in the Iraq War. Most of the Republicans avoided eye contact, treated the activists "as if there was a bomb in the flag," and pretended not to see them. For Hunt, this moment was strongly metaphoric as a performance of the unpatriotic refusal of responsibility for one's political choices.

Of course, any image, even irresistible ones, can eventually be bowdlerized, coopted and distorted, which begs the question: how do symbols change over time?

Shifting symbols

The dominant symbols of our time are a crucial aspect of the cultural terrain in which we work. The hammer and sickle was a potent symbol in prerevolutionary Russia. The sickle represented the 85% of the population who were peasants. The hammer represented the 10% who were industrial workers. In one simple and easily-drawn symbol, the communists had created something that almost everyone in the country could identify with, even if they had different interpretations in mind. Only later did that symbol become, for so many, a symbol of oppression. This is in the nature of symbols—as Kertzer (1988) points out, they are strategically ambiguous. Symbols unify diverse polities better than words precisely because of their ambiguity. But ambiguity provides an opportunity for subversion, inversion, cooptation, and reworking. Like good situationists, we can pilfer and poach these designs, and reuse them.

The "Peace Sign" is a classic example of a symbol's evolution. It is widely identified with pacifism or more generally "hippies," but its original intention was much more specific. Originally designed for the Campaign for Nuclear Disarmament in the UK, it is a combination of the semaphore symbols for "N" and "D." This sign was only about nuclear disarmament. The symbol was so catchy that it spread to the larger peace movement and became identified with the entire 1960s rebellion. Naturally its prominence and potency attracted a reactionary response: it was dubbed "chicken tracks" by pro-war pundits, the joke supporting the argument that only cowards would oppose imperialist war. But the reframing of this symbol has gone further in recent years: I have had several students, educated in fundamentalist religious schools, who were taught that it was not a peace sign at all, but rather a pagan or Satanist symbol. This fascinating inaccuracy reveals the importance for some movements to (in this case, literally) demonize and invert the meaning of a popular and powerful opposing symbol.

In our tactical work, it is hard to create entirely new symbols, although it can be done—we will read about the Survivaball™ in Chapter 5. It is often better to rework existing symbols such as the Statue of Liberty or Ronald McDonald that history or advertising dollars have made universally familiar, and put them in a new context that attracts attention and resonates with the public.

The action is (not always) in the reaction

Alinsky's claim that "the action is in the reaction" means that it is only when the authorities are provoked that things really get moving (1989). In fact, a saying often misattributed to Gandhi rings true: "First they ignore you. Then they laugh at you. Then they attack you. Then you win." During the early months of the Occupy movement, which started with an encampment near Wall Street in New York City in September 2011, the media did not acknowledge the encampments;

then their coverage was dismissive and mocking; but finally a coordinated wave of police attacks against tent cities occurred throughout the US. I ruefully asked my friends: "Does this mean we're about to win?" The idea that a reaction from the authorities registers activist impact on the cultural Richter scale is convincing, if not always true.

However, in the case of a properly designed decision dilemma, an action can loosen an unjust law or facilitate recruitment and create momentum, even if authorities are savvy and do not react or over-react.[22]

Unpredictability: surprise versus shock

In an analysis of the El Salvadoran civil war, a notorious right-wing Special Forces commander expressed grudging respect for his guerrilla opponents, the FMLN. He stated that in other Latin American countries, such as Peru or Colombia, guerrilla armies had one dominant political ideology, which called for one supreme military strategy that matched the ideology. A Maoist group might call for taking the countryside first and then laying siege to the capital; whereas a Trotskyist group might call for working in the urban centers primarily. All a government had to do was determine the guerrillas' ideology-based military dogma, and then execute a counterstrategy (Perdomo & Spencer, 1995: p. 10).

The Salvadoran colonel noted that the FMLN was unpredictable due to its polyglot nature. A coalition of five ideologically diverse groups, the FMLN could not be dogmatic. It had to devise strategy based on internal dialogue and external praxis—the tactics that worked best. By accident of history, the lack of one dominant ideology proved a crucial advantage. The FMLN was not predictable and thus harder to defeat. It may seem strange to refer to this example while discussing the work of nonviolent creative activist movements; however, the lesson still stands. Dogma that leads to repetition and predictability makes surprise impossible.

We must distinguish here between surprise and shock. Surprise is important at a tactical level. Taking the initiative, and making new moves can be advantageous. Surprise is also important for cultural work because it is the opposite of cliché. Cliché dulls the senses and bores the mind. Surprise activates us. Our synaptic network is momentarily disrupted when we are truly surprised, as our brain scrambles to figure out what is going on. This is not a sinister experience; it is a moment of openness and freshness, in which new perspectives, responses, and reflections are possible.

Shock is different from surprise although sometimes the two are conflated. Shock can be achieved by overwhelming the senses with horror or disgust through violent confrontational imagery. But such a strategy can be problematic since it is difficult to shock anyone anymore, and attempts to do so can result in unintentional cliché and eye-rolling by the observer.

The Enmedio Collective of Barcelona has proven the value of surprise in many of their artistic actions, but I will choose just one of these—a playful contribution to street protest. They inflated huge silvery balloons and floated them in the streets between the riot police and protesters. These reflective cubes, like huge politicized references to Andy Warhol's *Clouds*, added an element of fun and wonder to the confrontation. They were also a harmless and aesthetically pleasing way to absorb the shock of police baton charges, filling up the space so that it was harder for the police to attack.

In September 2014, the day after the New York City climate change march, the largest such march in history, another group took the balloon idea into the world of messaging. On this day, several thousand people participated in the Flood Wall Street action, wearing blue clothing and simulating a flood by filling up and blockading the area

Figure I.7 The Reflective Cube in action during the General Strike in Barcelona 2012. Action of Enmedio collective in cooperation with Eclectic Electric. Photo by Collective (CC) Oriana Eliçabe/enmedio.info.

Figure I.8 The "CARBON BUBBLE?" balloon being deployed in New York City during the climate change march. It was later deflated by the police after it was bounced off the head of the Wall Street Bull statue. Photo by L.M. Bogad.

around the symbolically potent Bull Statue, which was guarded by the police. The protesters had prepared several huge balloons similar to the Enmedio silver ones, but these were black and emblazoned with the words "CARBON BUBBLE?"—an energy-sector term indicating that oil companies' worth and stock values are predicated on their ability to continue extracting and selling global oil reserves. This problem is central to the political–economic conflict around climate disaster. As the enormous balloons bounced around, one was pushed towards the Bull Statue. The police grabbed hold of it and deflated it, but the image was already created, and it was as gripping and succinct as the concepts it symbolized, and recognizable to anyone who saw photos of the event over the media and internet (Smith, 2014). It hoped to provoke many curious internet viewers to search the term "carbon bubble" and learn about the issue.

Tactics versus strategy

In George Orwell's *Animal Farm*, the propagandist pig, Squealer, explains to the animals why the boar-dictator Napoleon has repeatedly lied while amassing power (2003: p. 36):

> **“ *(dancing with glee)* Tactics, comrades, tactics! ”**

Tactics are not only the lies of the powerful, such as the Stalinist swine above or the Machiavellian bureaucrat below:

GROSS: Why did you say that you hold a critical attitude towards Ptydepe and that you're only interested in the snack bar, when in fact you believe in Ptydepe and do everything you can to get it quickly introduced?
BALLAS: A matter of tactics.

The Memorandum, Vaclav Havel (1981: p. 11)

Tactics are also moves, feints, tricks, and techniques at the local or immediate level of conflict.

Sidney Tarrow (1998) describes modular tactics that can be easily reproduced across contexts and issues, such as boycotts, strikes, and demonstrations. Groups all over the world can pull common tactics from their action toolkits, and perform these modular actions globally, in solidarity and simultaneity.

However, sometimes, when a tactic achieves surprise and a real win, social movements rely on it too heavily, to the point of predictability. Leslie Kauffman points out that this elevation of tactic to strategy can be disastrous (2003). The nonviolent, diverse, and creative blockade of the World Trade Organisation summit in Seattle in 1999 was a triumph for the global justice movement. However, further attempts over the next few years to repeat that kind of blockade at other summits resulted in frustration. The authorities, embarrassed once, fortified the summits, militarized the sites, and infiltrated movements. This is tactical interaction; one side learns from the other's move and develops countermoves, and vice versa, in an agonistic–antagonistic relationship.

Strategic timing

The grassroots Association of Community Organizations for Reform Now (ACORN) scored an impressive victory in the East New York neighborhood of Brooklyn in the 1980s due to their sense of strategic timing. At the time, the banks in New York City were refusing to live up to their legal obligations to lend to the communities they were based in, resulting in *de facto* redlining. ACORN wanted to take over abandoned housing in East New York, and run it cooperatively for low-income families. But how to get the city government and banks to cooperate with this illegal, but just, activity?

The plan was to conduct civil disobedience—squatting in the unused homes, making them decent abodes, and then letting the city government evict the squatters repeatedly. This would point out the injustice and waste of the situation. However, this kind of spectacle would not be enough for an actual win. ACORN did their research, and waited for a time when one major bank was politically and financially vulnerable. That bank was heavily leveraged in order to absorb another bank, an act for which they needed government approval. This was the time to move.

ACORN members occupied the abandoned houses, were arrested repeatedly, but persevered. The city faced bad publicity for arresting nonviolent homeless people who were just trying to fix up and share abandoned and crumbling housing stock. The bank did not want to become the target of popular outrage for their refusal to grant loans to the working poor at this vulnerable time. ACORN leveraged the spectacle of this confrontation to embarrass the bank and the city. In the end, they won land, financing, and legal legitimacy from some of the world's most powerful institutions. That low-income housing cooperative still stands today. Guy Debord (1995) proudly claimed about his savvy generation of radicals: "We know how to bide our time." His meaning: it is not always the right time to storm the barricades, nor is it always prudent to keep your head down and wait things out. Observe and participate in your cultural environment and terrain unsentimentally and with as much clarity as possible. Praxis yields a sense of timing that is just as important in activism as it is in theatre.[23]

Eschew cliché

Cliché is the bane of any art form—from poetry to novels, films, and theatre. The reader or viewer skips past familiar figures of speech without engaging with the specific image. If there are too many clichés and too much predictability, the audience wanders off, either mentally, by daydreaming, or by voting with their feet during the intermission. Surprise, whether playful or jarring, is the antidote to cliché; but it can be hard to achieve in a world where so much has already been done. How can we design actions that are surprising while still on topic?

Example 1: The sensitive spycam

Reykjavik, Summer 2008: Surveillance cameras are going up in front of banks and state buildings. Those of us who are already jaded to the reality of constant electronic surveillance might be surprised that Iceland had only recently joined the ranks of the panoptic societies. It was still something that people were talking about and questioning.

A group of friends and I went out one night and climbed up the surveillance poles to point the cameras at the night sky. I had written a few thought bubbles on stickers; when stuck to the wall next to the cameras, it looked like the cameras were thinking "I'D RATHER LOOK AT THE STARS THAN SPY ON PEOPLE." The camera, with minimal trespass and no damage, was now cast as an anthropomorphic entity that had a greater social conscience and more sensitive yearnings than the security agencies that installed it. A short, sweet, and darkly silly vignette was quickly legible to passersby.

One can see how this idea could develop into a series of actions along the same theme, as the cameras continue to express themselves: for example, fastening an open book over a camera's lens, so it looks like its "head" is buried thoughtfully in a novel, and giving it a thought bubble that says "I'D RATHER READ CAMUS THAN SPY ON PEOPLE."

Naturally, after a few such incidents it would be relatively easy for the owners to fortify or guard the cameras from further pranks. But then this is the nature of tactical interaction: new actions will have to be thought up.

Example 2: On rats and context

In the US labor movement, it has become a popular, modular tactic to place a giant inflatable rat in front of a workplace that is being picketed. Over the years this has become effective shorthand for the savvy and labor-sympathetic—"Ah! This place is having labor troubles." However, the rat rarely has any words on it that explain what it means to the uninitiated. It also isn't very dynamic (thankfully, it's not a real giant rat, and therefore just sits there). I have seen the giant rat in places where the workers were not picketing at the moment, sitting alone and incommunicative. The rat needs some work to regalvanize it as a useful symbol against the bosses.

What if, say, you could infiltrate a giant inflated helium-filled rat on a leash into the Macy's Thanksgiving Day Parade? Float it where it isn't expected and doesn't belong, right next to Mickey and Goofy and the gang? That would cause some trouble and create a moment that was electrifying, and humorous or infuriating, depending on your position. In a new context, even an old symbol can be reinvigorated through transgression.

Sometimes the opposition will unintentionally rejuvenate an old symbol. In Berkeley a few years ago, a giant rat was on lonely sentry duty outside a car dealership, mostly being ignored, when someone slashed it. Now it was a point of interest. Who stabbed the rat? Will they be caught? What was going on at that car shop in the first place; a labor dispute? Is the rat recovering from its injury with the help of duct tape? The rat was temporarily interesting again, and a useful device for attracting attention to the actual problem, thanks to the slasher. However, we're not always lucky enough to get help from the opposition, so it's better to devise dynamic symbols.

There is no purity

Not in this universe under its current management or lack thereof. Movements that strive for purity—in ideology, form, or action—spawn monsters. One of the best ways to paralyze a movement is to insist on action that contains no ethical or political contradictions. Holding to that standard, the very electrons in your body should cease to spin around the nuclei of your atoms. And when it comes to purity of form, in an ongoing tactical interaction between a movement and its political dance partners or opponents, there is an inevitable blurring of boundaries and identities through contact and struggle. Your opponent is not a block of wood, and neither are you. You will learn from each other's moves. You will blend aesthetics, steal riffs from each other, and make them your own. You will coopt each other, in part or whole. Hip corporate marketers steal ideas from anarchist subvertisers and guerrilla artists, and vice versa. This is the nature of agonism, where opponents learn to be better fighters by fighting each other, as opposed to simply antagonism. There is no such thing as a total and final victory, nor is there complete defeat; there is no completely pure motive and no perfectly pure aesthetic. And that is OK.[24]

Anticipate and incorporate

It is vital as a tactical player to anticipate the response of your opponent and incorporate that response into your action in order to achieve maximum effect. The sit-ins of the civil rights movement are just one powerful example of this principle, in which the predictably violent response of the white police and mobs led to critical catharsis and the galvanization of the movement. But this principle applies to less-famous actions as well.

Effective tactical performance anticipates the (sometimes outraged or even violent) response of its opponents and incorporates that response into the strategic dramaturgy of the staged event. At its best, the American civil rights movement did this masterfully. The more predictable the opponent, the easier it is to seize the initiative and control the exchange and the imagery that unfolds for the greater public. This is a lesson for all practitioners of tactical performance.

Example: Haunting healthcare

Alameda, California, 2009: A town hall meeting is being held by a congressperson who supports the passing of the Affordable Healthcare Act, also known as "Obamacare." The pattern had been established previously that Tea Party members, "birthers," and "deathers" would show up to shout down the supporters of healthcare reform. To give them credit, for their relatively small numbers, they had very large, well-printed protest signs that could be read from afar, something protesters often fail to do.

I joined a group organized by artists Marc Pinate and Aryeh Shell to counter-protest this group. We dressed all in white, with white makeup, and appeared in ghostly form as the spirits of people killed by corporate healthcare. This was no satirical or ironic action. Each of us memorized the story of a specific, real American who had been denied coverage by their health insurance company and died as a result. We came to the area outside the building, moving slowly and with dignity, occasionally freezing in unison, and occasionally flinching in pain together according to our individual ailments.

People got out of our way, as you can imagine, and stood back to watch us. We began to speak *sotto voce* and many stepped closer to hear. Each of us told our story: our name, our job, our family, our premiums faithfully paid, our coverage denied, and our wrongful death. The Tea Party faithful followed their script. While holding their large signs denouncing the fictional "death panels" and "socialism," they yelled at us, calling us "communists" who wanted the government to control everything. We did not acknowledge their taunts, but continued with quiet, ghostly dignity to murmur our stories of hard work and lethal betrayal. We stayed in character. Again, we flinched in unison, which became a more powerful image with the Tea Party folk yelling at us.

Eventually, the Tea Party activists realized, on some level, that yelling at the suffering ghosts of dead people made them look like unfeeling antagonists. They were the bad guys in this scene and they didn't like it. They walked away.

So we followed them. For the rest of the protest we haunted them; the ghostly conscience they lacked, the critical perspective they were missing, completing the scene they created with some nuance. Basically, we ruined their day. But as we were washing off our makeup in the parking lot, one of them, a late middle-aged white man, came up to us and said, "Well, I gotta hand it to you. I don't agree with you, but that was some good theatre you all put on." He shook our hands (*HyPE-Speaking for the Dead*, 2009).

What we can learn from theatre for tactical performance

Tactical performance is different from "legit" theatre, but we can still learn a great deal from that medium, which has developed and refined itself over thousands of years. Many of the values espoused here apply also to the theatre: timing, surprise, strong visuals, compelling characters, dynamic tension, specificity, discipline, and rehearsal. I have already discussed how the theories of Aristotle, Brecht, and Boal apply to tactical performance. I will now examine some more values from the theatre world.

Theatre practitioners understand the importance of "earning a moment." If your play has a social message that you want to convey, it's a bad idea to start out with it, prating on self-righteously. People generally don't enjoy being preached to. These moments are earned through quality, engagement, surprise, and delight, which are achieved through a great deal of creative investment. Tactical performance is served well by this principle.

Specificity is a value of the theatre. Generalized acting (expressing that "I'm ANGRY!" with furrowed brows) is too vague a device to truly move an audience. Stanislavsky urged actors and directors to seek specificity in their acting choices (2008). They've learned to communicate a specific and accurate emotion—for example, the difference between the stinging grief of recent losses versus the dull ache of old ones. In activist sociodramatic action, this specificity is also a value. Generalized repeated actions that simply express the same idea in a modular way lose affect. Details, local forces, and masterful timing should be unique and specific to each action. Text, context, and subtext, and their interplay are all essential elements of any performance text. As the civil rights movement has taught us, rehearsal and discipline are valuable theatrical concepts. We can also learn a great deal from some of the great protagonists and playwrights of the theatre.

Earning a moment

Aristophanes' *Lysistrata*, written 2,400 years ago, provides a classic example of argumentation under pressure. Aristophanes was writing an anti-war play while his city-state Athens was embroiled in a decades-long war with Sparta; a war which it had started in the name of spreading democracy, and which it was losing. It was neither popular nor safe to write a play against the war; Aristophanes had actually been tried for treason for an earlier play lampooning a general. With *Lysistrata*, he created a farcical premise as a way to make larger points: the women of both warring city-states go on a sex strike for peace. High jinks ensue, but the final argument's structure is most compelling for our purposes. The women's leader, Lysistrata, confronting the diplomats of both states, makes her argument for peace in the following way:

1 We should both be united against foreign opponents. (Not the most progressive viewpoint but one sure to appeal to Hellenic patriots on both sides.)
2 Remember when we, the Athenians, helped the Spartans in a war long ago? They should be grateful. (It was an argument sure to please the actual audience of the show, Athenians.)
3 (And the kicker:) Remember when the Spartans supported us Athenians in that other war? We owe them a debt as well.

If Aristophanes had started with point 3, the Athenian audience might have turned ugly. Instead he warms them up with point 1, blatantly panders to them in point 2, and in that way earns the moment to say point 3. Aristophanes avoided legal trouble, and the play won the prize for best comedy that year and has lived on as a classic referred to by peace movements since.

Weapons of the weak

Brecht's *The Mother*, an adaptation of Gorky's novel set in Tsarist Russia in 1905, centers around a protagonist who serves as a model for dissident behavior. This poor and illiterate peasant woman uses the few innate advantages she has—street wisdom, powers of observation, and stubbornness—to develop from a passive victim of Tsarism into a revolutionary leader. The struggle is not romanticized as fun or safe: she is repeatedly beaten and hurt, and her son loses his life. However, she demonstrates the savvy use of the "weapons of the weak" and tactical action, while teaching that losses and defeats are part of the struggle.

Brecht famously claimed that art is not a mirror with which to reflect reality, but a hammer with which to shape it. Radical artists should trim their sails to take advantage of the cultural winds as they change direction, rather than simply waiting for those winds to blow the right way. The Mother models this behavior; for example, when she joins a line of patriotic Russian women donating their metal goods for the war effort. Rather than protest openly, she stands there with an absurdly small teapot just large enough to justify her presence, and ironically extols the virtue of the war, claiming that she hopes it goes on forever so her son can get promoted to sergeant. Several women leave the line in disgust; another gets the irony and is converted to the anti-war cause; and another also gets the irony, calls the Mother a "Red," and hits her in the face. All in a day's work for a revolutionary.

Irony and tactical deniability

Vaclav Havel's *The Memorandum* provides an example of tactical deniability. Havel was a dissident playwright under communism in Czechoslovakia, eventually imprisoned for his human rights advocacy. Havel wrote *The Memorandum* under censorship, but in the relatively warm period of the Prague Spring. The play uses darkly playful and pointed metaphor to avoid punishment.

In the play, a company that seems not to produce anything except food for its bureaucrats adapts a new language for better intra-office communication, called Ptydepe. Ptydepe is superior to the sloppy human languages that have evolved over centuries of hit-or-miss history. It removes all subtle nuance from language so that no shades of meaning or dual definitions remain to cloud clarity. There is one problem: the language is so dense and interminably complicated that no human being can actually learn or use it. Havel thus made a trenchant and funny critique of Marxism–Leninism while preserving deniability in the case of arrest or censorship—after all, the play works well enough as theatre of the absurd or a satire of petty office politics. Havel outlasted the regime, and went on to become the first president of the new post-communist Czechoslovakia, presiding over the peaceful division of the nation into the Czech Republic and Slovakia.

Translating aesthetics from the stage to the street

In street performance, it is important to delineate and energize the performance space. Without the trappings of the formal theatre to direct audience attention with fixed seating, focused lights, etc., performers must attract an audience to a space that has good sightlines, decent acoustics, and symbolic and practical significance. The piece should have a strong beginning that builds up and attracts the crowd, and a surprising and strong ending. Perhaps a barker with strong lungs can overpower the sounds of traffic to bring a crowd together. Or the use of shills, much as in a circus or a fairground, can attract attention to the affair. Shills can actively participate and bring people to the action, but even just silently standing and watching the action can direct attention.

To illustrate these principles, I will present the work of one of my students. Joe Ferreira, an undergraduate theatre major at UC Davis, created an intervention about the US National Security Agency (NSA) and surveillance. He appeared at the student union on campus in a conspicuous costume easily identified by the large lunchtime crowd: that of a Man In Black, or government agent, in dark suit, tie, and glasses. He held a large cardboard cone marked "NSA." As people walked by, he held the cone to his ear and pointed the wide part at them, using it as a mock listening device. He would then hold the cone to his mouth and bellow out whatever the hapless passerby had just said: "SHE'S GOING TO HAVE THE FALAFEL!" or "HE'S GOT A RASH!"

This was an elegantly simple, amusing, and gleefully obnoxious device to gather a crowd. Outside of the orderly space of a proper theatre, one must create and define a performance space, and create an audience out of the chaos of everyday life through transgression or playful provocation.

Once said crowd had gathered, the next phase of the performance could begin. Agent Joe's assistants, two Women In Black, appeared holding a large wooden sign that said "Celebrate Your Security!" while Joe performed a quick and pithy monologue about the issue of warrantless wiretapping. After he said the word "tapping," his assistants dropped the sign on the ground with a crash, leapt on it—and began to tap dance. This was a moment of surprise that paid off. The double use of a prop, as sign and dance stage—and its simultaneous double-entendre, tapping against tapping—earned Joe a moment to make his point. The crowd was visibly rapt and amused, and applauded at the end. An elegant action design and charming tone had overcome the many challenges faced by guerrilla street performers.

Creating a stage on the street where there is none continues to be a challenge. In 2012, in downtown San Francisco, a May Day protest began with participants stepping into Market Street and taking it over. David Solnit and many friends then chalked the outline of a huge sun with rays shooting out of it on the sidewalk. Demonstrators were then invited to help finish the work of art—coloring in the sun, and the slogans "RISE UP 99% LEVANTENSE 99%" in glorious yellow, orange, and red. This was fun, and many joined in on the art project. More importantly, the demonstrators were invited to write their own slogans on the individual rays shooting out from the sun. Soon personal and collective concerns such as "Living Wage," "No Fracking," and "Justice" appeared emanating out of the Sun of the 99%. Everyone was now invested in the image, having co-created it—and this was done quickly and beautifully because of the guidance of the artist's chalk lines. As soon as the painting was finished and dry with the help of the real sun, performers jumped onto its surface and begin a performance about the 1% versus the 99%.

Figure I.9 The May Day Sun Stage, on Market Street, San Francisco, 1 May 2013. The "stage" is outlined by an artist, then filled in by demonstrators. Photo by L.M. Bogad.

Figure I.10 The Sun Stage being painted by demonstrators, who then fill in their own personal political desires on the sun's rays. Photo by Mona Caron.

Figure I.11 A performance follows on the completed Sun Stage: a confrontation between the 1% and the 99%, with the author typecast once again as the spokesman for the 1% (in dark suit with microphone). The 1% giant is pulled down by the crowd at the end of the piece. Photo by Mona Caron.

This was an elegant example of a tactical performance that occupied the space, blocked the street, but also opened up the venue for collective expression along the theme of the protest. Finally, the performance defined and energized the space with a colorful and thematically relevant stage for street theatre.

Some fun false binaries

What follows are some categories with which to think about tactical performance. These categories are fluid and overlapping: hybrid forms are often the most impactful.

Air war versus ground war: classic strategy as a template for nonviolent action

Referring to military terminology in a book about creative nonviolent activism is neither advocacy for a military mindset nor a glorification or apology for military methods. I am merely suggesting a parallel between military air and ground power and theatrical and more conventional grassroots activism. Like the chess metaphor that launched the chapter, let us explore this comparison, take from it what is useful, note its inconsistencies, and discard what is unnecessary.

According to modern military theory, air war is very important for softening the enemy's defenses and making the job easier for ground forces to take territory. But air power alone cannot win. Bombing the enemy into submission doesn't work; an army must invade and seize the ground. On the other hand, while ground fighting is necessary for actual victory, it can be a long, hard, and slow slog without air support.[25]

With this in mind, it may be helpful to think of fantastic, spectacular pranks and guerrilla theatre actions as "air-war" actions. They soften the cultural terrain, draw attention to a problem, change some minds or at least weaken opposition, and galvanize discouraged supporters. However, a prank alone does not change a policy or the course of an election or social struggle.[26] That is the job of the more fundamental "ground war" equivalent: the hardcore, everyday organizing, in workplaces and communities, face-to-face. You have nothing without a ground game in social-movement organizing; but that air game can really help move things forward. These modes of action complement each other in peace, as they do in war.

As an example, the group Billionaires for Bush, was focused on "air power." Billionaires for Bush weren't out collecting signatures for petitions or giving people rides for a Get Out The Vote drive. They were in character, as ironic "billionaires" in absurd and fabulous costumes, dramatizing the problems of oligarchy and hypercapitalism for live television and internet audiences. That was their focus and they did it well. They might have benefitted from working in more direct coordination with "ground power" activist groups such as unions and economic-justice organizations, but that is a question I explore more in Chapter 4.

By contrast, most labor unions in the US focus on straightforward ground-war activities: organizing in workplaces, negotiating with employers, striking, and volunteering to help friendly electoral candidates. I provide a few examples in this book where labor organizing is assisted by creative air-war activities that help to dramatize picket lines, and to tell a union's story in a more convincing and charismatic way, which is important because a large portion of the public remains culturally hostile to labor unions.

Opening space versus occupying space

Sometimes it is crucial to occupy a public space—town square, public building, or campus—to call attention to the problem at hand by preventing business as usual, and making an unconscionable situation visible to those who are not aware. Some actions attempt to open up an occupied space to radical participation. The May Day Sun Stage described above is an example of an opening-space action. Although tending to be messier with less message discipline, these actions can be more playful and empowering, and can serve as prefigurative affirmations of the world we want to see.

Bricks versus clicks

Ideally, we can find a balance between "bricks" (the physical world and face-to-face activism) and "clicks" (online activism such as exemplified by the group MoveOn.org). The internet's connectivity is a tool to be used for any campaign; but not everyone is connected to it, and it functions best as a complementary aspect of a campaign in the streets. The aforementioned Billionaires for Bush were a good example of a strategy that combined bricks and clicks. They performed disruptive, live theatre and satirical confrontations in the streets that attracted attention from mass and social media, and directed traffic to their website, where clickers could learn more about the issues, and download materials that would help them to get into character and create Billionaire-ish confrontations on the streets of their hometowns. This savvy feedback loop between bricks and clicks provided a model for future action.

Independent artist–activists versus coalition with organizations

An ice cream truck downtown is giving away free popsicles! You line up and get one. The suited man standing on top of the truck cheerfully informs you that these new icy treats are made from the last few glaciers on earth. This promotion is part of his corporation's campaign to adjust public attitudes toward climate change. The glaciers are melting anyway, so they might as well melt in your mouth:

> **Enjoy! Go With the Floe!™**

The crowd smiles uncertainly and begins to ask questions. Some play along, showing that they "get it," and add to the joke with their own riffs. A few of the irony-deficient react with alarm and horror at our product. I tell them quickly, with a wink, "It's a joke." My goal as the corporate-shill character is not to actually fool anyone, but to give them a "Huh? Aha!" moment and then to play with them. Had we been standing on the street corner handing out flyers about climate change and earnestly advocating for a carbon tax, most people would have ignored or avoided us. Instead, we created a play space around a serious issue, facilitated dialogue, and garnered press coverage for our low-budget effort.

This was a project I worked on with the Center for Tactical Magic in 2007. We performed it in Davis, California, and later I did a solo version in Pittsburgh. We were lone glacier-popsicle distributers and activists, not beholden to any climate change organization. There were pros and cons to this. On the one hand, it was a fun experiment. On the other hand, it was too disconnected from any actual campaign to do something tangible about climate disaster.

There is a clear difference between tactical performances directly tied to the campaigns of social-movement organizations, and tactical performances that are the free-floating creations of independent artists. Both have their advantages. When working directly with a labor union or an anti-war group, creative artists can craft their performances in direct collaboration with activists with experience, insight, and a budget. They may even see direct results and modest victories from the campaigns. On the other hand, they are also responsible to a larger group that may not agree with or approve of their artistic decisions. This may feel like control and censorship, and often it is; but the larger group's concerns are usually justifiable, linked to resources, reputations, and an understandable reluctance to be misrepresented or sued due to the actions of a bunch of wild artists. Creative activism that is not directly tied to a social-movement organization may be free of restrictions, but is often distanced from a specific set of goals by which achievement can be measured. However, autonomous projects that do not answer to a union or environmental nonprofit organization enjoy the freedom to develop through experiment and uncensored imagination.

Inside the system versus outside the system

Activists argue about whether to work within or outside of the system of institutions and structures of power. Even Lenin suggested that the Bolsheviks participate in elections to the Tsar's Duma, an advisory body that was hardly democratic. Did Vladimir Ilyich not see the cooptative nature of the Duma, or the dangers of lending legitimacy to the Tsarist system by participating in it? Of course he did—but he noted that the Duma could still be a valuable platform for radical, disruptive, and denunciatory oratory. If elected Bolshevik Duma deputies were kicked out for their radical speech, so much the better. You don't have to be a Leninist to see his point: if there is an opportunity in society where participation can open up conversations or perspectives, it should be considered. Remembering that there is no purity in a dynamic and chaotic universe, we must remain flexible and look for openings where the mix of risks and rewards is tolerable and leans mainly in our favor.

Example: The parable of Sartre and Fo

This is the story of two radical writers and artists, both of whom were awarded the Noble Prize for Literature: Jean-Paul Sartre in 1964, and Dario Fo in 1996. Sartre refused the award; Fo accepted it.

Sartre already had a strict policy of not accepting official awards. He wanted readers to judge his work on its own merits and not to be influenced by prestigious institutional endorsements. Although he respected the institutional body, as a socialist he did not want to accept an award from a body that had become associated with the West in the Cold War. He did not want to be "rehabilitated" and "forgiven" for his radical politics, and accepted back into the capitalist fold. Even though he was unlikely to be coopted by this prestigious award, Sartre was concerned his reputation would be compromised. He refused the award and its substantial prize money (250,000 Swedish crowns), albeit regretting that he wouldn't be able to donate this sum to a good cause such as the Apartheid Committee of London (Sartre, 1964).

Dario Fo, on the other hand, accepted the award. The Vatican formally complained when his award was announced—noting that he had written many "dubious" plays that bitterly ridiculed the church's authority, along with the state, capitalism, and even reformist social democracy. Fo was every bit as radical as Sartre. Yet he donned a tuxedo, bowed to the Swedish King, gave a clever and gracious acceptance speech, and donated most of the $1 million prize to children's causes, and the defense fund of three political prisoners whose plight he had taken up in one of his plays (Bohlen, 1997). Why did Fo trade with an establishment that he had battled for most of his life? Perhaps he felt he could accept the prize without being coopted, and leverage its prestige and remuneration for the support of his causes.

I'm not choosing sides. These examples provoke us to think about the larger question of what is at stake in an issue, and whether our interests are better served by working inside or outside of the systems of authority. We are, after all, tactical agents, and not strategic powers. We must be flexible, and use our best judgment, particularly since we live in a world where there is no purity or higher Platonic Forms. Indeed, the Nobel Prize dilemma underscores how flexibility and well-exercised judgment can result in diametrically opposed actions that serve a common cause. Sartre felt too much was at stake in the Cold War for him to join the West symbolically, and he may have been right. Fo may also have been right at a later time and in different circumstances when he calculated that his causes stood to gain more than would be lost by his acceptance of the award.

Proactive versus reactive

When considering the affects of an action by an artist–activist, much depends on whether it is proactive or reactive. Reactive tactical performances make incursions into or react to the scheduled events of opponents, such as protests during the annual assembly of global powerbrokers like the World Trade Organization (WTO) and Group of Twenty (G20). There are reasons for this kind of protest. Such events draw media coverage, which protestors can poach to draw attention to their movements and worldviews. Turning a WTO meeting into a "WTF?" experience might accomplish activist ends. However, it may be helpful for practitioners of tactical performance to examine if they are too consistently reactive, seeing opportunities only in gatherings of strategic opponents and spending massive resources to fly thousands of activists to the opponent's well-guarded and isolated meeting places. Such a strategy can lead to redundancy, clichéd action, and dwindling public interest.

There is another problem with these protests. The authorities know you are coming. Predictability is dangerous, and groups protesting at these events will confront massive fortification, legal battles, infiltration, and preemptive arrest.

Sometimes it is better tactically to be proactive—to create an action of your own choice, ground, and terms. This may involve infiltration of the strategic power's hometurf when uninvited and unexpected. A classic example of this kind of action is the guerrilla musical created by the Billionaires for Wealthcare (B4W), a spinoff group of Billionaires for Bush. B4W wanted to advocate for a "public option" to be included in the Affordable Healthcare Act—a government-run healthcare program that would compete with private programs without replacing them. Americans would have a choice between this public option and the many private healthcare corporate plans, and this would provide the opportunity for competition between paradigms for the hopeful improvement of both. But how to call greater public attention to this complicated policy issue without spending tremendous money on ad campaigns?

Example 1: The guerrilla musical

October 2009, Washington DC: The America's Health Insurance Plans conference. Republican pollster Bill McInturff is about to give his speech laying out strategies for fighting the passage of Obamacare. McInturff is a well-respected strategist who led the successful effort to torpedo Hillary Clinton's attempts to reform the American healthcare system. As he is just beginning his speech, a voice from the back (Andrew Boyd's) yells out "Thank you for all the good work you do!" McInturff demurs good-naturedly, and then a woman stands up, says "No, thank YOU!" and begins singing, with a clear and strong musical-theatre quality voice, to the tune of "Tomorrow" from the musical *Annie*:

> **For killing the public option**
> **And crushing any hope of its adoption**
> **Thank you sir!**

The spectators laugh, perhaps thinking this is a fun demonstration of affection from a supporter. However, a man stands up now and sings the counter-voice to this positive avowal of love:

> **But what about competition?**
> **It's an old American tradition**
> **So I've heard . . .**

Something is clearly going on here. The security guards begin to move towards the singers, but we have established a sing-aloud argument in classic musical-theatre tradition. Now a third singer stands. How many singers are there? What's going on here?

> **SINGER 3: When Olympia Snowe**
> **Said no**
> **It croaked? Right?**
> **SINGER 2: No the option's not dead**
> **SINGER 3: Or Red!**
> **SINGER 1 (the "conservative"): Explain! (Who let these people in here?)**

More singers are now standing and joining in with the finale, just as the main singers are being led out by security. The final trill of the final line comes from Singer 1, who has apparently been converted to the progressive cause through the power of song, exactly during her last few moments in the room:

> **ALL: If we get a public option**
> **We can sniff out waste just like a Daschund**
> **Costs come down**
> **SINGER 1: Hey, those "costs" are my profits!**
> **ALL: The option!**
> **The option!**
> **The public wants options**
> **Without it it's a give-away**
> **SINGER 1: Right! To us! Am I in the right room?**
> **ALL: The option!**

The option!
The public wants options
Without it it's a corporate give-a-waaaaaaaaay!!!! ”

One small suggestion I gave was that the first singing voice had to be a positive one—heralding McInturff as a personal hero and savior. Why? Because this sacred and special moment, this first moment of the Holy Weird in which someone stands up and starts belting out a song during a closed corporate meeting, was precious and could not be squandered. If someone stands up and starts denouncing the speaker, security guards and viewers recognize the theatre as "protest" and begin instantly to shut it down. However, starting with an unexpected reversal created a moment of synaptic misfire in which the minds of viewers wondered—What is happening here?—before recognizing the action as a protest. "Well, maybe this woman really does love her hero so much she wrote a funny song for him," many might have thought. This confusion provided just enough time for the song to be completed before security escorted out the singing activists, creating a charming and good-humored spectacle for the television audience later.

The performers used social camouflage, which simply means they dressed and groomed for the part. Counterculture signifiers such as tattoos, alternative clothes, or piercings can undermine blending-in during this kind of action. It is a matter of choosing the right costume for the success of a performance. This is not a universally fair concept, and in a racist society those who present as white have easier access to social camouflage. In this case, the performers all looked corporate and normative, and it worked.

Of course, some of the socially camouflaged activists never revealed themselves. They stayed in the role of amused and confused conference-goers, and started to film the musical from different angles on their smartphones as if out of personal interest. After the event was over and the singers had been ejected, they sauntered out, and downloaded and edited their footage, before sending it to major media outlets in time for nightly news broadcasts. Sending out preedited video improves the chances that it will be aired since the final product will be clean and amusing, and media workers need do little with it before broadcast.

This was certainly the case for "Public Option Annie." The video that resulted from the action described above appeared on MSNBC, CNN, and other media outlets, along with running commentary. CNN host Wolf Blitzer thoughtfully introduced the segment with a few seconds of the "real" Annie singing the "real" song to provide a cultural cue to viewers (*Billionaires for Wealthcare*, 2009). Rachel Maddow of MSNBC is visibly amused throughout her Annie segment, quoting her favorite line of the song, chuckling, and offering asides throughout (*Liberals Sing Opera,* 2009). The lesson is: if you can amuse media gatekeepers, you have a much better chance of being covered.

Some background information: the original plan was to use an entirely original song for the action. It was only in the last few days of the secret planning that the collective decided that it was much better to simply take a song that was universally known, change the lyrics, and roll with it. Tactically it was the right choice—one that draws deeply on the history of oppositional performance, echoing the time-tested methods of the Industrial Workers of the World, who changed the lyrics of well-known church and folks songs to support their One Big Union. You can go back much further: to the Middle Ages when peasants during carnival changed the lyrics of hymns, making them subversive and irreverent. The advantage is that of attraction, using the cultural momentum that the popular song has already earned—everyone instantly "gets it," and can hum along. The transgression of invading a private space with an opposite political ideology, and then delivering a transgressive reworking of a beloved song, provides the *frisson* necessary to get past the barrier, earn a moment, and make a point to a much larger viewing audience than would otherwise be possible.

The public option was not included in the Affordable Healthcare Act, which was passed after an immense political battle. Nevertheless, "Public Option Annie" provides a useful example of the guerrilla musical at work. By using playful transgression, proactive tactics, and well-executed theatrics, this project grabbed a lot of attention for its cause while using minimal resources. As action organizer Marco Ceglie noted, it also demonstrated a flattering contrast in image between the movement and its opponents. This joyful and fun image of progressives with good pipes cheerily singing witty lyrics was designed to evoke negative recent images of enraged, combative Tea Partiers shouting down, threatening, and spitting at their opponents. The main strength of this piece was its proactive nature—it did not simply go to an expected spot, but chose its own time and place, and made a surprising intervention.

A far more somber example of proactive action is the "patrols" conducted by Iraq Veterans Against the War (IVAW). Conducted in major American cities, these patrols had an electrifying effect, and were highly effective because the activists acted on their own terms, non-violently ambushing the public. IVAW is a group of military veterans and active-service members who organize support for veterans, and mobilized opposition to the Iraq War and occupation.[27] IVAW provides a strong example of proactive tactical performance. They create their own events at the location, date, and time of their choosing, all coordinated to make their point.

Example 2: IVAW and Grandmothers for Peace

While IVAW has done a wide range of actions across the US, I focus here on the street theatre they designed to increase public awareness about the realities of the war. In New York, San Francisco, and many other major cities, IVAW has staged "patrols" in full battle gear, minus the guns. They move in squad formation according to their actual training and experience: they shout, "aim" and "fire," fall victim to the enemy, and retrieve and carry their wounded comrades. Civilian supporters, acting as "plants in the audience," play the part of the "prisoners" who are forced to kneel or lie down, and be bound, blindfolded, and have plastic bags put over their heads. Sometimes IVAW squads carry them away. Called Operation First Casualty (*IVAW Takes Manhattan*, 2007), these actions represent visceral experiences of urban guerrilla warfare to a sheltered public. Conducted on crowded shopping days in San Francisco's trendy Union Square, downtown Washington, and Times Square, these patrols give the public a small, diluted taste of what it might be like to live under military occupation (Montgomery, 2009). IVAW de-romanticizes war by exposing citizens to its reality—demonstrating instead of describing, and performing rather than making speeches.[28]

There is one Brechtian element to these performances: the lack of actual or even replica guns. The veteran's uniforms and behavior are authentic, but using empty-hand, stiff-armed gestures instead of guns serves several purposes. Firstly, it prevents armed and deadly police response, and panic from the civilian audience. Secondly, it creates a strange moment of cognitive dissonance, or synaptic misfire that stimulates thought. What is going on here? They're not actual soldiers. They can't be because they're lacking the most important thing soldiers have—their rifles. So what are they doing? Their aim is to encourage people to think, not to harm or terrify them.

The IVAW draws credibility from the authenticity of their combat experience; they are actual veterans who, in many cases, have sacrificed more for their country than critics who brand dissidents as unpatriotic. They have put their lives on the line in war, and do the same in the name of peace.[29]

IVAW's authenticity as war veterans offers some protection against recrimination. Similarly, Grandmothers for Peace were able to disrupt the military's recruitment process effectively and with a measure of safety because their members are revered and elderly. The Grandmothers for Peace, also known as the Grannies, are a group of women senior citizens who were opposed to the Iraq War. On 17 October 2005, they presented themselves at the high-profile military recruiting station at Times Square, New York City, to enlist in the army. Their declared intention: they did not want any more young Americans to die in a wrongful war, and since they were closer to death of natural causes, they offered to sacrifice themselves instead. The military recruiters refused to let them in, and when they sat down on the entry ramp, the police arrested them (Shepard, 2008). News coverage of the arrest and subsequent trial helped spread word of the Grannies' action and their opposition to the war.

The Clown Army performed a similar action in Oakland in the US, and in Leeds in the UK; swarming recruiting stations and clownishly volunteering to enlist. In both actions, after being ejected from the premises, they set up their own Clown Army recruiting stations with a cardboard box and a misspelled banner in front of the actual recruiting station, causing the military recruiters to shut down for the day rather than endure ridicule. Arguably, the Grannies' action was even more effective. They did not fit the mold of the typical protester or absurdist street performer. By earnestly leveraging their own identities as elderly women and choosing a high-profile location for their action, the Grannies made a conspicuous intervention with few resources. Of course, the Grannies exploited their identity for tactical purposes, much like the Madres of the Plaza de Mayo in Argentina (Hernandez, 2012).

Hybridity

Hybridity is the sweet spot of artistic activism. Occupy space, and open it up to playful participation. Coordinate a "combined forces" campaign with the air power of theatrical spectacles combined with ground-power campaigns to yield maximum benefit. Think about the two-handed strategy of the eco-anarchist Dutch group, the Kabouters or "Gnomes." With one hand they provoked and critiqued the old oppressive order, while with the other hand they helped to build a new and better society.

Measuring efficacy in tactical performance: how many widgets of social change did we make today?

A metric of efficacy in any creative action is elusive, and this is troubling. How can we help social movements win if we can't measure the impact of different tactics? This isn't a science, and often the data is qualitative rather than quantitative. The success of some actions are more recognizable than others, depending on your goals. For example, if the aim is to change the conversation around an issue in the mass media, then a media survey before, during, and after your action will provide insight. Yet activists usually lack the funding to run polls and surveys to test how their actions have affected the outlook and behavior of consumers, voters, or other groups. However, we can at least have the goal of measurement in mind, and we can acknowledge several definitions of efficacy. To complicate matters, success is not always about direct victory—the dictator steps down, the corporation divests, or the law is passed.

Outside of rare situations where there is clear victory or defeat, it is even more difficult to measure the efficacy of a tactical performance.[30] The regulation of public protest and the privatization of public space as privately owned malls replace America's increasingly mythical Main Street makes tactical performance a necessary aspect of the progressive movement in the US. Tactical performance remains a vital avenue progressives can use to surprise and engage their fellow citizens and stimulate public dialogue with creativity and visions of a better world. Tactical performance effectively spoke truth to power during the Bush regime, and has pressed for progressive social change under the Obama administration in the same way the Federal Theatre Project operated during the FDR Presidency. To those who fear that playful, activist street performance trivializes complex issues, I would reply that our mantra is: "serious but not solemn."[31] Satirizing figures and structures of power spans the history of civilization. Sometimes you need to take a situation seriously enough to make fun of it.

Alternative efficacy definition #1: The choir needs love too

One of the central arguments against radical street performance is that it "preaches to the choir." This criticism endures in the face of countless creative actions that entered contested spaces and engaged, and possibly converted, countless citizens who were opposed, uncommitted, or neutral to the issues at hand. But creative performative dissent is still valuable even among those who are already sympathetic to the performers. A committed and joyful group action can create energized networks for future campaigns. These performances enable activists to create visions of the world they are striving for, and not just to illustrate the conditions they oppose. Social movements need shared worldviews and agendas, and they thrive on shared stories and folklore. Outrageous events and the stories they spawn serve a significant purpose within movements—bonding people through shared risks and absurd experiences, and facilitating the recruitment of new members by making activism joyous, creative, and participatory.

Alternative efficacy definition #2: Performing coalition on the site of conflict

Beyond winning policy victories, tactical performance can help to expand social networks of activists through risky and dramatic experience. It can help to build coalitions between groups with different interests, as they put themselves on the line at conflict sites in true performances of solidarity. When the drag queens of Church Ladies for Choice performed satirical pieces at abortion clinics, their work achieved several results. Firstly, they burst the bubble of terror and shame carefully crafted by anti-abortion protesters. Secondly, they raised the morale of clinic workers enduring these protests (Cohen-Cruz, 1998: p. 90–99). But they also made a public display of solidarity right on the picket line, between themselves and the women confronted by protestors as they tried to gain entry into clinics. These activists proclaimed a clear nonverbal message: we are different, and we have different personal issues, but we have a common opponent—the fundamentalist extreme right—and we are here to stand (and even kick-line dance) with you. This use of performance to unify diverse forces is crucial in our global justice movement, a movement of many different movements, with its slogan of "One No, Many Yeses"—a mantra that unifies without undermining diversity.

Alternative efficacy #3: Modeling creative, engaged citizenship

Nonviolent creative civil disobedience mixes the strategies of Mahatma Gandhi and Martin Luther King with Harpo and Groucho Marx.

The resulting brew is complex and potent. The tragicomic slapstick of creative civil disobedience, with repressive authorities unwittingly assuming the role of Punch, also plays a part in the carnival. Even beyond creating converts for collective action, civil disobedience has the profound potential to model citizenship—citizenship with a small "c" that is creative, active, informed, involved, and willing to spend time and energy to shape the policies of a republic. Groups such as ACT UP and the Yes Men demonstrate that citizenship entails more than production, consumption, or voting. Their performances show that it can be fulfilling, empowering, and even enjoyable to throw oneself into an action in an effort to interrupt the hegemonologue of a corporation or a government.

The culture of apathy is sustained by a passive, subliminal culture of fear—fear of "the Man," sanction, fine, imprisonment, "getting on a list," and even ridicule. These fears are sometimes justified, and to be fair the experiences of some radical street performers have confirmed those fears. But for others, fear itself is combatted through energetic, creative, and disruptive defiance. Another mode of citizenship is possible—indeed another world is possible—and the former can lead to the latter. Mass performance stretches the range of imagined behavior in public space. In a society in which public space is increasingly privatized and regulated, this alone is a valuable service. Ironic street performance, in which the performers say one thing and mean another, calls on a deeper democratic concept—the potential of citizens to create, rather than simply consume. Ironic work calls on the unsuspecting passersby to decode, engage, and actively get the joke—and maybe even to banter back. It answers hegemonologue with dialogue.

The very different but contemporaneous activist–theorists Guy Debord and Augusto Boal each expressed a desire for a more participatory and playful life, both for its own sake and for breaking down oppressive structures. Debord denounced the "society of the spectacle," and Boal called for disempowered spectators in society to become "spect-actors." J.C. Scott (2014) recently called for "anarchist calisthenics" in everyday life; creative participation in tactical performance may help to build the existential muscle mass necessary for more autonomy.

There are many more definitions of efficacy. I hope that the reader will contribute his or her own definition to any discussion that this book may help to spark.

A quick guide to this book's infrastructure

The rest of this book is laid out as follows:

Part I: The Question of Carnival

1 *Chapter 1: Tactical Carnival: dialogism and social movements*
Demonstration is such a common aspect of activism that it has become the form by which a social movement presents itself to the public. This can be detrimental to the movement since many aspects of demonstrations are clichéd and alienating to a general audience. That problem has inspired a celebration of the idea of "carnivalesque protest," drawing on the oft-quoted theory of Mikhail Bakhtin. This chapter criticizes conventional demonstration and the oversimplified deployment of Bakhtin's carnivalesque, illustrating how new movements may become just another clichéd and ineffective form.
Bakhtin's medieval carnival "had no footlights" or distinctions between the masses and the performers. However, the footlights are now global and digital, and all is seen as performance for an audience. Can this still be considered carnival? And if not, is that theoretical elision or confusion a flaw that impacts the entire practice of current "carnivalesque" protest?
This chapter looks at examples of both conventional and "carnivalesque" demonstrations, theorizing the form of a third genre—innovative, surprising, unapologetically performative, and confrontational, but participatory and dialogically conversant and engaged with movements around the world.
2 *Chapter 2: Clownfrontation and clowndestine maneuvers: the Clown Army and the irresistible image*
A critical–ethnographic examination of the key case study of the Clandestine Insurgent Rebel Clown Army (CIRCA), a historical meme and organization, from its founding in 2003 to the present moment. As a co-founder of the group, I examine its founding concept and theory, internal dynamics, and development over time. CIRCA was infiltrated by the police in the UK after its first year of action, but it also successfully intervened in a slew of actions, and in some cases influenced the public conversation around issues of globalization and climate disaster. It was a flawed project, but one worthy of examination.

Part II: The Struggle for Public Space: Outflanking authority, upstaging the establishment

3 *Chapter 3: Reclaim the Streets: tactical interaction and urban mallification/mollification in New York City*
An inside-out examination of the group Reclaim the Streets (RTS) in New York City, of which I was a member. RTS engaged in street theatre, unpermitted street parties, and a creative cat-and-mouse game with the police for ten years. It contested public space for protest and launched prefigurative gestures for a more humane and sustainable city. Under pressure and infiltration, the group morphed, changing its tactics over the years. I follow those moves with a critical eye. RTS championed important issues of urban life, such as gentrification, zoning, and the protection of parks and gardens from corporate development (newly relevant given the major protest movement provoked in Turkey by the state's attempt to destroy a park). A study of RTS also sheds light on the relationship between movements and police, the fraught relationship between activists and local communities, the politics of social-movement groups, creative planning methods, the importance of using masks, and how the law is often selectively enforced.

4 *Chapter 4: Breaking Conventions, Breaking into Conventions (From the WTO to WTF?)*
Beginning with a tactical examination of the vast and diverse protests around the Republican National Convention (RNC) in New York City in 2004, this chapter opens a larger conversation about the pros and cons of protesting at large corporate or state events such as the RNC, the Democratic National Committee (DNC), the World Trade Organization (WTO), and the International Monetary Fund (IMF). The 2004 RNC protests were a classic example of a local victory that did not change the result of the national election. This chapter discusses the performative strategies of the Republican Party as well as the groups that made up the Counter Convention, and evaluates which actions were successful and which failed. Ultimately, the reactive nature of convention protests is examined in a larger, global sense.

Part III: Eschew Cliché!: on the value of surprise

5 *Chapter 5: Critical Simulacra and Tricknology: Oil Enforcement Agents, Yes Men, and Survivaballs*

An exploration of the advantages of playful surprise, impersonation, imaginary regulatory agencies, and Swiftian technology that preserves the wealthy in the event of eco-collapse. (The technology is a Survivaball™, a globe that surrounds a person with a personal ecosphere, and costs only $4 million.) I provide a behind-the-scenes view of the creation of these media spectacles as a practitioner, writer, and performer, and celebrate their dramatic impact. However, I also note their limitations as media spectacles that merely complement a successful campaign's efforts. A non-violent social-justice campaign, I argue, benefits greatly from this kind of surprising and playful symbolic action, in the same way that a military campaign benefits from air power. However, along the same metaphorical line, without a "ground game" of community organizing, these spectacles cannot provide a victory all by themselves.

6 *Chapter 6: All the News We Hope to Print: the creation and mass distribution of progressive prank papers*
An account of the creation of several major prank newspapers: a fake *New York Times*, *New York Post*, and *International Herald Tribune*. The theory, tactics, and techniques of these three projects are examined in this chapter. Although they all looked the same and successfully stimulated policy debate and attention to social problems, they were all quite different in rhetoric, legal strategy, goals, and distribution tactics. All three had strengths and weaknesses that I will elucidate. These case studies open up larger questions concerning the advantages of prefigurative, hopeful projects versus Swiftian dystopic ones (such as the aforementioned Survivaballs).

Part IV: Serious but Not Solemn

7 *Chapter 7: Crisis In Califorlornia: creative protest at the University of California*
A case study examining the role of creativity, theatrics, satire, and irony in the student protests that happened in my own university system during the recent budget and tuition crisis.

8 *Conclusion: earning moments for the movement*
An overview of the principles and theories laid out in the previous chapters, this chapter will also point towards the new developments and directions for tactical performance. These developments include the use of game theory to outmaneuver authorities, and the creation of actual games—radical participatory video games and role-playing games.

We will first examine that staid staple of social-movement performance; the public demonstration. How have our predecessors and contemporaries experimented to renew that now predictable form, and make it surprising, exciting, and inspiring again?

Notes

1 However, recently restrictions have tightened for unions in the US. They are not allowed even to directly advocate boycotts or "secondary boycotts."
2 In the recent movie, *Selma* (2015), a fictionalized Dr King acknowledges to his SNCC rivals and allies that his group uses "drama" as part of an overall strategy.
3 The movement, influenced by the training methods of "New Gandhians" such as James Lawson, worked with both the idea of "ahimsa" or passive resistance, and "satyagraha" or more active and interventionist pacifism. "Creative disruption" and above all "disciplined disruption" of everyday structural oppression were considered vital.
4 This action can range from donating resources to the movement, to lobbying, to actual front-line participation; its impact is to provoke masses of people, in a wide range of ways, to act on behalf of the cause.
5 For Martin Luther King's own comments about the need to dramatize issues, see *The Papers of Martin Luther King, Jr.* (2005: p. 434). On civil rights performance discipline, see Lewis (1999) and *Citizen King* (2004).
6 For example, the movement benefited from Dr King's prominence as a leader, orator, and powerfully symbolic figure, but often local leaders thought their efforts were eclipsed and even sidetracked when King came to their cities.
7 John Lewis, a congressman who was a member of the Nashville Student Movement, renders this pledge of conduct with only slight variations. "DO NOT: 1. Strike back nor curse if abused. 2. Laugh out. 3. Hold conversations with floor walkers. 4. Leave your seat until your leader has given you permission to do so. 5. Block entrances to stores outside or the aisles inside. DO: 1. Show yourself friendly and courteous at all times. 2. Sit straight; always face the counter. 3. Report all serious incidents to your leader. 4. Refer information seekers to your leader in a polite manner. 5. Remember the teachings of Jesus Christ, Mahatma Gandhi and Martin Luther King. Love and nonviolence is the way. MAY GOD BLESS EACH OF YOU" (Lewis, 1999: p. 98). Another version of the discipline reads similarly: "No aggression, no retaliation. No loud conversation, no talking of any kind with anyone other than ourselves. Dress nicely. Bring books, schoolwork, letter-writing materials. Be prepared to sit for hours. Study, read, write. Don't slouch. No napping. No getting up, except to go to the bathroom, and then be sure there is a backup to fill your seat while you're away. Be prepared for arrest. Be prepared to be taken to jail" (Lewis, 1999: p. 93).
8 Interestingly, while groups trained at important centers like the Highlander Center in Tennessee for these actions, and prepared to launch them in a coordinated manner, the sit-ins were actually launched by four black men in Greensboro, North Carolina. They had not prepared or trained but

spontaneously chose to sit in on 1 February 1960. This took civil rights organizers by surprise, but fortunately they were prepared and were able to follow this brave and spontaneous act with the coordinated campaign as planned (Lewis, 1999: p. 91–92).

9 Indeed, this presents the *cute cat for progressive causes viral meme problem*. Sometimes a video carefully constructed by activists to spread on the internet gets a few thousand hits, while a simple video of a cute cat doing cute things attracts millions of views. The challenge becomes: how to create something as appealing as the cute cat, to harness that virality for a progressive cause? Or do politics inherently make a video less likely to become viral? Can we radicalize the cute cat? The experiment continues.

10 Hoffman's life story serves as an example of the "air war" and "ground war" duality in activism. Having been a showboat prankster for the New Left for many years, he was arrested on a drug charge and went underground from 1974 to 1980; during this time he changed his name to Barry Freed and became a hardworking, door-to-door organizer in upstate New York in the ultimately successful drive to save the Saint Lawrence River. Hoffman lived both sides of this duality—high-flying cultural pranks and grassroots organizing, and his perspective for activism deepened in the last years of his life.

11 The Kabouters, who won five seats in the Amsterdam City Council in 1970, found it difficult to reconcile countercultural grassroots action and practical engagement with state power.

12 "Birddogging" refers to the relentless pursuit of a targeted official, so that wherever they go—around the nation or even the world—the protest follows them.

13 Steve Kurtz:

> The oldest contradiction of the avant garde is: how do you pay for what you're doing? The only place you can get money is from the very infrastructure you're criticizing and trying to change and sometimes to topple. That's the downside. It's harder when you're younger, but then when you get older it's easier because you realize how complicit you are. Complicity time is a huge slice of your pie and resistant time is this tiny sliver, which you're always trying to increase. If you drink coffee, if you flush the toilet, you're complicit in energy and water policy. You're enveloped in the system. And then you go to work, I don't even want to talk about that! But when you accept complicity, see it clearly, it becomes an enabling moment. Then you can grow that resistant bit of the pie chart that's working in a different direction. Going to the different institutions, now you can say we're talking about a negotiation. We rarely get big art grants, or we get one-time ones like Cultural Capital. So you go and negotiate with the institutions. It took us a while to build up the cachet for this. We have a lot of social capital now, they want that, and we want their economic capital. We try to get as much as we can get. They want an alibi for being a democratic and not elitist institution. Any minoritarian artist has to deal with that. It gives them cover. That's what you're trading. You just have to evaluate the trade each time and decide, is it worth it? We can go in, come out with a lot

> of capital and then redistribute it. That's how we pay for these projects. We extracted the institution's money and redeploy it. We get legitimation as well, social capital. It cycles. So you can continue to find ways.
> (Kurtz, 2014)

14 Interview with the author, 3 December 2014. All other quotes from Conant are from this interview.
15 Here, "policy" refers to the policies of states, corporations, and other strategic institutions.
16 The seizure of Alcatraz actually had some legal basis. The federal government had declared it surplus property in 1963, and the 1868 Treaty of Fort Laramie stated unused federal land would be returned to native peoples. If nothing else, invoking this treaty revealed once again that the US government has a consistent record of ignoring treaties signed with native peoples.
17 The occupation resonates through the years. Native Americans still host an "unthanksgiving" sunrise ritual on the island at dawn on every Thanksgiving, with permits from the government.
18 Their website can be viewed at: www.storybasedstrategy.org
19 The symbolism of the Boston Tea Party endures even though many current patriots would not approve of breaking and entering and felony property damage in defiance of the state. In fact, the US government has recently increased the punishment for this activity under the Patriot Act and RICO (the Racketeer Influenced and Corrupt Organizations) statutes. Some activists have received longer jail sentences for property damage under these laws than they might have received for manslaughter.
20 This story is such a strong example it is discussed in Ben Shepard's *Play, Creativity, and Social Movements* (2011), *Beautiful Trouble* (Boyd & Mitchell, 2012a), and *No Billionaire Left Behind* (Haugerud, 2013).
21 Interview with the author, 24 March 2009. All other quotes from Jenna Hunt are from this interview.
22 See Boyd & Mitchell (2012b).
23 Conservative activist James O'Keefe secretly recorded interactions with public figures in campaigns, purportedly to reveal illegal activities. In 2009, his undercover recordings with members of ACORN seemed to implicate them in criminal activity. However, he had actually edited them in a way that completely fabricated a false impression and in fact no such conversations had taken place. Despite ACORN's good work, public and private funding for it dried up and the organization was driven to bankruptcy. O'Keefe was later arrested for his rogue surveillance activities. An investigation by the California Attorney General's office absolved ACORN of any illegalities.
24 Lenin said: "we must strive to be as radical as reality itself." Had he lived up to that slogan, he may have been less authoritarian and more willing to accept ideas from rivals. Ultimately, his mark on history might have been less tragic.
25 A similar parallel is used in American football, with passing referred to as the "air game," and running as the "ground game." Conventional electoral commentators sometimes use these terms to refer to television commercials versus door-knocking tactics, etc.

26 Sarah Sobieraj expounds convincingly on the danger of overemphasis on media-centered activism in her book *Soundbitten* (2011).
27 See the IVAW webpage at: http://ivaw.org/
28 Other creative actions by IVAW include: carpeting a gas station with thousands of toy soldiers, one for each American casualty; "occupying" the US Archives Building; and "freezing" en masse in Union Station, Washington D.C. (*Iraq War Veterans Raid Gas Station*, 2008).
29 Indeed, one protestor was charged and trampled (a hoof crushed part of his face) by a mounted policeman while protesting outside one of the political debates of the 2008 presidential campaign.
30 Steve Kurtz of CAE has an incisive take on the issue of efficacy:

> First of all, there's the microperspective—qualitative standards, we don't use quantitative, scale is not our issue, ours is the quality of the experience for the people we deal with. If they're engaged we say we did a great project. If you had to put a number on it, the amount of time a person usually spends on an artwork is 20 seconds, or a video installation—about two minutes! We did a lot of research on that. You have to keep the video installations to short length. If people are hanging around, 10, 20, 30 minutes or coming back, we know we are reaching them. This worked with Free Range Grains, and Flesh Machine, and Cult of the New Eve. With Flesh Machine, people stayed all night, they were engaged, they were actively figuring it out. That's a success, qualitatively. If it's 10, 100, 200 people, it doesn't matter to us. On the macrolevel—this is where it gets all messed up. This is where the individualist philosophy gone right wing acts as a sabotaging force—"You alone are responsible for changing a cultural dynamic or huge institution." No artwork has ever done that. Ever! This is a way to corral people and put them in a place of inaction. As if the only way you can change things is by how you consume and how you vote. And to think a single artwork can change things is absurd, ridiculous—it's all about what the *aggregates* of cultural action do *over time*. It depends what the *whole movement* does, the collective action. That's how you judge whether you're contributing. Not as one little action. I give a salute to the sixties not a lot for things but—I do for one thing—for work like that of the Situationists, the Diggers, and the Provos. They understood that you cannot have a political movement without a cultural movement. If you're going to get that movement train going you have to have both tracks. If you only have one of those tracks, the train ain't gonna run. It's gonna come apart. We're building that cultural track.
>
> (Interview with the author, 20 November 2014)

31 My thanks to Hilary Ramsden for this phrase.

References

Alinsky, Saul (1989) *Rules for Radicals: A pragmatic primer for realistic radicals.* New York: Vintage.

Aristotle ([335 BCE] 1997) *Poetics*. New York: Penguin Classics.

Billionaires for Wealthcare Guerilla Musical "Public Option Annie" on CNN's Situation Room. [Digital video.] YouTube. 27 Oct 2009. www.youtube.com/watch?v=_fZrZbJaVDo

Boal, Augusto (1979) *Theatre of the Oppressed*. Trans. Charles A. and Maria-Odilia Leal McBride. London: Pluto Press.

Bogad, L.M. (2016) *Electoral Guerrilla Theatre: Radical ridicule and social movements*, 2nd edition. London: Routledge.

Bohlen, Celestine (1997) "Italy's Barbed Political Jester, Dario Fo, Wins Nobel Prize." *The New York Times*. 10 Oct 1997. www.nytimes.com/1997/10/10/world/italy-s-barbed-political-jester-dario-fo-wins-nobel-prize.html

Boyd, A.; Mitchell, D.O. (2012a) *Beautiful Trouble: A toolbox for revolution*. New York: OR Books.

Boyd, A.; Mitchell, D.O. (2012b) "Put your Target in a Decision Dilemma." http:beautifultrouble.org/principle/put-your-target-in-a-decision-dilemma (accessed 28 Oct 2015).

Canning, D.; Reinsborough, P. (2010) *Re:Imagining Change: How to use story-based strategy to win campaigns, build movements, and change the world*. Oakland: PM Press.

Citizen King (2004) Documentary Film. Directed by Nolan Walker and Orlando Blagwell. [DVD] US: PBS Home Video.

Cohen-Cruz, Jan (ed.) (1998) *Radical Street Performance*. New York: Routledge.

Conant, Jeff (2010) *A Poetics of Resistance: The revolutionary public relations of the Zapatista insurgency*. Oakland: AK Press.

Critical Art Ensemble (2015) *Tactical Media*. Online Project List. www.critical-art.net/TacticalMedia.html (accessed 15 April 2015).

Crowley, Amanda (2002) *Public Art Action Coalition: Public announcement*. Online 10 Mar 2011. http://publicartaction.net/tarndanyungga/

De Certeau, Michel (1984) *The Practice of Everyday Life*. Trans. Steven Rendall. Berkeley: University of California Press.

Debord, Guy (1995) *The Society of the Spectacle*. Trans. D. Nicholson-Smith. New York: Zone Books.

Duhamel, Philippe; Pearson, Nancy (eds.) (2004) *The Dilemma Demonstration: Using nonviolent civil disobedience to put the government between a rock and a hard place.* Minneapolis: Center for Victims of Torture. www.newtactics.org/en/TheDilemmaDemonstration (accessed 5 Feb 2011).

Fraser, N. (1997) *Justice Interruptus: Reflections on the "postsocialist" condition.* London: Routledge.

Haugerud, Angelique (2013) *No Billionaire Left Behind: Satirical activism in America.* Stanford: Stanford University Press.

Havel, Vaclav (1981) *The Memorandum* [Stageplay]. New York: Grove/Atlantic.

Hernandez, Vladimir (2012) "Argentine Mothers Mark 35 Year Marching for Justice." *BBC News*. 29 Apr 2012. www.bbc.com/news/world-latin-america-17847134

Hudema, M. (2004) *An Action a Day: Keeps global capitalism away*. Toronto: Between the Lines.

HyPE-Speaking for the Dead – Public Health Care NOW! Posted by Marc Pinate. [Digital video] YouTube. 2 Oct 2009. www.youtube.com/watch?v=eMkRIdWyXBE&list=UURWEIBtV63b2Mg56btVNXWg (accessed 6 Feb 2015).

Iraq War Veterans Raid Gas Station. Produced by IVAW. [Digital video] YouTube. 11 Nov 2008. www.youtube.com/watch?v=6nnx2Wv4T1o (accessed 17 Oct 2015).

IVAW Takes Manhattan – Operation First Casualty. Produced by IVAW. [Digital video] YouTube. 31 May 2007. www.youtube.com/watch?v=2WvIaDeNIbk (accessed 19 Oct 2015).

Johnson, Troy R. (1996) *The Occupation of Alcatraz Island: Indian self-determination and the rise of Indian activisim*. Illinois: University of Illinois Press.

Kaufmann, Leslie (2003) "A Short, Personal History of the Global Justice Movement." In E. Yuen, D. Burton-Rose and G. Katsiaficas (eds.), *Confronting Capitalism: Dispatches from a global movement*. Brooklyn: Soft Skull Press.

Kennedy, R. (2014) "The Civil Rights Act's Unsung Victory and How It Changed the South." *Harper's Magazine* (6) p. 39–40.

Kertzer, D.I. (1988) *Ritual, Politics and Power*. New Haven, CT: Yale University Press.

King, Martin Luther (1964) *Why We Can't Wait*. New York: Harper & Row.

King, Martin Luther (2005) *The Papers of Martin Luther King, Jr.: volume V: Threshold of a new decade, January 1959–December 1960*. Clayborne Carson (ed.) Berkeley: Berkeley University Press.

Kurtz, Steve (2014) Interview with the author. 4 Dec 2014.

Lewis, J. (1999) *Walking with the Wind: A memoir of the movement*. New York: Harvest.

Meet the Press. Interview with Martin Luther King. *NBC*. 17 Apr 1960.

Liberals Sing Opera at DC Conference of Health Insurance Billionaires for Wealthcare – Rachel Maddow (2009) [Digital video] www.youtube.com/watch?v=-_fHKgxP6GA&list=PL34A2636E6B32D5EF&index=3 (accessed 20 Oct 2015).

Montgomery, David (2009) "Far From Iraq, A Demonstration of a War Zone." *Washington Post*. 23 July 2009. www.washingtonpost.com/wp-dyn/content/article/2007/03/19/AR2007031901558.html

Oppenheimer, M.; Lakey, G. (1965) *A Manual for Direct Action*. Chicago: Quadrangle Books.

Orwell, George (2003) *Animal Farm*. New York: Houghton Mifflin Harcourt.

Perdomo, Gustavo*; Spencer, David E. (1995) *Strategy and Tactics of the FMLN Guerrillas: Last battle of the Cold War, blueprint for future conflicts*. Prager.

* Gustavo Perdomo was a Colonel in the El Salvadoran Armed Forces, and at first published this book under a pen name, "Jose Angel Moroni Bracamonte."

Plato ([*c.* 380 BCE] 1992) *Republic*. Cambridge: Hackett Classics.
Sartre, Jean-Paul (1964) "Sartre on the Nobel Prize." *The New York Review of Books*. 17 Dec 1964. www.nybooks.com/articles/archives/1964/dec/17/sartre-on-the-nobel-prize/
Scott, J.C. (1985) *Weapons of the Weak: Everyday forms of peasant resistance*. New Haven: Yale University Press.
Scott, J.C. (2014) *Two Cheers for Anarchism: Six easy pieces on autonomy, dignity, and meaningful work and play*. Princeton: Princeton University Press.
Selma (2015) Film. Directed by Ava DuVernay. [DVD] US: Paramount.
Shepard, Benjamin (2008) "Review of Joan Wile's Grandmothers Against the War: Getting off our fannies and standing for peace." *Working USA*. 399401 (11.3).
Shepard, Benjamin (2009) *Queer Political Performance, Protest, and the New Community Organizing*. New York: Routledge.
Shepard, Benjamin (2011) *Play, Creativity, and Social Movements: If I can't dance, it's not my revolution*. New York: Routledge.
Smith, Heather (2014) *In the Protest-Icon Game, Polar Bear Beats Carbon Bubble*. Online 29 Sept 2014. http://grist.org/climate-energy/in-the-protest-icon-game-polar-bear-mask-trumps-carbon-bubble-balloon/
Sobieraj, Sarah (2011) *Soundbitten: The perils of media-centred activism*. New York: New York University Press.
Stanislavsky, K. (2008) *An Actor's Work*. New York: Routledge.
Tarrow, S. (1998) *Power in Movement: Social movements and contentious politics*. New York: Cambridge University Press.

Part I

The question of carnival

Chapter 1

Tactical carnival

Dialogism and social movements

> All Power to the Imagination!
>
> —Situationist International slogan

This chapter examines the most basic social movement performance form: demonstrations in public space. It questions the underlying goals and aesthetics of demonstrations, and posits the possible role of modified forms of Bakhtin's theory of carnival, and Boal's methods of dialogical performance, in the conception and creation of more dynamic and compelling actions. It posits and defines "tactical carnival," and two overlapping modes of public action—"occupying space" and "opening space"—and the pros and cons of using both modular, familiar forms and creative, disruptive, and chaotic forms of protest.

Washington, DC, 26 October 2002: A preemptive peace demonstration, responding to the Bush Administration's call for preemptive war on Iraq, is in progress. Hundreds of thousands have gathered for the largest anti-war demonstration here since the Vietnam War. Although the call to demonstrate was first made by International ANSWER, a group largely run by the Workers' World Party, the massive turnout includes people of many walks of life and worldviews, from all over the country and beyond. This diversity is encouraging for the potential growth of the peace movement.

International ANSWER has organized a very long series of orators, and while thousands of people in this massive rally cannot see the soundstage or hear the speakers, many stand quietly and listen to the amplified oratory, applauding and cheering when moved to do so, while others mill around, chat, and wait for the announcement that the march will begin.

However, at least one troupe of costumed performers called Absurd Response is not listening to the speakers. Instead, they move randomly through the throng, singing, dancing, and improvising with the crowd around them. They walk behind a banner that reads "ABSURD RESPONSE TO AN ABSURD WAR." These are the Perms for Permawar: eight alluring men and women wearing fluorescent colored gowns, opera-length gloves, and two-foot high Marge Simpson-type wigs. Each wig sports a brightly colored letter, which together spells "P-E-R-M-A-W-A-R." The Perms, also known as Bombshells for their glamour and pro-war orthodoxy, lead festive chants such as "We Need Oil! We Need Gas! Watch Out, World, We'll Kick Your Ass!" and "We Love BUSH! We Love DICK! All You Peaceniks Make Us SICK!"

The Bombshells are accompanied by dozens of other characters created around the theme of absurd response. A ghoulish trio, The Spirit of '76 Gone Wrong, costumed in pallid skin, bloody rags, and militarist trappings, carry drum, flute, and flag, which reads "OIL". As the comi-tragic, mute flautist, the gasmask on my face makes it impossible to play, but I keep trying, banging the flute against the air filter on my snout. Gibbering War Clowns bounce and pounce around the perimeter of the procession. A singing, stilt-walking Angel of Death[1] in a red dress hovers above. She plays a squeezebox, and hanging from her neck are a miniature skeleton and a sign reading "Death ♥s W." A slew of Billionaires for Bush are there as well, in their top hats, tuxedos, jewelry, and formal dresses, to ironically support the war effort and cheer their boy "W" onward.

Finally, the speakers on the stage are finished. The enormous march begins, and Absurd Response joins the parade. At one point, we are passed by an International ANSWER sound truck. ANSWER is as one-way in their communicative style as their name suggests. They are heavily amplified, overpowering the voices of those below them, as they shout old, plug-in chants such as "Hey, Hey, Ho, Ho, George Bush Has Got to Go!";"George Bush! You Can't Hide! We Charge You with Genocide!"; and "The People, United, Will Never be Defeated."

There is a palpable clash in style and worldview between Absurd Response, with its irony, satire, multivocality, and even ambiguity, and the monotonous monological chant of the sound truck. Before long, some new call-and-response chants emanate from the Absurd Response contingent, no longer merely mocking the warmongering

White House, but lampooning ANSWER's dogmatic, redundant, unimaginative style. These chants include: "Three Word Chant! (Four Words Are Better!)"; "March March, Chant Chant, Rhetoric Rhetoric, Rant Rant!"; "Bad Slogans, Repeated, Ensure That We're Defeated!"; and my favorite:

> **Hey, Hey, Ho, Ho—"Hey Hey Ho Ho" Has Got To Go!**

The people on the ANSWER sound truck, perhaps unwilling to break their rhythm or come up with a comeback, simply continue their own chants and drive down the street. A brief, instructive disruption has occurred. These groups have clashing approaches to the performance of demonstration, and to the role, if any, of the carnivalesque in protest.

This chapter is an exploration of performance aesthetics and tactics in social-movement activism. It focuses specifically on what social movements are most known for: demonstrations in public space. It draws on the praxis of the global justice movement, specifically in the US and mostly in New York City. This is a local effort meant to open the subject; I am not trying to arrive at final conclusions, nor to write from one locality in a way that creates generalizations about this incredibly diverse, dialogical, and decentralized movement. Finally, a look at social movement theory will help us understand the importance of the public demonstration and where Augusto Boal's Theatre of the Oppressed (TO) fits within the wider range of activist practice, at both planning and execution stages.

Building social movements

A social movement is a network of people engaged in sustained, contentious, collective action, using methods beyond established institutional procedures such as voting (Tarrow, 1998: p. 3). For example, the global justice movement, also known as "globalization from below" (Brecher et al., 2002), or the anti-globalization movement by its detractors, seeks to oppose the disastrous effects of corporate globalization while building progressive, constructive, and dialogical connections between the people of the world. Performance, both public and private, is a key element in the formation, sustenance, and building of such social movements.

Hidden transcripts and the cycle of contention

Movements often form slowly, through the daily building of social networks, a growing awareness of a collective complaint, and an increasingly articulated conceptual frame for taking action. Even in periods of repression, people can build networks for potential social movements through the clandestine creation and nurturing of a "hidden transcript" (Scott, 1990). Hidden transcripts are the highly articulated and stealthily nurtured worldview and grievance list of the oppressed. They are the stories, rumors, complaints, and utopian visions that a subculture or counterculture keeps alive for the historical moment when, because of shifts in political opportunities and constraints, substantial mass liberatory action becomes possible. While Scott refers in his work to truly abject and dominated people in total regimes such as slavery or medieval serfdom, the idea of a less hidden but still separate and partially coded transcript still applies in the development of social movement narratives in more open societies.

Alternative worldviews need an alternative space in which to be developed and shared. Nancy Fraser argues that the oppressed create "subaltern counterpublics" as an alternative to the dominant bourgeois public sphere because they need:

> [V]enues in which to undertake communicative processes that were not, as it were, under the supervision of the dominant group . . . to articulate and defend their interests . . . [and] to expose modes of deliberation that mask domination by absorbing the less powerful into a false "we" that reflects the more powerful.
>
> (Fraser, 1997: p. 81)

Through this communicative process, counterpublics can develop a collective action frame, or a way of looking at the world that argues that mass mobilization for struggle is both possible and necessary (Tarrow, 1998: p. 21). The development of sophisticated subaltern counterpublics, including the nurturing of hidden transcripts and/or collective action frames, is a necessary precursor to the launching of a powerful social movement.

An example of this is the development of the civil rights movement in the US. Though locked out of the halls of power and civil society in the South, this movement was able to nurture resistance based in churches, civic organizations, and their own press and allied cultural workers (musicians, artists, theatre-makers, et al.). They also built coalitions across region, race, and class, sustaining their struggle against American apartheid over the course of decades.

A "cycle of contention" begins when the incentives for contentious collective action are raised, and/or when the costs of such action are lowered for various reasons, such as when there is a perceived split in the elites, a weakening of the state's repressive apparatus, or a shift in the relative power of competing or allied forces, encouraging social movements to get active across an entire society (Tarrow, 1998: p. 24–25):

> [C]ontentious politics is triggered when changing political opportunities and constraints create incentives for social actors who lack resources on their own . . . When backed by dense social networks and galvanized by culturally resonant, action-oriented symbols, contentious politics leads to sustained interaction with opponents. The result is the social movement.
>
> (Tarrow, 1998: p. 2)

Social movements cannot preordain a top–down loosening of national policy in order to better facilitate their own actions, but they certainly have the agency to "seize the time" if they perceive a chink in the establishment's order or a Certeauan "occasion." When a historical opportunity for such collective agency presents itself, a cycle of contention may begin. To take advantage of the opportunity and to build group formation and cohesion, activists need to construct a cultural frame or a set of impassioned, shared meanings, which justify and motivate collective action. A cycle of contention gains momentum when social actors perceive that change is desirable, that the risks and costs of movement participation have lessened, and that the chance of victory has grown (Tarrow, 1998: p. 21–24). Without a sense of shared grievance, purpose, and possibility, an effective social movement cannot develop; but that sense of shared meaning, a role in history, and liberatory agency, can sustain resistance even when the tide has turned and danger has increased (Wood, 2003: p. 231–41).

Theatre of the Oppressed (TO) workshops can play a vital role during cycles of contention in helping members of a burgeoning movement to define their issues and explore possible solutions.[2] Whether participants are seasoned activists or people who have never engaged in overt political action, TO's Image Theatre techniques can help bring people together, in a common space, to creatively, nonverbally, and dialogically express and develop their perceptions of their world, power structures, and oppressions. TO's Forum Theatre techniques provide a relatively safe space, protected from the actual ramifications of reactive state repression, to experiment with possible contentious methods. This is oppositional praxis in action. TO's Legislative Theatre methodology can even help a movement to develop a parliamentary agenda. With its myriad variations, this body of practice can assist social movements in developing hidden transcripts and collective action frames.

Boal was not the first to call for decentralized, anti-authoritarian methods for building progressive movements. In fact, various methods of "rehearsing for reality" are a common staple of organizing manuals from way back.[3] However, these manuals generally call for activists to discuss overall strategy, and to role-play and rehearse only the moment of action, public performance, and/or confrontation. For example, nonviolence training teaches activists, through practice, how to stay calm, centered, committed, and nonviolent in the face of harassment or abuse. Theatre of the Oppressed expands the role of radical rehearsal for reality, helping people at any level of political commitment not only to rehearse direct confrontation with the state, but to use improvisatory performance to decide what their problems are, what they want, and what they are able to do about it.

There is a long history of theatre at the service of social movements. But Boal's unique, historic contribution is the inventive synthesis of these traditions with Freirian and anti-Aristotelian theory, and the established theatrical rehearsal techniques of sense-activation, improvisation, trust creation, and ensemble-building.[4] The result is a powerful dialogical tool for building a movement. Boal denounces globalization, not only as a process of economic oppression, but also as the imposition of a top–down monologue upon the entire world. Influenced by Freire, Boal calls for dialogical resistance (Boal, 1998: p. 251): a director or auteur does not dictate the activist performance, but rather a joker facilitates the creative collaboration of a group. Jokering is not unproblematic, of course, but TO strives to minimize hierarchy. In his first book, Boal (1979) articulated the ways in which his theatre consciously resists Aristotelian catharsis. This is ideal for social movements' development of collective action frames and tactical and strategic praxis. A social movement seeks to galvanize, to agitate, and to articulate dissent and dissatisfaction; the purgation of social complaint through catharsis is anathema.

Movements communicate with the greater public by using "culturally resonant, action-oriented symbols" (Tarrow, 1998: p. 2). The challenge with symbols is subtle: if a symbol is too conventional, tame, and general like the national flag, then it will not eloquently communicate the special identities and agenda that the movement wishes to project. However, if a symbol is so avant-garde that it is beyond what Baz Kershaw and others have called the "horizon of expectations"[5] then it will not resonate outside of the ranks of the movement's cognoscenti. The most effective new symbols do not solely evoke established symbolism, nor do they confound understanding. Rather, they stretch the horizon of understanding further; using, inverting, and twisting the given symbolic vocabulary, and challenging conventions while remaining intelligible. One American version of the Gay Pride flag, which uses the pattern of the US flag but changes the thirteen stripes to six rainbow-colored stripes, is an example of a movement symbol that is recognizable yet unique and pointedly eloquent—a "repetition with a critical difference" of an established and widely recognizable sign. This is a symbol of a movement that insists on equality and full citizen rights for its adherents, while publicly defying heterosexist norms. The symbol represents a struggle in the national context and challenges unmarked assumptions of what it means to be American. At the same time, after decades of usage, this same flag, and the Pride Flag in general, has changed in meaning—being used by corporations for pinkwashing marketing campaigns, for example.

The border fence between the US and Mexico has become a grim symbol that must be inverted or subverted in order to energize the movement for immigrant rights. In a large May Day march for immigrant rights in San Francisco, some artful activists mounted a large corrugated metal "border wall" on wheels, and pushed it slowly down the street. It blocked the path of the march, and it moved slower than the marchers—an obstacle! But there was an opening in the fence, and the wall was festooned with slogans such as "Welcome to USA" and "Noone is Illegal." The activists loudly and cheerfully welcomed everyone to "cross the border" through the opening, and hundreds of marchers did. This participatory, playful, mobile art installation acknowledged the border issue and envisioned a reality in which people can move as freely as capital across the NAFTA-deregulated, militarized border where so many have died in the desert.

Creating efficacious movement symbols is a subtle challenge. This includes not only creating logos or images, but crafting and enacting charismatic symbolic actions, and performing movement identity in public demonstrations. Public actions are not only symbolic: they may also have direct impact upon the state or infrastructure. Either way, they inevitably have a symbolic component, and movements should consciously design that element to their advantage.

Figure 1.1 May Day demonstration for immigrant rights, San Francisco. Demonstrators push a "border fence" along the parade route, inviting marchers to pass through the opening in the wall and be welcomed into the US. Photo by L.M. Bogad.

Figure 1.2 The other side of the "border fence." Photo by L.M. Bogad.

Repertoires of contention

The "repertoire of contention" is the set of oppositional tactics that movements creatively accumulate over the course of many struggles (Tarrow, 1998: p. 20–21). These tactics evolve over time as movements interact with their often-hostile environment. Some tactics become outdated; at other times, variations are invented. A new tactic can initially be incredibly disruptive, catching one's opponents by surprise. The first mass demonstration in Tsarist Russia must have been quite a stressful shock to the monarchy, which explains their ill-advised and heavy-handed violent response. The first sit-down strike in the US, by the United Auto Workers in Flint, Michigan in 1936–37, was a powerful innovation in the repertoire of contention and resulted in an important victory for the labor movement; the UAW won recognition and its first contract. Gandhi's philosophy and techniques of nonviolent resistance confounded the British Empire, and the American civil rights movement achieved similar successes with its own version of those techniques. In the US and Europe, the New Left caught their opponents unaware with spectacular, symbolic pranks that disrupted what they saw as the oppressive activity of the state, drew media attention to their social issues, and provoked the imagination and sympathetic ire of many spectators. The Kabouters, for example, broke into many abandoned houses and vacant office buildings across the Netherlands, using whimsical humor in art and street performance to soften the shock of their illegal actions as they squatted in the buildings to protest about the desperate housing shortage. They succeeded in gaining the sympathy of Dutch people of all ages and most classes, who were all affected by this shortage. Eventually, they forced the state to address the housing problem, including the legalization of a number of Kabouter squat-communes (Bogad, 2016). While such tactics can boost the efficacy of social movements, if overused they lose a great deal of their effect. The state develops counter-tactics for containing and minimizing their potency, including what the Dutch Left, quoting Marcuse, bitterly referred to as "repressive tolerance." For this reason, some activists feel that prearranged, routinized civil disobedience arrests have lost much of their bite.[6]

One of the major turns in the history of the repertoire of contention is the development of modular tactics, or tactics that can be transferred across boundaries of context, complaint, location, and identity. The public demonstration is an example, spreading across many national borders and tried by almost every social movement to date. Modular tactics have great utility: when an action is needed, the local groups of a movement across a country, or even internationally, can do the same type of action on the same day. The advantages are not to be underestimated. For example, if a corporation knows that the result of pushing one union too far may be not one local strike, but a national strike with sympathy strikes against their subsidiary firms in other countries, they will think twice before escalating a conflict. Examples of coordinated global modular action include the demonstrations against the US build-up before the invasion of Iraq on 15 February 2003, in which an estimated 10 million people across the world took part; and the Lysistrata Project, in which hundreds of groups in many countries performed the ancient Greek play as an anti-Iraq War statement (see www.lysistrataproject.org). The set of theatre games and methods of the Theatre of the Oppressed can be thought of as a potential modular form of resistance: because books describing the practice have been widely translated and TO centers and groups operate all over the world, TO actions could be launched on several continents at once.

Modular action also carries with it some risk of routinization; it can become reductionist and mechanistic. However modular it may be, an action must be adapted to local needs, dangers, cultures, and legal and sociopolitical contexts. This is reflected in a hard-won bit of wisdom shared among experienced TO jokers and theorists: TO facilitators must remember that TO techniques are meant to serve the local, specific, and ever-changing needs of "spect-actors," and not the other way around. As a modular tactic in the repertoire of resistance, TO remains valid only as long as groups adapt and change its form.

Many activists fall in love with a particular tactic, and start to confuse that increasingly redundant tactic with strategy. As noted in the Introduction, strategies are comprehensive, complex plans for a long-term campaign, projecting power onto space and time; whereas tactics are immediate actions. Tactics can be the building-block elements of a strategy; on the other hand, they may simply be the only options available to a player that lacks strategic power. New tactics need to be constantly innovated to feed a movement's evolving strategy. States and corporations innovate, too! The tactical interaction between social movements and their opponents is an agonistic dance of competing innovation. As one tactic is used, the police may develop another tactic that disrupts or neutralizes that tactic. Yet another tactic will have to be innovated to respond to that response, and so on. A movement that maximizes the creation and circulation of new tactics and employs praxis-oriented experimentation and reflection on those methods is a movement that will remain flexible and unpredictable.

De Certeau on tactics

Michel De Certeau critiqued the faux-military approach to the question of strategy versus tactics. He noted that, in social conflict, strategic players such as states or corporations can decree and enforce laws, poison environments, and transfer resources on a massive scale, etc. They can surveil and infiltrate in order to dominate the landscape, with a monopoly of legal force, a steady income of taxes and profits, and a cadre of professional experts with whom to work. In this framework, dissidents and activists are tactical players, inheriting a landscape or playing board they did not design, and a legal structure or rulebook they did not write. They must adapt to their environment and subvert it through wily pseudo-obedience that in fact corrodes authority and sustains a subculture of dissent. J.C. Scott refers to these methods as the weapons of the weak, and the arts of resistance under domination (1985). This is not just a question of a movement using tactics, but of yielding the strategic level of conflict, and accepting an overall position of tacticality.

The dominated build this subculture, this private transcript, this repertoire of resistance in the backstage of history, awaiting an *occasion*, or an opening for greater action, to strike at a grander level. They cannot create these occasions, such as the Tsar losing a war, but they can be prepared, or unprepared, to strike when one arises, depending on how deliberately they have sustained their culture of resistance in the interim. In this reading, tactics are not just a local aspect of strategy, but tacticality is itself a position in society—that of the subjugated, who lack great power but retain agency, and who are perhaps nimbler and wilier than their strategic counterpart.

This Certeauan perspective, projected over long stretches of time, contradicts the very idea stated above that tactical players have inherited a playing board and a rulebook over which they have no influence. The tactical players of earlier generations have, through corrosion, *la perruque, détournement,*[7] etc., impacted the shape and structure of the inherited landscape, and the rules in their actual application. This impact is gradual and barely visible, like erosion, or a molecular process we may call *dissensmosis*. Daily ongoing resistance that causes a repressive law to be loosely enforced in practice may not seem like much of a victory. However, at a tactical level it has real impact and import. It is the duty of every dissident or subject to continue this work in daily life; to employ tactical agency to poach upon and whittle away at the strategic power structure.

Many progressive political thinkers, such as Adolph Reed, Jr., critique the embracing of tacticality on the left, or at least the academic left.[8] It is all well and good to be secretly subversive, but don't tangible strategic structures need to be overthrown, occupied, or replaced for a better world to come into existence?

This is a fair point. A movement's approach to tacticality comes down to its relationship with power—is the aim to take strategic power, or to change it, as the Zapatistas and many other groups in the global justice movement hope to do? A radical movement's desired relationship and approach to world-changing power defines its attitudes both to the formulation of individual tactics and strategies, and to the assumption or rejection of a more fundamental position of tacticality.

But what model of movement organization encourages maximum creativity, tactical innovation, and experimentation? Movements are structured with different forms of leadership (if any), and varied structures and processes for internal dialogue (within its own membership) and external dialogue (with other movements, potential coalition partners, sympathetic figures in government or other institutions, and opponents). These differences result in different sorts of public demonstrations. Analyzing a movement's performance at a demonstration is one of many ways to consider the character of a movement.

Public demonstrations

Why do movements spend so much time and effort organizing public demonstrations? Some feel that the public demonstration is obsolete—that public space no longer exists, or that power is now too fluid and dispersed to be contested by gathered masses of people. There are so many other tasks for activists: direct action, recruiting door-to-door, fundraising, lobbying, training, reflecting, theorizing, writing, and building counter-institutions at the grassroots level, to name a few. There are many conflicting and overlapping motivations for public demonstrations. Here is a non-exhaustive list, with each item accompanied by the tactical emphasis that is most beneficial to further the particular goal:

1 To collectively express dissent on a specific issue, in order to influence the state, other elites, and the larger public, or at least to embarrass the state and put mass opposition to state policy on the public record. The more important this is to the group, the more *the coherence of its message* matters.[9]
2 To express the strength of the movement, both for internal confidence-building and as a general warning for opponents. If this is important to the group, then *successfully organizing a big turnout* is of the essence.
3 To recruit new members and grow the movement. If this is important to the group, then *the event they create should be attractive or charismatic.* Even if the issue is deadly serious, there should be something about the time spent and the physical movement through space that inspires desire and defiant joy. An atmosphere of serious play, of ludic experimentation with freer ways of being, may be ideal, but concerns about going past a broader public's horizons of expectations or understanding may complicate this.
4 To define collective identity for a group, subculture, or movement. Since demonstrations alone rarely change public policy or power structures, they arguably should serve a countercultural purpose, to build cohesion and sustain resistance. When development of a countercultural identity is important to the group, then *the style of the demonstration* matters a great deal. Organizers and participants may ask themselves: What is the mood at the demonstration? Is the composition of the group diverse or homogenous? What culture is being created and expressed in the space? How are people's bodies costumed and gendered, and how do they move in the space? What is the dramaturgy of the space—the blocking, timing, tone, composition, and design? What is the role of art and creativity? Is the emphasis toward individual identity or collective identity, or toward a non-dualistic mix and interplay of the two?
5 To convene the movement for targeted direct action. The anti-abortion movement, for example, has gathered people from all over the US to shut down abortion clinics in some localities. The pro-choice movement has responded in kind, gathering masses of activists to protect access to those clinics. The global justice movement regularly convenes to disrupt and protest at the proceedings

of state and corporate globalization agencies such as the World Trade Organization. If this goal is important to the group and the target is well defended, then it helps to have *a diverse organization that is trained to implement a diversity of tactics* in the space. Currently, the phrase "diversity of tactics" has degenerated into shorthand for breaking-windows versus not-breaking-windows. However, I use it in its original sense—an actual wide variety of tactics of many kinds, used thoughtfully, and tailored to the specific political moment.

6 [Insert your motivation here.]

These different priorities are always competing and overlapping with each other. The previously described friction between International ANSWER and Absurd Response reflects a conflict between priorities at a demonstration. International ANSWER valued coherence of message the most while Absurd Response valued creativity, style, and opening up a joyful, countercultural space. These two approaches parallel two overarching models of public demonstration, which I will refer to as "occupying public space" and "opening public space." Almost every public demonstration shows elements of both models in a tensive, dialectical mixture. When the two styles clash in the same place, the result is often an instructive disruption that reveals underlying assumptions.

Instructive disruptions: occupying versus opening public space

Demonstrations that occupy public space typically preprint thousands of identical signs and ask people to hold them high while they stand, listen, and march together, chanting the same chants at the same time, in order to keep their message absolutely clear. However, this uniformity can be boring and uncompelling. Dramaturgically, this sort of action may have been seen so many times that viewers react to it in the same way that they react to any cliché—by tuning out, even when they wish to pay attention. A mass of social actors fades into the background like blurry extras from central casting.

But there is something else that is unappealing about this style of demonstration in its extreme form. Generally speaking, there is no process whereby the average participant can contribute creatively to the dramaturgy of the protest. The underlying ideology of this sort of gathering is monologic, with a mass of spectators listening to a few elevated and amplified leaders. The clear division between speakers on a podium and the audience stands in sharp contrast to Boalian concepts of dialogism and spect-actorship.

However, this sort of demonstration does occupy a public space to serve a unified purpose and a clear message. Just because it is monologic, it is not necessarily authoritarian. It also requires no special effort to attend, so if one is really tired from work or life, all one has to do is show up.

In contrast to the occupying-space model, with its very clear message and control of space for unified dissent, is the opening-space model. This model attempts to open a space for collective and individual, do-it-yourself creativity, generally organized around a certain loose theme, such as Absurd Response to an Absurd War. Sometimes the group will even bring extra costumes (e.g. plastic Billionaire top hats) to offer to people who didn't have the time or energy to bring their own. Sometimes the event is enjoyable enough to refresh and re-energize participants after a long workday, enacting the slogan "we need bread but we also need roses."

The opening-space message may get confused, lost in the fun, or there may not even be a central message. Far from a liability, Naomi Klein (2002) considered such semiotic variety in protest desirable, at least in the case of the anti-corporate movement, which reflects a coalition of diverse agendas. The chaos is accepted in the hopes that the event as a whole will nevertheless hold together. I would add that, beyond the pleasure of the moment, these unpredictable and participatory actions can help create a joyous counterculture that can sustain long-term participation in a movement. Also, sometimes an idea can be conveyed through the opening of a creative space more powerfully than it could through conventional debate.

Some public actions have no explicit, verbal political content besides the action itself; they are not clearly open-space or occupying-space models. For example, a Critical Mass action disrupts car culture and exerts pressure for non-polluting urban public transport by the "organized coincidence" of hundreds of people riding their bikes on the streets at the same time. These actions can polarize by angering and inconveniencing car-users. However, activists have consciously accepted polarization as a necessary aspect of directly confronting what they perceive as an unsustainable and unacceptable urban infrastructure and system of priorities that have gone unchallenged for too long. While this action delivers the monologic message of an occupying-space model, its participatory design borrows from the opening-space model, especially during Halloween Critical Masses, when pirates, monsters, and superheroes of all shapes and sizes convene for the ride.

In some contexts, different motivations for demonstrating can coexist in a mutually reinforcing way. A group may realize that they can more clearly communicate their agenda if the greater public and passersby actually feel compelled to stop and pay attention. They may thus make their demonstration interesting and entertaining, which, in turn, also serves the purposes of recruitment and of performing the movement's countercultural identity. The activists will then feel pressure to be innovative and to keep creating new material: this is the same challenge that career comedians face in order to avoid becoming stale.

Both occupying-space and opening-space models have the option of using a variety of aesthetic strategies. What are the ramifications of using the strategies of humor or irony as elements of protest in both models?

Humor and irony

> [T]he weird and clownish forms . . . get on the nerves of the Establishment. In the face of the gruesomely serious totality of institutionalized politics, satire, irony, and laughing provocation become a necessary dimension of the new politics.
>
> (Marcuse, 1969: p. 64)

Not only can laughter poke fun at grim authorities, it can also help the laughers to get through the strains and tensions of everyday life and movement activity. Humor can also add to the efficacy of a demonstration as people are often more likely to stop and listen if they are entertained.

It is important to note that the opening-space model has no monopoly on the use of humor in protest. The use of humor takes different forms for the two models. For opening the space it means the encouragement of a festive and ridiculous theme for the event. The result may be a less organized type of humor, one that does not have a single point of focus, a sort of simultaneous and chaotic variety show. On the other hand, occupying-space protests may attempt to choreograph and coordinate complex and surprising humorous performances, organizing the space to direct audience focus as is desired.

Andrew Boyd (2002) argued that irony has become a tool for a highly motivated new generation of activists. Inverted meanings and sarcastic satire can surprise people and stimulate reflection. By throwing several simultaneous meanings at recipients, irony may cause passersby to do interpretive work, puncturing their assumed frame of reference to let new light shine in. There is always the risk of losing spectators if the irony is either too simplistic or too abstruse. There is no way to control the creative consumption of irony by all individuals, but performers may nevertheless play with the audiences' sensibilities, trying to anticipate possible misfires. We are playing on the cultural horizons of expectations of the public, on the edge of novelty and familiarity; if our work is too "out there," it falls beyond that horizon and is illegible. We hope to push those horizons outward into stranger and more thoughtful interpretation by putting our work right on the edge of the horizon. Let the viewer of our guerrilla pranks and zaps metaphorically strain their eyes, crane their necks a bit, and then say "Ah! I *see* . . ." and enjoy the joke.

An example of the use of irony in an opening-space action: on the day after Thanksgiving, New York City's Union Square is traditionally filled with booths of people selling freshly baked goods. On this day in 2002, members of Absurd Response staged a Bake Sale for the Military in Union Square. While activist Kate Crane held out a tray of (delicious) missile-shaped gingerbread cookies, I called out for people to "Give 'Til It Hurts Someone Else." As concerned citizens, we hawked our wares, calling out to the passing crowd to please help our charity, to dig down deep, to do their part, because a lot of missiles were about to be expended by the government in the first few minutes of impending war, and if we could sell 1,200,000 cookies we would be able to buy one replacement missile for the rubble-bouncing second wave.[10]

A small mob of Billionaires for Bush and a trio of joyfully ultra-rightist Missile Dick Chicks accompanied the bake-sellers. The latter were dressed in red, white, and blue wigs, showgirl outfits, and makeup, with enormous missiles jutting out from their crotches. They performed tightly choreographed numbers rewording songs such as "These Bombs Were Made for Dropping" to the tune of "These Boots Were Made for Walking." The idea of selling cookies on the street fit the bake-sale context; the cruise-missile phalluses waving proudly in unison did not. The charity drive rhetoric was familiar; the premise of the Pentagon being strapped for funds and in need of volunteer help was not. People hesitated, cocked their heads, watched, listened, and walked on. Some approached us. Of those, most played along, responded wryly, and were rewarded with a missile-cookie and some anti-war mobilization literature.

However, there were three concerned, apparently anti-war people who asked, "Are you serious?!" We responded in character, playing out the irony as blatantly as possible, and while this seemed to reach them they were still shaken up enough by the spectacle to need our straightforward assurance that we weren't serious. I stayed in character and handed them the anti-war literature, and this finally gave them the relief they were looking for. The literature served as a catchall for anyone who wasn't comfortable with the irony, while also giving them an internet link for anti-war event schedules and locations. This was hardly an act of Invisible Theatre! Nevertheless, our choice of irony in a protest with lots of swirling, absurd signifiers around us did confuse a few people.

That Christmas, Absurd Response dressed as war-mongering elves and stormed fabulous megastores such as Macy's, adding to the holiday shopping experience with rousing carols of "Jingle Bombs." About sixty elves sang while riding escalators and skipping through upscale shopping aisles singing:

> **Jingle Bombs, Jingle Bombs, jingle all the way,**
> **Disobey the U.S.A. and we'll blow you away, hey!**[11]

The intent was to remind folks that the bombing was about to start, with bright smiles and a reflection on how this perhaps clashed with the meaning of the holiday. Some people were amused, some were offended, and store managers and mall security were mobilized to eject the elves to the next store.

Protests that use irony and other forms of humor are engaged in a balancing act between novelty and familiarity. Public reactions to them are not predictable. They may help a movement reach people in a more engaging way, but can threaten the clarity of a movement's message. On the other hand, an emphasis on unity of message, of being "on point," can suppress the multivocality of a diverse movement.

Unity meets diversity

As noted earlier, the occupying-space model has the strength of emphasizing a movement's unity. However, when the movement is composed of a coalition of various interests and identities, "unity" is a false and fragile façade that can ultimately detract from the movement's integrity and efficacy: hence, unity itself must be redefined. When actual power relations within a group are unequal, it deepens the oppression to maintain the pretense of a Habermasian space where all are free to speak as equals (Fraser, 1997). As Kelly Moore and Lesley J. Wood argue, coalitions are strongest when they do not claim a unity of interests, priorities, or tactics, but rather acknowledge their diversity while emphasizing the spirit of cooperation for the tasks at hand (2002: p. 30).

The US global justice movement was an example of a complex array of loosely coordinated affinity groups and blocs of activists who gathered at non-hierarchical "spokes-council" meetings to plan actions. The decentralized affinity group model is not just ultra-democratic dialogism for its own sake. The consensus process that affinity groups use to make decisions, when flexible and not fetishized, can result in greater efficacy even if it takes more time than an authoritarian central committee. Starhawk (2002) argues that the decentralized aspect of the movement made it much more capable during the Battle of Seattle against the World Trade Organization (WTO) in 1999. The movement nonviolently swarmed the city, the WTO was disrupted despite the violent police response, and the existence of mass opposition to corporate globalization in the US was on view for a global audience.

When affinity groups meet at spokes-councils, the emphasis on dialogue is not purely idealistic but is vital for planning intelligent action that acknowledges the heterogeneity of the movement. At the spokes-council meeting for the massive 15 February 2003 anti-war demonstration in New York City, representatives for the Carnival Bloc made an important negotiation with the People of Color Bloc. Both groups were planning to gather at the main branch of the Public Library, and then to move out in the direction of First Avenue where the rally was taking place. However, the City of New York, with the help of a Bush Administration lawyer, had successfully banned marching against the war that day. The rally was permitted, but there would be no legal way to march in the street in order to get there.

The Carnival Bloc, which included opening-space groups such as Reclaim the Streets, Glamericans, and Missile Dick Chicks, had a history of ignoring anti-democratic rulings forbidding them from demonstrating in public spaces. For reasons of privilege or motivation, this bloc was mostly made up of people who were willing and able to incur some risk of arrest in this situation. The People of Color Bloc, however, included many who could not afford to be arrested because of job, income, family, or legal status. At the spokes-council meeting, it was agreed that the People of Color Bloc would set out for the rally first, staying on the sidewalks and following traffic signals. After they had traveled far enough away that they would not be embroiled in any mass arrests, the Carnival Bloc would set out on its path, following its agenda of taking over a street or a neighborhood and playing music and dancing, despite the permit ban. In a movement with more totalizing, reductionist unity, or which took orders handed down from a central committee, such a dialogue might not have occurred, and one group's needs might have been subsumed by the other.

Working with a diversity of tactics is more complex than having a central command, but it is also more dynamic and flexible. Organizers of occupying-space protests may be more inclined to emphasize or impose unity than those that attempt to open space. However, in the planning stage of either type of event, a movement can engage in open dialogue between blocs so that diversity of interests, tactics, and identities are acknowledged and respected. Pre-action TO workshops may also be of use in acknowledging and dealing with these differences.

Tactical carnival

Standing in contrast to set-piece conventional demonstrations, recent creative protest, with its do-it-yourself ethos, emphasis on collective and individual creativity, and free-flowing multivocality, is often described as *carnivalesque*. Kauffman asserts that:

> [T]he central idea behind the carnival is that protests gain in power if they reflect the world we want to create . . . a world that is full of color and life and creativity and art and music and dance. It's a celebration of life against the forces of greed and death . . . not unlike creating a community garden.
>
> (Kauffman, 2004: p. 380–81)

The opening-space model overlaps in many ways with the practice of carnival. The global justice movement, for example, often convenes in massive, festive, creative street protests, and has consciously theorized itself using terms such as "Carnival Against Capital" (Notes From Nowhere, 2003: p. 185). This type of engaging, ludic protest encourages people to enjoy, and to imagine other possible worlds. The attempt to remove the performer–audience divide follows Bakhtin's notion that carnival is liberatory and subversive because it "does not know footlights." (Footlights, at the foot of the classic stage, formed a clear boundary between stage performers and audience.) Calls to action for this carnivalesque model do not only list a series of angry complaints, but also solicit contributions to a counterculture fantasia, or a human community garden. The Glamericans came to protests in maximum glam-majesty to decorate public space with themselves. The Rock Stars Against the War assumed alter-personas, boarded their tour bus, and turned protests into hard-partying, no-sleep adventures.

This form of protest, invoking the carnivalesque, has not only been used to oppose capitalism. The grassroots, independent groups in Eastern Europe who undermined authoritarian Communist power using absurdist, carnivalesque mass protests were a key, unsung element in the collapse of Soviet power in several of the Warsaw Pact countries (Kenney, 2002).

Carnival is as much for the benefit and social change of the activists as it is for any spectators who will hopefully become spect-actors. The serious play is meant to inspire desire, collective stories, group cohesion, and identity formation—making a movement that has denser social networks and is more sustainable and adaptable through hard times. Even setbacks and misfires will be fed back into the creative process to help generate new ideas for the movement. As Stephen Duncombe argues:

> This is praxis, a theory arising out of activity . . . An embodied theory of mass activity is competing against the idealized theory of capitalism that celebrates the self-gratifying individual . . . Direct action groups . . . consciously try to create these theory-generating, lived experiences as part of our politics . . . Protest becomes a breathing, dancing example of what a liberated public space might look like. A lived imaginary.
>
> (2003: p. 15–16)

But are these protests carnivalesque in the Bakhtinian sense? Are they liberatory simply because the footlights are removed? Is this purely an opening-space model?

Bakhtin and the carnivalesque

Mikhail Bakhtin (1895–1975), a Russian literary scholar and philosopher who struggled in obscurity under the reign of Stalin, and whose major works were only published in the last fifteen years of his life, celebrated the carnivalesque, mass-participatory freedom, and anti-authoritarian laughter that he found in the writings of Rabelais. He also refers to the medieval European carnivals that preceded Lent in the Christian calendar, during which mask-wearing mobs partied, drank, blasphemed, and broke every rule of those strict societies for just a few allotted days:

> Carnival does not know footlights, in the sense that it does not acknowledge any distinction between actors and spectators. Footlights would destroy a carnival, as the absence of footlights would destroy a theatrical performance. Carnival is not a spectacle seen by the people; they live in it, and everyone participates because its very idea embraces all the people. While carnival lasts, there is no life outside it. During carnival time life is subject only to its laws, that is, the laws of its own freedom.
>
> (Bakhtin, 1968: p. 7)

The "carnivalesque," and its liberating qualities for the "lower orders" of society, includes abuse and laughter, which degrade at the same time as they renew. Grotesque realism exaggerates the material body and the "lower bodily stratum," inverting the hierarchies of elite taste and decorum, and the symbols of hierarchy. This is a frenetic, celebratory, and ideologically ambivalent performance mode which breaks down the bodily boundaries of the idealized bourgeois individual, "polluting" and collectivizing the human condition in a joyous, outrageously humorous demonstration that has some potential for rebellion (Bakhtin, 1968).

Bakhtin theorized the carnivalesque as a mode of being and as a social ritual wherein laughter and ribaldry, emphasis on the undifferentiated masses, bodily functions, and symbolic inversion of the social order created a liberatory space even in the most repressive societies. Bakhtin perhaps romanticized the power and nature of carnival, but in the Stalinist context in which he was writing, who could blame him? It is questionable whether medieval carnival ever totally over-rode individualism and hierarchy. Carnivals have even created moments of displaced abjection where the peasants unleashed horrific pogroms upon unarmed minorities such as Jews or Roma. Later theorists have argued that carnival is situational—that, depending on the historical moment, the balance of forces, and opportunities, it can either be a liberatory moment of rebellion or a safety valve that actually serves the long-term stability of the given social order (Stallybrass & White, 1986: p. 16–19; Kertzer, 1988: p. 144–50). J.C. Scott agrees that carnival is situational, but he does emphasize that it was a tactical "opening" that was hard-won by the oppressed through cultural conflict, and provided a convenient regularly scheduled occasion for signifying and trouble-making. Franco's regime outlawed carnival as one of its first repressive actions after winning the Spanish Civil War, something that Scott (1990) interprets as a sign of its potential liberatory power. Finally, theorists such as Michael-André Bernstein (1983) have leveled a harsh critique both against Bakhtin's theories and those who find hope for current rebellions in them.

There are important differences between modern oppositional performances that evoke the carnivalesque and the phenomenon that Bakhtin was exploring. Feudal carnival was a calendrically circumscribed event, tied to the harvest and religious schedules of agrarian-Christian societies still influenced by their pagan pasts, and the event itself was part of a commonly shared cultural and religious vocabulary. The oppositional, carnivalesque protests of today take place when and where the protestors choose: sometimes in reaction to "establishment" events, sometimes not. The old carnivals, with their coded mockery of church and world-turned-upside-down iconography, were ideologically ambivalent. The twenty-first century carnivalesque protests may be ideologically complicated, ironic, and multivocal, but they still tend to be more focused and specific in their social critique than most feudal carnivals. In this sense, there is more tactical agency in contemporary carnivalesque protest, drawing on a narrower, more specialized appeal than the all-community carnival of feudal times. While those who dance, sing, and party in current street protests may share an experience of the joyous and outrageous carnivalesque, the entire society does not take part, sharing the ritual as members of the same culture. Thus there is an inherent performer–audience divide in current carnival protest. It is not purely participatory. The footlights are the television and laptop screens of the remote viewers. Pundits and protesters alike evaluate the events, either on the street or through the mass media. For these reasons, I would distinguish between Bakhtinian carnival and what I call the *tactical carnival* of today.

This is also not purely an opening-space proposition. Tactical carnival involves a dialogue and dialectic not only between individual activist groups, but also between the modes of occupying space and opening space. Similarly, during the initial performance of the anti-model, TO's Forum Theatre is more controlled than freewheeling open-space protest, but then the scene is opened up for spect-actor improvisatory intervention. Theatre of the Oppressed contains both strident critique of power and improvised glimpses of the future in which the participants would like to live. The techniques of TO that increase the level of dialogism and spect-actorship can be very useful for the strategic dramaturgy of the tensive negotiation that is the public demonstration.

To be truly tactically flexible and sustainable for a diverse coalition with different interests, resources, and vulnerabilities, and to effectively engage with an ever-inventive and vigilant state, tactical carnival must negotiate and fuse techniques from various modes: a huge demonstration that scatters into a citywide radical costume ball; a creative and ironic engagement with passersby resulting in earnest direct action; or dozens of diverse columns converging at City Hall for an extended session of Legislative Theatre.

Tactical carnival has developed as a tactic in the toolbox of the burgeoning global justice movement. This movement has been more accurately described as a "movement of movements" due to its great diversity in geography, identity, and ideology. "One No, Many Yeses" is one of its main slogans. As connections and coalitions are forged between Bolivian miners, American anti-corporate activists, Polish organic farmers, Zapatistas and Argentinian *piquiteros*, etc., organizers have coordinated a celebratory form of protest that involves unpermitted street parties and processions that occupy public space, both to assert movement identity and importance, and to disrupt state or corporate events and daily business. Movement organizers and writers use the term *carnival* to label these explicitly oppositional events, at which flamboyant costumes, dance, puppets, tricksterism, samba bands, and other musical groupings can all be seen. They also seem to refer to ideas about carnival that may, to some scholars, seem romantic or overly idealist: nevertheless, what is fascinating is that they are attempting to deploy the ideal of carnival in a practical, experimental way on the street, to create a new, twenty-first century carnival that is neither calendrically nor spatially circumscribed by the state, but declared and embodied by a movement that identifies itself as global, anti-corporate, and anti-authoritarian.

I posit that the goals of tactical carnival are:

1 To declare and occupy a joyous, participatory, and semi-anonymous, relatively safe place for power inversions/subversions. "Celebrity"

has been explicitly denounced in some movement literature, in favor of the relative egalitarian anonymity of the mass. These spaces are also meant to be non-dogmatic and non-sectarian; a more open place for wider participation. The hope is that more people will join the movement when a space for joyful participation is opened up.

2 To put a friendly face on the movement as a way to interrupt what I refer to as the *hegemonologue* of the corporate media and state rhetoric, which demonizes activists as crazed, nihilistic hooligans (Bogad, 2004). The idea is to insert images that at least partially disrupt or disharmonize the barrage of negative images (for example, a clown kissing a riot shield juxtaposed with the usual images of street melee and property damage), and to replace the usual "story of the battle" (street fights or vandalism), with the "battle of the story" in which colorful and creative costumes, dance, music, performance, and improvised interactions give a new look at the movement and its agenda.[12]
3 To interrupt another aspect of the hegemonologue: the rhetoric of the inevitability of corporate globalization (or as Margaret Thatcher famously put it, "There Is No Alternative"), by demonstrating that better alternatives are possible.
4 To experiment with new ways to play with and around power. The idea is to develop less obvious and predictable ways to interact on the street with agents of the state, corporations, and passersby. Much of the creativity is intended to dispel fear and tension during confrontations involving a massive police presence, for example.
5 To create a celebratory culture of active defiance, as an alternative to everyday life, and in response to a widespread frustration that many participants feel regarding their official relegation to the role of consumers of culture and spectacle rather than creators/spect-actors.

"Carnival" has been an explicit referent for the global justice movement and many of its actions, even if Bakhtin would not recognize these events as Rabelaisian. On 18 June 1999, the opening day of the G8 summit in Cologne, Germany, a "Carnival Against Capital" was declared by the movement as an "international day of action, protest, and carnival aimed at the heart of the global economy" (Ainger, 2004: p. 33). This proposal identified capitalism as the "root of our social and ecological problems, and was taken up by the People's Global Action network, translated into seven languages, and distributed by email and post to thousands of groups worldwide" (Notes From Nowhere, 2003: p. 184). On that day, in the financial district of London, 10,000 people gathered in the street, playing "volleyball with inflatable globes and danc[ing] to samba rhythms in the spray of a waterspout from a damaged fire hydrant" (Ainger, 2004: p. 33). In order to avoid being penned in by the police, to keep moving, and to add flair to the event, organizers distributed color-coded masks to participants: a note inside the masks suggested that the wearers follow the flags that matched their masks when the time came. Sure enough, at one moment, colorful flags went up and soon streams of masked revelers were running, following the flag-bearers through the narrow streets of the financial sector of London. This was a remarkable way to set up an action that gave the advantages of both central, creative vision, and free-flowing, optional participation (Notes From Nowhere, 2003: p. 176–77). Bizarrely, it has since come to light that one of the planners was a police agent who maintained his "cover" even while testifying in court later (Monbiot, 2015). Of course, this event had not been permitted by the state, and the ideology of the gathering asserted itself through direct action as the day progressed:

> . . . by the end of the day a group of the protesters had invaded and trashed the ground floor of the London International Financial Futures Exchange, three McDonalds had their windows broken, two people had been run over by police vans, and riot police were charging in. The sight of anarchy hitting the world's largest financial center prompted newspaper headlines that denounced the protesters as "evil savages," an ignorant "unwashed horde" hell-bent on turning a "carnival into a riot" . . . the carnival-goers in London – the majority of whom had been nonviolent in actions and intent – were members of a far larger, invisible but international constituency organizing around a common enemy: globalization.
>
> (Ainger, 2004: p. 33)

This Carnival Against Capital was not limited to London. Simultaneous protests of similar nature took place "against global capitalism, the international financial system, and corporate power . . . in 43 countries around the world" (Ainger, 2004: p. 33). For example, in Nigeria, a Carnival of the Oppressed brought:

> nearly 10,000 Ogoni, Ijaw, and other tribes together in closing down the country's oil capital, Port Harcourt . . . meanwhile

> in Köln, the Intercontinental Caravan, made up of 400 Indian farmers and other activists from the global South, plan[ned] to conclude its tour with a Laugh Parade, but police detain[ed] 250 of them before they [got] the chance to guffaw at the G8.
>
> (Notes From Nowhere, 2003: p. 185–87).

In fact, this global event was so disturbing that the FBI listed Carnival Against Capital as a terrorist group in their memo of 11 May 2001, four months before the Al Qaeda attacks of 11 September of that year (FBI, 2001). This is strange, as Carnival Against Capital was not an organization but rather a concept: a call to action, and an invocation of the idea of the subversive and celebratory carnivalesque that resonated around the world for the global justice movement.

There are many other examples of this movement's invocation of the idea of "carnival" for its actions. The famous anti-World Trade Organization protests that shut down Seattle in 1999 were also conceived, in part, as carnivalesque, with colorful costumes, giant puppets, dancers, marching bands, and people dressed as sea turtles and butterflies, playing and interacting with more conventional union members and other activists. The protest against the Free Trade Area of the Americas (FTAA) conference in Quebec in 2001 was also dubbed a Carnival Against Capital. There is a neckerchief, designed by John Jordan and sewn by Argentinian women textile workers who took over their own factory during the financial collapse in that country, that is worn by some activists, and became regulation gear for members of the Clown Army. Produced in red, yellow, pink, and orange, the neckerchief boasts a smiling face printed on one side, and can be worn with the mass-produced smile covering the lower half of one's face. On the other side, a pattern of a chain-link fence covers an unhappy face, so the wearer has the choice of looking free and happy or fenced-in and sad. A mass of people, filling up a public space, dancing or playing games, and making music while wearing these masks, creates an effect that is ideologically unclear, yet eerie. Written on the neckerchief's edges in four languages is a passage that defines Carnival:

> **"We will remain faceless because we refuse the spectacle of celebrity, because we are everyone, because the carnival beckons, because the world is upside down, because we are everywhere. By wearing masks we show that who we are is not as important as what we want, and what we want is everything for everyone."**

This passage shows some of the key ideas that the global justice movement embraces from their creative interpretation of the carnivalesque. The idea of masked anonymity is advantageous for concealing identity from the authorities. It is also a way to celebrate the undifferentiated mass, and combat the cult of personality by the mass media and pop culture. This reflects the Bakhtinian distinction between the carnivalesque of undifferentiated bodies, versus the discrete, separate, and closed-off bourgeois individual imagined by mercantilism and capitalism. Anonymity also serves as a tool for tactical players; lacking the strategic power of the state or corporations, anonymity enables protestors to maneuver, play, and perhaps escape, while in full view of the authorities (De Certeau, 1984). The demand for "everything for everyone" echoes the millenarian, utopian poetics of the Rabelaisian carnival, also expressed in the "hidden transcripts" of the oppressed of many peasant cultures (Scott, 1990), and the rhetoric of the Diggers[13] (Hill, 2002). "The carnival beckons" this celebratory movement to action.

Many groups were formed with the goal of contributing art, festive costumes, and music to these carnivals. One group explained their savvy theorization in their name: Tactical Frivolity. Musical bands are a crucial aspect of these gatherings; one such group playfully named itself Reclaim the Beats, after the seminal movement group, Reclaim the Streets. The choice of music varies, but there is a great deal of influence from the carnivals of Brazilian and Caribbean communities, showing that tactical carnival is not only motivated by a reference to medieval European traditions. While the now-defunct Seattle-based Infernal Noise Brigade played a postmodern blend of "drumline, taiko, Mughal and North African rhythms, elements of Balkan fanfares, breakbeats, and just about anything else" (Infernal Noise Brigade) and dressed in paramilitary uniforms, the UK-based Rhythms of Resistance stated:

> Whilst people often refer to us as a "Samba Band" we actually have more affinity with the Afro Bloc parading drum bands that emerged in the mid-70s in Salvadore, Bahia in Brazil. Bands such as Ile Aye and Olodum formed as a political expression of black awareness, resisting economic exclusion. Coming out of some of the poorest urban communities, Afro Blocs became a mobilising focus on picket lines and marches. The growth of Schools of Samba both in Brazil and all over the world since the 80s is largely a result of the commercialisation of this culture of resistance.
>
> (Rhythms of Resistance website)

Having declared their inspiration from the Global South, they connected this music to the goals of global justice, playing as "a force of resistance and source of self-confidence" for themselves and for others. They also shared the history of their group, proclaiming the tactical power of their music:

> Rhythms of Resistance formed as part of the UK Earth First action against the IMF/World Bank in Prague in September 2000. A Pink and Silver carnival bloc, focused around a 55-piece band, detached itself from a march of 67,000 and outmaneuvered police resources defending the IMF annual summit. With an international "black bloc" and a large contingent from the Italian movement, "Ya Basta," three diverse forms of direct action worked towards a common goal and resulted in the shut down of the IMF summit.
>
> Building on the success of S26 [the Prague protest], more bands are forming, playing the same rhythms and with the same approach. The Electric Blue band formed in Amsterdam for the Rising Tide Actions against the Cop6 Climate Conference in November 2000 and joined together with 10 drummers from Rhythms of Resistance to form a 65-piece band.
>
> With bands forming across Europe and beyond (at least 2 in the US), an international network of percussive resistance to the march of capitalism is now emerging.
>
> Street carnival is the vital component of protest and life and fun – use your imaginations, connect and network, build instruments and costumes, learn our tunes and distribute them noisily through the world!!
>
> (Rhythms of Resistance website)

Rhythms of Resistance exemplifies the anti-capitalist movement's awareness and appropriation of culture and tactics across borders of nationality, race, class, and privilege. Just as globalization enables capital and goods to circulate around the world, traditions and innovations of resistance are also shared. The same internet technology used so well for commerce allowed the global movement to coordinate the Carnival Against Capital in 43 different countries.

From the text on their website, it is clear that Rhythms of Resistance, which inspired groups in other countries, embraced the idea of carnival as a positive and uplifting mode of defiance and advocacy. They also performed their music at protests in order to foster group "confidence," defiant joy, and to make the protest a good time for all joining in.

Why was carnival so important to this "movement of movements"? As conceived by Bakhtin, carnival does have an edge. It suggests a possibility of riot or rebellion—that licensed foolery might escalate into outright revolt. This was an encouraging idea. J.C. Scott (1990) acknowledged that medieval carnivals, far from serving as a mere "steam valve," could be tactical in the ways I have outlined above. Moreover, social movements have a desire to search for historical ancestors, continuity of struggle, and heroes. They draw inspiration, legitimacy, and heritage from the distant past, and identify with a tradition of defiance. Importantly, some modern anarchists are drawn to the idea of carnival because it appeals to their egalitarian ideology and participatory, do-it-yourself ethos. Bakhtin is eagerly echoed in the key movement text *We Are Everywhere: The irresistible rise of global anticapitalism* (Notes From Nowhere, 2003). In the "Carnival" section of that book, under the heading "Participate, Don't Spectate," the Bakhtin passage about footlights is quoted in full, followed by these words:

> Passivity disappears when carnival comes to town, with its unyielding demand for participation . . . It is a moment when we can break free from the alienation that capitalism enforces in so many ways . . . Carnival denies the existence of experts, or rather, insists that everyone is one . . . it demands interaction and flexibility, face-to-face contact and collective decision-making, so that a dynamic and direct democracy develops – a democracy which takes place on the stage of spontaneously unfolding life, not raised above the audience but at ground level, where everyone can be involved. There are no leaders, no spectators, and no sidelines, only an entanglement of many players who do their own thing while feeling part of a greater whole.
>
> (Notes From Nowhere, 2003: p. 177–78)

This idealistic view that in carnival the mass is actively involved and no one is passive appealed to a movement that viewed the mainstream media with great skepticism, being influenced by Guy Debord's concept of the deadening, pacifying, and self-perpetuating "society of the spectacle" (Debord, 1995). This worldview encourages and practices a participatory, do-it-yourself form of political action and communication. Many members of the movement, while not explicitly anarchist, do embrace the term coined by the movement in Argentina: "horizontalist." This egalitarian idea of *horizontality* calls for minimizing the concentration of power of any single person or group. Bakhtin's idea of the carnival, although critiqued by scholars, is strongly consistent with such ideological desires and agendas. To distinguish carnivalesque protest from the carnivals that occur in Rio de Janeiro or Notting Hill (London), the Notes From Nowhere collective declared:

> What carnivals remain in most parts of the world have themselves become spectacles – specialist performances watched by spectators – with police lines and barriers placed between the parade and audience. Thus the vortexed, whirling, uncontrollable state of creative chaos is shoehorned into neat straight lines and rectangles. A visit to many contemporary carnivals sanctioned by the state (such as Carnaval in Rio de Janeiro, or the Notting Hill Carnival in London), where consumption and corporate sponsorship has taken over from the creativity and spontaneity is enough to illustrate how carnival under capitalism has lost its vitality. But carnival has been with us since time immemorial and it has always refused to die. Reappearing in different guises across the ages it returns again and again. Freed from the clutches of entertainment, the anticapitalist movements have thrown it back into the streets, where it is liberated from commerce for everyone to enjoy once again.
>
> (2003: p.177)

This passage reveals how important the concept of carnival is to some movements, and how it has influenced how they organize and perform in public space in critical contrast with (an activist's perception of) events such as Rio's Carnaval.

Tactical carnival differs from the form idealized by Bakhtin just as much as these commercialized street parades. It is not a yearly event that fits into an agrarian calendar and a Christian feudal worldview and system of power; it happens when and where the movement calls for it, though often in reaction to corporate or state events such as meetings of the G8 or WTO. Far from being a day of state-licensed foolery and excess, it is often unpermitted by the state, triggering police repression. Tactical carnival comes from a complex, global coalition of social movements, and defies ideological generalization. However, its laughter, while ambivalent and self-mocking, is not as ambivalent as Bakhtin's carnival. It is joyful, but it is also satirical laughter, coupled with a political critique, and therefore not as universal as Bakhtin's interpretation.

In short, tactical carnival espouses not just the "World-Turned-Upside Down" concept described by scholars of medieval European carnival, but rather the slogan "Another World Is Possible." The difference between these two phrases is the difference between a temporary inversion of power and substantial progressive social change. This slogan, "Another World Is Possible," has been used on movement proclamations and banners around the world. Its resonance with "One No, Many Yeses" reflects the open, radical, and prefigurative gesture of tactical carnival.

Scholars of carnival may disagree with the global justice movement's interpretation of the carnivalesque. They may disparage an uncritical reading of Bakhtin, and might argue that this uncritical interpretation undermined the movement's actual praxis around the world. Others may claim that this reading of carnival is not historicized rigorously enough, or is a wholesale acceptance of Bakhtin's ideas, or that carnivalesque protest is no longer relevant in any case. However, it is unquestionable that the idea of carnival helped to inspire and galvanize the theory and action of a global, anti-authoritarian, anti-capitalist movement. This global movement was determined to build and sustain its own cultures, in defiance of the homogenizing corporate monoculture that is spreading so rapidly. These oppositional cultures developed a new concept of carnival. This concept, influenced by older ideas but moving beyond Bakhtin, developed new parameters and tactics through activist praxis. The movement aimed to reclaim the carnival for its own purposes and agendas, against the society of the spectacle and the hegemonologue, in pursuit of sustained, deeply oppositional, creative, and egalitarian activism.

Notes

1 Tannis Kowalchuk, Co-Artistic Director of North American Cultural Laboratory.
2 For readers unfamiliar with Boal's Theatre of the Oppressed, see Boal: *Theatre of the Oppressed* (1979); *Games for Actors and Non-Actors* (1992); and *Legislative Theatre* (1998).
3 Such sources include: *A Manual for Direct Action* (Oppenheimer & Lakey, 1965); *War Resisters League Organizer's Manual* (Hedeman, 1981); *Students Against Sweatshops* (Featherstone, 2002); *An Action a Day* (Hudema, 2004); *Organizing for Social Change* (Bobo & Kendall et al., 2010); *Beautiful Trouble* (Boyd & Mitchell, 2012); *The Activist's Handbook* (Shaw, 2013); *The Earth First! Direct Action Manual* (Earth First!, 2015); and many more.
4 Innovators of these methods include the Piven Theatre Workshop and Viola Spolin.
5 See Kershaw's *Theatre Ecology* (2009); *The Radical in Performance* (1999); and *The Politics of Performance* (1992); see also J.H. Johnson's *Listening in Paris* (1996).

6 As for the end of cycles of contention, there are many ways in which movements can meet their end. In *Globalization From Below*, Jeremy Brecher, Tim Costello, and Brendan Smith list the possible paths to the demise of social movements as: schism, repression, fading out, leadership domination, isolation, cooptation, leadership sell-out, and sectarian disruption (2002: p. 30).
7 *La perruque*: repurposing one's employer's resources for personal use. *Détournement*: rerouting or hijacking mainstream culture for countercultural purposes.
8 For example, see Reed (2000).
9 In "Absurd Responses vs. Earnest Politics," Shepard aptly cites McAdam's six specific publics to which social movements must seek to speak in order to create change: "1) potential recruits, 2) those working within the movement, 3) potential coalition partners, 4) media outlets, 5) public opinion, and 6) policymakers" (Shepard, 2003).
10 This, of course, was a play on the well-known bumper-sticker slogan: "It'll be a great day when the schools have all the money they need and the military has to hold a bake sale."
11 The protest jingle's lyrics were written by Kate Crane.
12 D. Solnit, interview with the author, 2 July 2005, and Canning & Reinsborough (2010).
13 The Diggers were a radical egalitarian movement who formed in England in 1649.

References

Ainger, K. (2004) "A Global Carnival of the Dispossessed." In E. Yuen, D. Burton-Rose and G. Katsiaficas (eds.), *Confronting Capitalism: Dispatches from a global movement* (p. 33–35). Brooklyn: Soft Skull Press.

Bakhtin, M.M. (1968) *Rabelais and His World*. Trans. H. Iswolsky. Cambridge, MA: MIT Press.

Bernstein, M. (1983) "When the Carnival Turns Bitter: Preliminary reflections upon the abject hero," *Critical Inquiry*, Vol. 10, No. 2: 283–305.

Boal, Augusto (1979) *Theatre of the Oppressed*. Trans. Charles A. and Maria-Odilia Leal McBride. London: Pluto Press.

Boal, Augusto (1992) *Games for Actors and Non-Actors*. London: Routledge.

Boal, Augusto (1998) *Legislative Theatre: Using performance to make politics*. London: Routledge.

Bobo, K.; Kendall, J.; Max, S. (2010) *Organizing for Social Change*. California: Forum Press.

Bogad, L.M. (2004) "The Counter Convention: American grassroots satire and the 2004 presidential elections." Conference Paper. Association for Theatre in Higher Education, Toronto, 1 Aug.

Bogad, L.M. (2016) *Electoral Guerrilla Theatre: Radical ridicule and social movements*, 2nd edition. London: Routledge.

Boyd, A. (2002) "Irony, Meme Warfare, and the Extreme Costume Ball." In

R. Hayduk and B. Shepard (eds.), *From ACT UP to the WTO: Urban protest and community building in the era of globalization*. London: Verso.

Boyd, A.; Mitchell, D.O. (2012) *Beautiful Trouble: A toolbox for revolution*. New York: OR Books.

Brecher, J.; Costello, T.; Smith, B. (2002) *Globalization From Below: The power of solidarity.* Cambridge, MA: South End Press.

Canning, D.; Reinsborough, P. (2010) *Re:Imagining Change: How to use story-based strategy to win campaigns, build movements, and change the world*. Oakland, CA: PM Press.

De Certeau, Michel (1984) *The Practice of Everyday Life*. Trans. Steven Rendall. Berkeley: University of California Press.

Debord, G. (1995) *The Society of the Spectacle*. Trans. D. Nicholson-Smith. New York: Zone Books.

Duncombe, S. (2003) "The Poverty of Theory: Anti-intellectualism and the value of action," *Radical Society: Review of Culture and Politics*, Vol. 30, No. 1: 11–17.

Earth First! (2015) *The Earth First! Direct Action Manual*, 3rd edition.

FBI (2001) Statement for the record, Louis J. Freeh, Director, Federal Bureau of Investigation, on the threat of terrorism to the United States before the United States Senate Committees on Appropriations, Armed Services, and Select Committee on Intelligence. Retrieved from: www.fbi.gov/congress/congress01/freeh051001.htm (accessed 23 June 2003).

Featherstone, L. (2002) *Students Against Sweatshops: The making of a movement*. New York: Verso.

Fraser, N. (1997) *Justice Interruptus: Reflections on the "postsocialist" condition*. London: Routledge.

Hedeman, Ed (1981) *War Resisters League Organizer's Manual*. New York: War Resisters League.

Hill, C. (2002) "Levellers and True Levellers". In S. Duncombe (ed.), *Cultural Resistance Reader* (p. 17–34). New York: Verso.

Hudema, M. (2004) *An Action a Day: Keeps global capitalism away*. Toronto: Between the Lines.

Infernal Noise Brigade. [Webpage.] http://infernal noise.org (accessed 26 Oct 2015).

Johnson, J.H. (1996) *Listening in Paris: A cultural history*. Berkeley: University of Southern California Press.

Kauffman, L. (2004) "A Short, Personal History of the Global Justice Movement." In E. Yuen, D. Burton-Rose and G. Katsiaficas (eds.), *Confronting Capitalism: Dispatches from a global movement*. Brooklyn: Soft Skull Press.

Kenney, P. (2002) *A Carnival of Revolution: Central Europe 1989*. Princeton, NJ: Princeton University Press.

Kershaw, B. (1992) *The Politics of Performance: Radical theatre as intervention*. London: Routledge.

Kershaw, B. (1999) *The Radical in Performance: Between Brecht and Baudrillard*. London: Routledge.

Kershaw, B. (2009) *Theatre Ecology: Environments and performance events.* Cambridge: Cambridge University Press.

Kertzer, D.I. (1988) *Ritual, Politics and Power.* New Haven, CT: Yale University Press.

Klein, N. (2002) "The Vision Thing: Were the DC and Seattle protests unfocused, or are the critics missing the point?" In R. Hayduk and B. Shepard (eds.), *From ACT UP to the WTO: Urban protest and community building in the era of globalization.* London: Verso.

Lysistrata Project. [Webpage.] www.lysistrataproject.org (accessed 26 May 2004).

Marcuse, H. (1969) *An Essay On Liberation.* Boston, MA: Beacon Press.

Monbiot, G. (2015) "Did an Undercover Cop Help to Organize a Major Riot?" *The Guardian*, 1 Aug 2015. www.theguardian.com/commentisfree/2014/feb/03/undercover-officer-major-riot-john-jordan

Moore, K.; Wood, L.J. (2002) "Target Practice: Community activism in a global era." In R. Hayduk and B. Shepard (eds.), *From ACT UP to the WTO: Urban protest and community building in the era of globalization.* London: Verso.

Notes From Nowhere (2003) *We Are Everywhere: The irresistible rise of global anticapitalism.* London: Verso.

Oppenheimer, M.; Lakey, G. (1965) *A Manual for Direct Action.* Chicago: Quadrangle Books.

Reed, A. (2000) *Class Notes: Posing as politics and other thoughts on the American scene.* www.nytimes.com/books/first/r/reed-class.html (accessed 28 July 2015).

Rhythms of Resistance. [Webpage.] www.rhythmsofresistance.co.uk (accessed 26 Oct 2015).

Scott, J.C. (1985) *Weapons of the Weak: Everyday forms of peasant resistance.* New Haven: Yale University Press.

Scott, J.C. (1990) *Domination and the Arts of Resistance.* New Haven, CT: Yale University Press.

Shaw, Randy (2013) *The Activist's Handbook: Winning social change in the 21st century.* Berkeley: University of California Press.

Shepard, B. (2003) "Absurd Responses vs. Earnest Politics," *The Journal of Aesthetics & Protest*, Vol. 1, No. 2: www.joaap.org/1/BenShepard (accessed 26 Oct 2015).

Stallybrass, P.; White, A. (1986) *The Politics and Poetics of Transgression.* Ithaca, NY: Cornell University Press.

Starhawk (2002) "How We Really Shut Down the WTO." In R. Hayduk and B. Shepard (eds.), *From ACT UP to the WTO: Urban protest and community building in the era of globalization.* London: Verso.

Tarrow, S. (1998) *Power in Movement: Social movements and contentious politics.* Cambridge: Cambridge University Press.

Wood, E.J. (2003) *Insurgent Collective Action and Civil War in El Salvador.* Cambridge: Cambridge University Press.

Chapter 2

Clownfrontation and clowndestine maneuvers

The Clown Army and the irresistible image

Run Away From the Circus–Join the CIRCA!
—Clandestine Insurgent Rebel Clown Army recruiting slogan

CIRCA is the only army in the world in which General Strike outranks Private Property.
—Colonel Oftruth, Clandestine Insurgent Rebel Clown Army

This chapter examines the global phenomenon of tactical carnival through the G8 protest in July 2005, with a further focus on the Carnival for Full Enjoyment in Edinburgh on 4 July, as participated in by the Clandestine Insurgent Rebel Clown Army (CIRCA). I will draw on press clippings, videos, interviews with CIRCA members, movement literature and my own experience, in the persona of Colonel Oftruth, as co-founder and participant/observer, to examine how CIRCA theorized and actualized its participation in the tactical carnival at the 2005 G8.

Carnival for Full Enjoyment, Edinburgh (Scotland), 4 July 2005: Police in black riot gear stand shoulder to shoulder. Their clear, body-length plastic shields form a wall across the city street. They have just used those shields to shove people down the road and assert control of the space. Visors are down. Heavy boots and hulking full-body armor add to their imposing appearance. They are poised to preserve public order.

The police are confronted by a disorderly gaggle of men and women in chaotic facepaint, second-hand military gear, and clownish, garish pink and green frills. These are the tricksters of the Clandestine

Insurgent Rebel Clown Army, or CIRCA. Far from being intimidated, the CIRCA folk seem overjoyed to see them, and hail them as friends and playmates. The clowns scrub the policemen's boots with their feather dusters. They breathe on the shields to fog them up, and then polish them.

Althusser wrote that interpellation is key to the articulation of power; when the policeman hails you with a "Hey, you!" and you acknowledge the hailing—"Who? Me?"—you are already caught in the power relationship (1971). This applies to any standard response to policing: fight, flight, or freak out. CIRCA clowns resist interpellation. They neither flee nor fight. They stay and play.

One of the main rules of improvisation theatre is the idea of "yes, and"—one never negates a performing partner's idea or proposition, but rather agrees and adds a new creative suggestion to the mix. The rebel clowns jump about, following each other in an agreeable "yes, and" ethos of improvisational frolicking in front of the police line. They simply refuse to acknowledge the very clear and stark NO of the police cordon, asserting their own ridiculous and enthusiastic YES AND over and over with each moment. Finally, one trickster, aptly named Trixie, kisses one of the police shields. Her kiss is so enthusiastic and vigorous that she smears her clown makeup and lipstick all over it. She then goes from shield to shield, all the way up the phalanx-line, kissing and leaving a smeary mark on each one. The police stay in formation. Some are disturbed, some impassive, and some amused by these paradigm-shifting kisses. One says "Step away from the shield, please," while another can clearly be seen to be smiling (Young, 2005).

Trixie needs to reapply her lipstick in order to continue her loving assault, and while doing this she is asked by Zoe Young, a CIRCA videographer, why she is doing what she's doing. "Because I love them!" she declares in a high-pitched voice. "I love the police! They're our friends." She then runs off to continue kissing.

Trixie draws smiley-faces on the shields with her lipstick while cheering "Yay!!" Soon she is writing "Yey!!"[1] on some of the riot shields, while the other clowns cheer. Images of her kisses and lipstick happy faces are broadcast and printed all over the world the next day. There is a marked gender element to this interaction—the male clowns aren't kissing any shields, but they are scrubbing away solicitously, saying things like "Oh, it's a mess, it's very bad—don't worry! I'll clean it, you won't get in any trouble!"

Soon the clowns form a line facing the police, and begin a motion-sound performance in unison. Bending at the hip with arms and hands

Figure 2.1 CIRCA clownbattants confront the riot police, Edinburgh, 4 July 2005. Photo by Matthew Dutton.

extended, they utter "Shhhhh," and then make a "Whooo" sound while standing straight. Through group improvisation, they are acting out an ambivalent, absurd gesture, simultaneously kowtowing to and shooing away the police. After five or six repetitions of this movement, the clowns begin jumping up and down, yelling "Yippie!"

At this precise moment, the police line breaks. They pull away, form two files, and jog away down the road at double time. The clowns briefly run alongside them, and a great cheer rises from the watching nonclown protesters and bystanders. Once the police are gone, a celebration begins in the street.[2]

It is prudent at this point to note that the police line may not have been broken by clown magic. A few blocks away, the clowns I was dancing with, in a more strategic intersection, were baton-charged. However, in this happier example, one can imagine the rear-rank conversation between the officers, or by walkie-talkie with headquarters:

"Look, we've become sucked into some kind of performance art here, and we'd really like to go elsewhere so we can fight crime . . . well, look, to be fair, our training doesn't include improv theatre . . . requesting permission to withdraw."

The improvisation of the clowns made such a poetic moment possible; where it appeared that fearless silliness and serious play could dispel the intimidating power of the state. As one clown said, "They loved us so much, we asked them to go away, and they did." This was not "street theatre" *per se*, but a form of improvisatory and creative direct action.[3] The clowns immediately began to fill the authority gap created by the policemen's withdrawal—power abhors a vacuum, after all—by directing traffic, including police wagons, with feather dusters, and giving passing vehicles the CIRCA Clown Salute (the thumbing of one's nose with a big smile: eventually, after several weeks, police were seen giving us this salute). Then the clowns continued playing games in order to hold the space.

This absurd face-off between two groups of masked, uniformed performers—police and clowns—occurred during the Carnival for Full Enjoyment on 4 July 2005. This tactical carnival was not a state-sanctioned ritual (as in a cultural steam-valve occurring, like *Mardi Gras*, within recognized temporal bounds based on the agrarian calendar). Rather, it was a festive and defiant event declared by members of the global justice movement. While in part a response to the G8 summit happening a few miles away at the fortified, remote country resort, Gleneagles, the carnival was not purely negative and reactive in character. It was an attempt to open up a space for anti-authoritarian, egalitarian and participatory celebration without state permits or sanction. With slogans such as "No Wage Slavery," "No Benefits Slavery," "No Army Slavery," and "No Debt Slavery," the Carnival for Full Enjoyment claimed to represent workers of all descriptions—"Flex, temp, full-time, part-time, casual, and contortionist workers, migrants, students, benefit-claimers, New Dealers, work-refusers, pensioners, dreamers, duckers & divers." In a press release, organizers urged workers to "Phone in Sick and Join the Carnival":

> **"Bring drums, music, banners, and imagination for action against the G8 that expresses our resistance in work, out of work and wherever we live. Assert our desires for FULL ENJOYMENT with fun in the city and begin to make capitalism & wage slavery history . . . On 4 July we can take action and experience—if only temporarily—what life could be like if we got the bosses off our backs."**

The announcement then evoked the joy of carnival with an anti-corporate twist:

> The Carnival for Full Enjoyment involves both local people and people from round Britain and beyond. We are making it a carnival because life should be more fun for those of us who labour in underpaid insecure jobs, in casual and agency work, or on 'New Deal' schemes. There should be more joy for the unemployed trying to survive on a few quid a week and for those of us juggling childcare and debt . . . Get together with friends and set your sights. Bring what you'd want to find, and most of all bring imagination and passion. Diversity and creativity is our strength . . . Our purpose is to oppose those who devastate our communities through economic exploitation. We will make clear our resistance to organisations which thrive on the poverty and debt in which many of us find ourselves. Because our society is mainly based on using people to make money for others, there are many such organisations to choose from.
>
> We are in favour of direct action because marching around with placards can be safely ignored by those who control exploitation. We advocate direct action against the institutions which exploit the majority . . . We invite workers from Standard Life and all other corporations to join the Carnival. Take an extended lunch-break, phone in sick! Join us in opposing casualisation, the intensification of work, attacks on pensions and conditions . . .
>
> *The carnival is a celebration of how good life can be, and at the same time a statement against those who spoil it for the majority.*
>
> (Carnival for Full Enjoyment, 2005; my italics)

The organizers explicitly presented the carnival as an anti-capitalist, anti-authoritarian event with links between local workers and activists, and a larger global movement. The carnival was to be a rejection of state authority (significantly, no permit was requested for this event), an affirmation of the joy of unified resistance (particularly resistance to the regulation of everyday behavior in privatized and controlled public space), and an alternative to the staid tactic of "marching around with placards."

The carnival was also seen as an opportunity for direct action to disrupt the proceedings of corporations and "business as usual" in the city. Authorities mobilized a massive police force in Edinburgh to protect banks and corporate offices from vandalism or nonviolent disruption such as sit-ins, and to prevent the reveling, disorderly crowds from blocking the streets. The government trucked in 10,000 uniformed officers from across the UK to respond to this threat to security and public order. Police filled the streets, blocking intersections, surrounding, searching, arresting, chasing, breaking up large groups of protestors and keeping them separated. Among protestors, there was a great deal of game-playing, samba bands, festive costumes, dancing, and revelry, and even a huge anarchist black cat puppet that spooked police horses. There was plenty of fleeing, regrouping, cat-and-mouse tactics, and on one street a scuffle between protestors and police.

Tactical carnival is partly a response to more conventional and institutionalized models of social-movement protest. The goal here is to open up public space with do-it-yourself group and individual creativity, rather than to merely occupy it with uniform marching and chanting while holding signs. This opening of public space for a freer and more festive direct action is one of the main goals of CIRCA.

CIRCA: the Clandestine Insurgent Rebel Clown Army

Figure 2.2 Recruiting card. Courtesy of the Laboratory of Insurrectionary Imagination.

CIRCA was formed in London in the autumn of 2003 when co-founder John Jordan proclaimed the existence of an army of "rebel clowns" who were to storm Buckingham Palace during a state visit by President George W. Bush. To make this vision a reality, several of us responded to the call, bringing training, inspiration, and creative agendas to the mission. We were armed with feather dusters, helmeted with colanders, and motivated by a clownish call for action, upon which the whole day of improvised foolery would hang. (This would serve as the model for CIRCA actions in the future—declaring a farcical central premise that would motivate a loose plan). Our first premise: CIRCA was elated to hear that a fool would be allowed back into the royal palace after so many centuries, but we were dismayed to find out it was the wrong kind of fool. So we mobilized.[4] As the *The Scotsman* reported:

> They had the unmistakable air of clowns with a purpose. They were, it turned out, the Clandestine Insurgent Rebel Clown Army, protesting at what they called the "auspicious news that, for the first time in 500 years, a fool is being allowed back into the Palace on official business."
>
> "Do you want a leaflet?" one inquired, thrusting it into my hand before marching off.
>
> A footnote explained that official court jesters were discontinued in the English court in 1638 when King Charles I sacked Archie Armstrong for a gibe against the Archbishop of Canterbury.
>
> The leaflet stated CIRCA's case, which appeared to be all for fools, but Dubya, it said, was "a false fool" whose "desire to spread global misery" had disqualified him from the job.
>
> Their demands were simple. If the Royal household did not rescind his invitation, they would "muster forces and prepare an assault on the palace" – custard pies at the ready. And with that, they set off, drumming loudly, across the square and towards the Palace.
>
> ("Clandestine Clowns," 2003)[5]

CIRCA was seen all over the city, marching with surprising military precision, turning on a dime and responding to Colonel Oftruth's calls: "Right—Sneer!" or "Left-spit!" The militarized slapstick—right column obediently spitting on left column's shoulder, then apologies all around, entertained crowds as we marched through major train stations. We dragged behind us our huge cardboard clown cannon, and a caisson filled with hundreds of lovingly painted pink pretzels. We set up the cannon, aiming it at targets like the Esso building—the UK version of Exxon. Shaking our fists in warning at the security guards and riot police protecting the target, we set up the *lazzo* or clown routine. As tension grew and a crowd gathered, we gloated about the devastation the cannon would cause as we laboriously loaded it and trembled with excitement, covering our ears. Once enough spectators had gathered, we pulled the pin! A pink pretzel shot out of the muzzle, sailed through the air about four inches, and fell to the pavement. We cheered in triumph! Then we reassembled in ranks and marched off, spitting and sneering on command.[6]

We marched behind Beefeaters for an admittedly easy visual joke. We attracted a great deal of attention from the international media, fielding questions on the street from reporters and more importantly from other protesters and passersby. There was something about our ridiculous intensity and quality, and our attention to detail in costumes, routines, and shtick that earned appreciation. "At least someone put in some effort!" was a typical comment we heard.

Confronted with several rather large, burly fellows on one street corner, I must confess that I indulged in the lowest kind of displaced abjection, always a danger during carnival. "WE HATE CLOWNS," said one ham-fisted gentleman. I said, in a bright tone, "well, at least we're not MIMES!" The giant considered this and said, "yeah, fair enough," and off we marched. Sorry, mimes—the only group lower than clowns in the cultural hierarchy.

We came upon a group of earnest activists doing a die-in. This simulation of mass death was once a shocking tactic, but was now, in our view, a worn, undynamic cliché. Colonel Klepto (Jordan), with a devilish gleam in his eye, said to me "Let's tickle them! Let's go and wake them and help them get up!" I suggested we just move on: I was less in *bouffon* mode. We later came upon a silent candlelight vigil in Trafalgar Square—and slowly and quietly backed away so as not to disrupt the reverent atmosphere with our absurdity. We do respect a diversity of tactics!

When we finally reached the park across from Buckingham Palace, we spontaneously went into faux-commando mode. We hit the ground, wriggling forward silently in the autumn leaves. We gave each other hand signals to stop or move forward. I should mention at this point that our uniforms were festooned with neon-bright pink and lime fuzz and fluff. As crowds gathered to watch our pseudo-sneaking, Colonel Oftruth stood up and began to hide behind a single leaf in his hand.

His comrades followed on point. A police helicopter swooped above us. Oftruth held the leaf over his head for cover. We marched toward the palace, delivered our manifesto about the true nature of the wise fool, denouncing the destructive false fools inside, cheered rousingly and withdrew back to the streets. The first day of action of the Clown Army was complete.

CIRCA was a motley group of radical artists, activists, military veterans, and actual clowns. We were a mix of hardcore activists facing burnout and hoping to do something rejuvenating; anti-war military veterans who could provide real training in formation drilling; clowns who could share actual clowning techniques; and a few radical performers and artists who had wanted to bring these hybrid forms together for creative direct action. The originators included Jordan, who had the initial spark of the idea, Jen Verson, Zoe Young, Theo Price, Matt Trevelyan, Hilary Ramsden, and myself; many others joined in the months that followed, bringing a wide range of skills.

Our training methods, which developed over time, included games from clowning and *bouffon* traditions, improvisational theatre, and performance art exercises from the Viola Spolin method and other traditions, as well as noncompetitive games, nonviolent civil disobedience, and horizontalist organization and communication. I modified some Theatre of the Oppressed exercises to add to the mix.

As we practiced and drilled in the parks of London, and gathered for costume-sewing parties, our group ethic, aesthetic, and sense of comradeship grew. We worked out some comedic routines, but also created war-related, *bouffon*-style deformities of which our clowns were grotesquely proud. In response to expected searches by police, we thought of ridiculous things to stuff our pockets with—flower petals (great for throwing in the air), toy soldiers, gum balls, bubble blowers, etc.

Later that autumn, CIRCA marched on the Greet the Buyers event in London, a meeting between corporations and the US-installed interim regime in Iraq, at which the privatization of Iraq's assets would be negotiated. The weather was stormy and hail fell from the sky. The streets were no less turbulent. Colonel Klepto was arrested. When his pockets were searched and the contents itemized, the police had to go through the whole list of absurd objects, culminating in a wind-up toy of a wanking bobby. The clowns marched to Klepto's rescue, arriving at the police station to perform strange clownish group movements in the lobby. My costume had disintegrated in the hailstorm, but I stayed in formation in clown mode as best I could. When kicked out of the police headquarters, we decorated the front of the building with festive ribbons. Matt Trevelyan, a brilliant Rabelaisian clown and free spirit, lost his trousers, as most clowns eventually do. The police came outside with large video cameras and spotlights, usually an intimidating move. Unfazed, we posed for the cameras as if shooting a grotesque, *bouffon* music video.

One policeman demanded that Trevelyan put his trousers back on. In a classic, performed example of the value of over-obedience and over-identification with hierarchy, Trevelyan slavishly agreed with the officer. The officer was right, he pleaded. It was shocking, SHOCKING that his trousers were in the wrong place. He then held his trousers out at full arms-length, shoulder height, and attempted to leap into them. He continued to attempt this impossible feat, apologizing profusely the entire time, while the police watched. Again and again, he jumped; again and again, he failed to land in his own trousers. The key to much clowning is needless exertion. Trevleyan had found a way to follow this guideline while mocking authority. It was a beautiful moment. When he finally pulled on his trousers, the clowns roared with victorious joy.

This kind of over-obedience in the face of oppression has been used in more serious circumstances, for example Communist rule in Poland. Tricksters of the Orange Alternative would stage laughably absurd events in celebration of Lenin—everyone wearing red, eating only red foods, and cheering wildly while an orator read a particularly staid and dated Lenin speech. The events were so excessively obedient, the secret police were unsure exactly what to do (Kenney, 2002). The Orange Alternative, in turn, picked up some of their symbolism and prankster moves from the Orange Free State of the Kabouters of the Netherlands.

Since 2003, CIRCA has been seen occupying the city of Leeds (UK); attempting to attend the Republican National Clown Convention in New York City as members of the Big Top Delegation; and disrupting daily operations at US and UK military recruitment centers by attempting to enlist, and then setting up Clown Army recruitment centers on the pavements outside. In both Leeds, UK, and Oakland, California, the recruitment centers shut down for the day in response to the clowns' theatrics.

With its horizontalist organizing model, CIRCA practices a form of nonviolent direct action that joins collective buffoonery with satirical performance. CIRCA moves *en masse* in tight-knit gaggles of ten or twelve, marching in accurate pseudo-military formation. Abruptly, they then break off into total clownarchy, engaging in antics and improvisation with passersby. Suddenly, and with no cue, the rebel clowns travel like a tightly clustered school of fish, all making the same sound and gesture, then changing direction simultaneously and making an entirely different sound and gesture. (This is called "fishing.") CIRCA's unpredictability and constant, collective shape-shifting come from hours of group practice and training. In their huddled and cuddled group movements, CIRCA evokes the carnivalesque mass as opposed to the idealized, individualistic, and discrete/discreet bourgeois body. CIRCA collectively embodies the neo-Bakhtinian concepts of Notes From Nowhere:

> The pleasures of the body have been banished from the public sphere of politics and the excitement of the erotic pushed into the narrow private confines of the sexual realm. But carnival brings the body back to public space, not the perfect smooth bodies that promote consumption on billboards and magazines, not the manipulated plastic bodies of MTV and party political broadcasts, but the body of warm flesh, of blood and guts, organs and orifices.
>
> During carnival the body sticks its tongue out as far as it can, it laughs uncontrollably, sweats and farts as it dances in the heat of other bodies. It's a body that refuses the static images of itself developed by capital, frozen in immortal youthfulness, aloof from natural cycles of eating and shitting, being born and decomposing. In carnival the body is always changing, constantly becoming, eternally unfinished. Inseparable from nature and fused to other bodies around it, the body remembers that it is not a detached, atomized being, as it allows its erotic impulse to jump from body to body, sound to sound, mask to mask, to swirl across the streets, filling every nook and cranny, every fold of flesh. During carnival the body, with its pleasures and desires, can be found everywhere, luxuriating in its freedom and inverting the everyday.
>
> (Notes From Nowhere, 2003: p. 175–76)

While CIRCA members rarely excrete on the street, they do move in groups and in ways that celebrate the group (mass body) over the individual, and earthiness and silliness over commercial standards of beauty and respectability:

> We see innovative forms of action as key for building dynamic social movements, but realize that the psyche is as important a

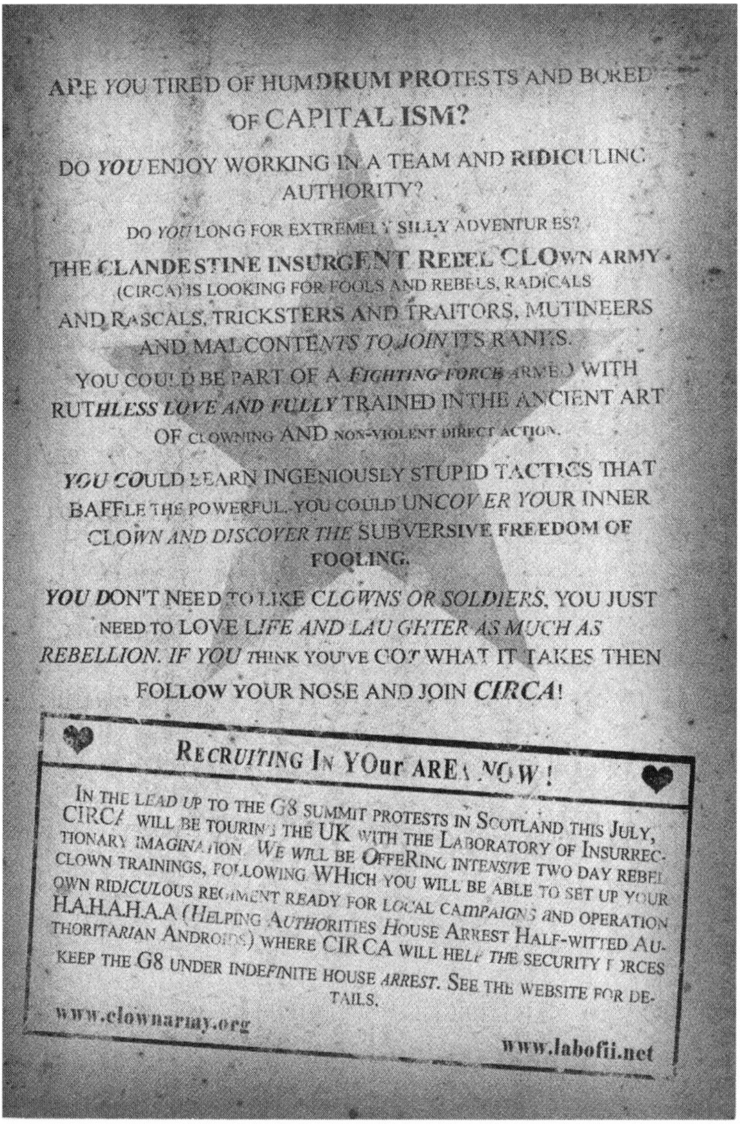

ARE YOU TIRED OF HUMDRUM PROTESTS AND BORED OF CAPITALISM?

DO YOU ENJOY WORKING IN A TEAM AND RIDICULING AUTHORITY?

DO YOU LONG FOR EXTREMELY SILLY ADVENTURES?

THE CLANDESTINE INSURGENT REBEL CLOWN ARMY (CIRCA) IS LOOKING FOR FOOLS AND REBELS, RADICALS AND RASCALS, TRICKSTERS AND TRAITORS, MUTINEERS AND MALCONTENTS TO JOIN ITS RANKS.

YOU COULD BE PART OF A FIGHTING FORCE ARMED WITH RUTHLESS LOVE AND FULLY TRAINED IN THE ANCIENT ART OF CLOWNING AND NON-VIOLENT DIRECT ACTION.

YOU COULD LEARN INGENIOUSLY STUPID TACTICS THAT BAFFLE THE POWERFUL. YOU COULD UNCOVER YOUR INNER CLOWN AND DISCOVER THE SUBVERSIVE FREEDOM OF FOOLING.

YOU DON'T NEED TO LIKE CLOWNS OR SOLDIERS, YOU JUST NEED TO LOVE LIFE AND LAUGHTER AS MUCH AS REBELLION. IF YOU THINK YOU'VE GOT WHAT IT TAKES THEN FOLLOW YOUR NOSE AND JOIN CIRCA!

RECRUITING IN YOUR AREA NOW!

IN THE LEAD UP TO THE G8 SUMMIT PROTESTS IN SCOTLAND THIS JULY, CIRCA WILL BE TOURING THE UK WITH THE LABORATORY OF INSURRECTIONARY IMAGINATION. WE WILL BE OFFERING INTENSIVE TWO DAY REBEL CLOWN TRAININGS, FOLLOWING WHICH YOU WILL BE ABLE TO SET UP YOUR OWN RIDICULOUS REGIMENT READY FOR LOCAL CAMPAIGNS AND OPERATION H.A.H.A.H.A.A (HELPING AUTHORITIES HOUSE ARREST HALF-WITTED AUTHORITARIAN ANDROIDS) WHERE CIRCA WILL HELP THE SECURITY FORCES KEEP THE G8 UNDER INDEFINITE HOUSE ARREST. SEE THE WEBSITE FOR DETAILS.

www.clownarmy.org

www.labofii.net

Figure 2.3 Recruiting card reverse side. Courtesy of the Laboratory of Insurrectionary Imagination.

> site for struggle as the street. CIRCA believes that a self-destructive tendency within many social movements is forgetting the inner work of personal liberation and transformation. This is an area our rebel clown trainings work on deeply, while also providing creative tools to confuse and befuddle authority.
>
> (CIRCA, 2005a)

As CIRCA members Isabelle Fremeaux and Hilary Ramsden describe in their essay "We Disobey to Love: Rebel clowning for social change," CIRCA training sessions aim to guide participants towards discovering and developing their own clown persona, learning to work together in groups without leaders, and joining freely and fearlessly in improvisation under pressure (2007). Finding one's inner clown involves coming up with a name, sensibility, physicality, and costume and makeup style. But it is also a much longer and deeper process that involves a great deal of thoughtful and playful exploration. Putting on makeup before an action is crucial to the transformation—the entry into one's alternate clown persona. This celebration of individual creativity and identity through the development of one's own clown enables CIRCA members to express themselves in the moment and mode of carnival while still sharing a larger group identity.

CIRCA aims to open up the spaces in which they move; to shift the paradigm or change the rules of behavior and engagement. They hope to bring the tactical carnival with them wherever they go, transforming confrontations into harmonic improvisations in the key of clown through absurdist cues and gestures. The spirit of playfulness can often be infectious, and civilians may be induced to play improvised games in the street. For example, several dozen clowns happen upon a speed bump and treat it as a unsurpassable obstacle, drawing on passersby to help them to climb over it, requiring a great deal of teamwork. The makeup and costumes of a mass of rebel clowns evoke a range of responses. CIRCA hopes their open vulnerability and fearlessness will prove infectious in the carnival spaces they create as they navigate the city. As the clowns greet police as "friends" and fail either to melt away in fear or raise tension with anger, a paradigm shift in the confrontation ensues.

The true challenge is to stay "in clown" even when conventional power relationships assert themselves. In a different neighborhood during the Carnival for Full Enjoyment, a small gaggle of rebel clowns was dancing in the streets with a samba band when they were attacked, at the blow of a whistle and a cry of "CHARGE!," by a rank of baton-waving policemen. The clowns, in a sophisticated, embodied reference to the teachings of Sun Tzu and Von Clausewitz, scattered and fled at top speed. Colonel Oftruth experimented with clown-rout shtick, cheerfully confiding to confused bystanders while running away: "We must be very dangerous!" (Note: Big clown shoes are a strong fashion choice, but impractical for such moments.)

CIRCA follows the egalitarian spirit of horizontalism and tactical carnival in its organizing model. While as many as 150 clowns were in Edinburgh at one time (and the sight of that many rebel clowns marching in perfect rank and file was a bizarre and mind-opening vision in itself), CIRCA is divided into "gaggles" of 10 or 12 clowns, analogous to the "affinity group" model of the direct-action movement. In groups of this size, members are working with people they know and trust. They develop models of group decision-making where every voice can be heard. When larger groups of clowns need to gather, they form a Clown Council where chosen spokesclowns (!) sit in a ring and speak for, and in constant consultation with, their own gaggles, who sit behind them in wedges. This basically follows the horizontalist model of organization, with the addition of makeup and red noses. To reflect our egalitarian ideology and disrupt police procedures of hailing, interpellation, and command, when police approached and demanded "Who's in charge here?" we would respond: "HE IS!" while pointing at a dog, a tree, a man watching us from a balcony above, or the sun.

Attitudes about carnival differed among CIRCA activists. Matthew Trevelyan, at some group meetings, read quotes directly from Rabelais' *Gargantua* (1936), which he found particularly inspiring and relevant. On the other hand, Jennifer Verson refused to accept the term carnival to describe CIRCA's efforts, denouncing its connotation as an escape valve for societal dissent.

Radical Origami and the caravan

> The moment we choose love we begin to move towards freedom, to act in ways that liberate ourselves and others. That action is the testimony of love as the practice of freedom.
>
> (bell hooks, 2005)

During the G8 campaign, CIRCA's central gaggle, including its co-founders, traveled throughout the UK in a biodiesel-fueled van, bearing the banner with the words "LABORATORY OF INSURRECTIONARY IMAGINATION." The laboratory was the umbrella organization of the tour, including the anti-consumerist group, Church of the Immaculate Consumption. When CIRCA pulled into a new city, the group would set up a performance space, and give a free show that included puppetry, performance art, and video presentations, all around the themes of civil disobedience, the G8, and rebel clowning. *The Aberdeen Press and Journal* describes CIRCA's activity:

> The Clandestine Insurgent Rebel Clown Army believes "nothing undermines authority like holding it up to ridicule" and takes on capitalism armed with red noses, tickling sticks and custard pies. During last year's meeting of the European Social Forum in London it employed tactics such as urban climbing across the entrances of banks and games of street tag around department store makeup counters. The group, which was set up to protest against George Bush's visit to Britain in 2003, is recruiting in Glasgow and Edinburgh this week ahead of G8 and held two sold-out training sessions in what it calls "subversive play" in Aberdeen's Tunnels nightclub last week.
>
> ("It's Iffy Miffy," 2005)

During the recruiting-tour performances, clowns gave out Radical Origami papers, designed by Jordan and Fremeaux, in the shape of a heart and covered with movement-oriented quotes. In the course of the show, the audience was taught how to fold the heart into various objects: dunce cap, megaphone, and French fries container. Jordan's design included a mischievous bit of biting the hand that feeds you. When the paper was folded into a cone, the words "funded in part by the British Arts Council" appeared on the tip. When it was time for the audience to use the cone as a megaphone, Jordan instructed them to rip off the tip so they could shout their desire through the cone. This was nicely symbolic—the state sponsorship label removed to amplify the voice. He called this the "radical rip-off" (CIRCA, 2005b).

During the intermission, organic French fries were distributed to all, and CIRCA explained to the audience that the fat from the fryer was recycled to power the biodiesel-fuelled van. Thus the possibility of a fossil fuel-free world was exemplified in CIRCA's practice, and playfully incorporated into the performance. After the performance, CIRCA announced that it would train interested locals in rebel clowning and nonviolent civil disobedience. We used the press and media to publicize these trainings, which resulted in a few radical soundbites and jokes:

> Self-styled "red nose rebels" are to run a clown school in Birmingham teaching protesters how to picket the forthcoming G8 summit with a funny face. The Clandestine Insurgent Rebel Clown Army is holding a two-day training weekend aimed at "making clowning dangerous again." Graduates will travel to Scotland in July to take part in non-violent direct action aimed at keeping the world leaders meeting at the Gleneagles golf complex under "house arrest." The organization claims to be composed of genuine clowns who have "run away from the circus" and "escaped the banality of kids' parties." The training course, to be held next month, will include tuition on civil disobedience, learning to be spontaneous and "finding your inner clown." "With greasepaint we give resistance a funny face," the group said. "Alone, clowns are pathetic figures but in groups and gaggles, brigades and battalions, they are extremely dangerous. We are reclaiming the art of rebel clowning." . . . The training course will be held at Decoy Arts, Green Street, Digbeth, from 10am to 6pm on June 4 and 5. Places will be limited to 50. They are free but must be booked.
>
> ("Clowns to Go On Warpath," 2005)

With this training tour, our CIRCA caravan served as a seeder group, starting CIRCA gaggles in each city that would then continue to train and practice on their own. Naturally, police agents tried to infiltrate groups during the training workshops, but they were usually easy to detect. Rather than be bothered by this infiltration, we gave the infiltrators useful tasks like sewing costumes, thereby putting the tax money spent on their salaries to good use. This was fair, because they were usually not very good clowns![7]

By the time of the Clown Council in Edinburgh ahead of the G8, a total of about 150 clowns, in a dozen gaggles from all over the UK, Ireland, Belgium, Italy, France, and Spain, gathered together to debate and discuss a plan of action.[8] We were all surprised by the large size of the gathering, as battalions and brigades arrived from many different cities. The BBC, which had embedded reporters in the British military during the Iraq War, asked if they could embed some reporters in our "army." After some debate and concern about how much access to give reporters, we agreed. The reporters made clown costumes and covered us fairly in the documentary, *G8, Can You Hear Us?*

CIRCA's main focus was on direct action in public space. However, it also hoped to speak through the media by generating absurd quotes and images critical of G8 policies and capitalism. These were messages not being enunciated by the celebrities of the Live Aid concert. (It may be for this reason that Bob Geldof was quoted as saying he didn't want a "bunch of guys dressed as clowns" showing up and ruining his show.) In order to spread this critique, CIRCA organized an absurdist "press conference" for 1 July 2005. The press release, written with the earnest absurdity of clown-logic, hoped to highlight CIRCA's concerns about the social movement being coopted by Labour Party leaders reportedly planning to join in the Make Poverty History march in Edinburgh. CIRCA also wanted to call attention to their biodiesel-powered van and the possibility it raised for a fossil fuel-free future. (Of course, recent research has made it clear that biodiesel recycled from food grease is a fine marginal method for replacing gasoline, but is not a long-term solution.) The press release read:

> **CLANDESTINE INSURGENT REBEL CLOWN ARMY (CIRCA) ANNOUNCES ITS FIRST G8 CAMPAIGN PRESS CONFERENCE**
>
> **FREE CHIPS TO BE DISTRIBUTED TO THE MEDIA . . .**
>
> **To the Media and Press:**
>
> **Please meet us at 12:30 pm on Friday 1st July at our lovely caravan . . . At this briefing, we will explain our immensely important role in support of the Make Poverty History march. We will then demonstrate the techniques of radical clowning with which we will protect the march—and we will receive an honorary salute from the cannons at Edinburgh Castle, showing the Queen's approval for our campaign.**
>
> **Free chips will be served! The chip fat will power our biodiesel van to Gleneagles! If you eat the chips you will help our movement move forward!! Hee hee hee!!!**
>
> **With all due respect, CIRCA**

In our accompanying communiqué, we hoped to call attention to the threat of cooptation of this grassroots radical movement by celebrities and politicians with different agendas:

> **To all our rebel friends in the global justice movement . . . We share your compassion and desire to TRULY make poverty history . . . We know the G8, far from being thanked for "forgiving" these illegitimate debts, should beg forgiveness from the Global South for their ongoing crimes and depredations . . .**

CIRCA hoped to make a clear distinction between direct action and lobbying for change from the powerful:

> **We of CIRCA thank YOU, our friends here at this march, for being part of a beautiful and loving nonviolent social movement to achieve true justice . . . for of course it is only through social movements that real social change can happen—not from begging the politicians or corporations to behave more nicely.**
>
> **BUT . . . the CIRCA Advanced Intelligence Team has discovered a grave threat to our powerful movement, just as we are all gaining momentum and making our demands for profound change heard. It has come to our attention . . . that SEVERAL CRIMINAL, ANTISOCIAL ELEMENTS are trying to HIJACK and CO-OPT our MOVEMENT! They are HERE, AMONGST US, these DANGEROUS EXTREMISTS, and they MAY even be marching in this very demonstration!!! They are GORDON BROWN (MP), the financier of the invasion of Iraq, whose £5 billion War Reserve Fund could, instead, fully immunize EVERY CHILD in the developing world for two years, who has stated explicitly that aid will go down as much as debt is relieved for a net change of ZERO, and that recipient countries will have to restructure their societies to make them even more vulnerable to the market. HILLARY BENN (MP) may also be present, wearing his pretty "development" mask over his true face of privatization and plunder. BEWARE! If you see Brown or any of his Errorist henchmen, please report them to the clown patrol nearest to you on the march, and keep your distance.**

We also hoped to reinforce the historical connection between the massive movement converging on Edinburgh and the greater global justice movement:

> **CIRCA has mobilized to PATROL and PROTECT our movement, so that it is not HIJACKED by these ghoulish buffoons. Our movement's unique accomplishment is the creation of a grassroots politics WITHOUT professional politicians and parliaments (as they have said in Bolivia, Argentina, Ecuador, Chiapas, and beyond, "Que se vayan todos! (Out with them all!)" We must not let these brown-nosing interlopers mislead us on our own march! . . .**
>
> **With love, laughter and red-nosed resistance,**

Colonel Oftruth, General Confusion
Clandestine Insurgent Rebel Clown Army

The actual press conference began with CIRCA feeding organic chips to the media (when most of them balked, with one journalist expressing fear that the chips were laced with LSD, Colonel Oftruth gleefully threatened to mash the chips into the camera lenses, and was sure to hand-feed each reporter until they all relented).[9]

A demonstration of CIRCA's parade skills followed, as an entire battalion marched directly into (and behind, and on top of) a tiny phone booth. CIRCA then demonstrated its fishing movement, and explained the premise of Operation HAHAHAA (Helping Authorities House Arrest Half-witted Authoritarian Androids), in which CIRCA planned to help the security forces with their ongoing house arrest of the G8's leaders—the ultimate "dangerous, anti-social, criminal elements" in the Gleneagles resort. The press reported on this with some choice quotes and commentary on police readiness for violence that seemed strange in juxtaposition to the descriptions of CIRCA:

> Protesters rallying against the G8 summit this summer are planning to cause chaos—by sending in an army of anarchist circus clowns.
>
> Anti-capitalists hatched the bizarre plan to antagonize police during the Gleneagles summit. The group, which calls itself the Clandestine Insurgent Rebel Clown Army (CIRCA), said it planned to "help" keep law and order. A spokesman said, "We are launching Operation HAHAHAA—Helping Authorities House Arrest Half-witted Authoritarian Androids—during which we will help the security forces keep the G8 under indefinite house arrest." CIRCA, which has been involved in a number of protests

> in the past, will use props such as tickling sticks and custard pies to harass police officers. The move is part of a concerted plan being co-ordinated by anarchists from Dissent Network, which will include disrupting transport.
>
> A spokesman for the Association of Chief Police Officers in Scotland said specialist units will be on hand with the estimated 30,000 demonstrators expected in Scotland for the event.
>
> ("G8 Anarchists," 2005)

And *The Sun* chimed in:

> . . . They have vowed to travel from across Britain to the event between July 6 and 8 and put world leaders 'under house arrest.' CIRCA has invaded buildings like army recruitment centers, harassed police and tried to recruit people for "civil disobedience training" in recent years. And a spokesman last night urged other demonstrators to clown around. He said: "You could be part of a fighting force armed with ruthless love and fully trained in the ancient art of clowning and non-violent direct action. You could learn ingeniously stupid tactics that baffle the powerful. You could uncover your inner clown and discover the subversive freedom of fooling." The clowns face a battle to even get near world leaders as 10,000 police will be on duty and a five-mile fence is going up around the famous hotel where the event is being held . . .
>
> (Herbert, 2005)

This typical CIRCA action premise used clown logic, assuming the best of the worst, by offering help to the lovely people of the security forces gathered at Gleneagles, grateful that they too realized how dangerous the G8 was to the future of the world.

Following the demonstration of parade skills, CIRCA then read its communiqué and scattered in all directions. The next day, several papers, including the *Daily Record*, *Daily Express*, and *Daily Star*, quoted our communiqué, which enunciated amid a great deal of ironic silliness a serious critique of the G8's actual policies and responsibility for the debt of the Global South, along with the disarming CIRCA claim that they would "amuse, bemuse, but never bruise." As Colonel Oftruth, I was often responsible for providing the kernel of truth throughout our clownish madness, by writing and orating our communiqués to the press. In this case, it was good to see policy points quoted along with accounts of madcappery. The *Daily Star* of 2 July noted:

> as thousands of protesters set up camp in the capital, clown leader Colonel Oftruth said: "The only real way to end poverty, in the global south or in the suburbs of Edinburgh, is to stop the great eight's amusingly anti-social habits."
>
> ("Fears of a Clown," 2005)

And the *Daily Express* drew a longer quote:

> The Clandestine Insurgent Rebel Clown Army took to the streets to brand Gordon Brown and International Development Secretary Hillary Benn "dangerous extremists."
>
> The army's spokesman, who identified himself only as "Colonel Oftruth," said: "The only real way to end poverty is to stop the great eight's amusingly anti-social habits, their rather nasty slapstick routines of kicking the poorer nations with war, arms sales, and bullying trade policies, manipulating their markets and plundering their resources while dangling the crumbs of debt forgiveness."
>
> (Swanson, 2005)

Our intent was to change the hegemonic discourse around the impending global justice demonstrations, reversing the rhetoric of criminalization and "anti-social elements" to where we felt it better applied, and making points about troubling policy issues while wearing the red nose. The red nose was an ambivalent tool here—it both amplified our voice by attracting attention and made us more absurd. Getting the balance just right was the challenge. Our mandate was to attract attention as a bizarre novelty item and then to flip the tone of the performance at just the right time to make the point. We did not always succeed, but we had our moments.

"Earned media" is a term that refers to media coverage that is not purchased as advertising, but free news coverage received by pitching a good story or press release to journalists. There is a parallel between activists' earned media and the idea of "earning a moment" for serious political critique with a theatrical audience. CIRCA actions were a hybrid of creative direct action that blocked roads or disrupted meetings in a festive way, combined with indirect action that used spectacular absurdity to attract press and media coverage to a radical critique of serious issues. It was a classic example of serious play.

Press coverage of CIRCA served to disrupt the hegemonologue that depicted protesters as violent and dangerous. Even in right-wing newspapers that were hostile to the movement's agenda, quotes and photographs of CIRCA members provided a cognitive dissonance to the reactionary storyline. On one such page of the *Daily Mirror*, under the huge headline "RIOT POLICE . . . 1 ANARCHISTS . . . 0: G-Hate aggro kicks-off as cops crush violent protesters," and next to a photograph of a beaten protestor, is the image of Trixie kissing the shield of a smiling policeman, with the subtitle of "KISS AND MAKEUP: Member of the Rebel Clowns plants smacker on cop riot shield." The *Daily Mail* also showed a picture of Trixie's kiss next to a photograph of a female protestor being arrested by heavily armored police, and this image was reproduced in American newspapers as well (Moore & McGregor, 2005; Madeley & Macaskill et al., 2005; Johnson, 1996). These images may have disrupted the constant barrage of dehumanizing rhetoric about protestors, if only from the jarring juxtaposition of the visuals above the denunciatory text. A reader might have wondered (if only for a split second): if these protesters appeared to be clowning around and kissing shields, why were they being beaten and arrested?

The image of Trixie kissing the riot shield, shown on the cover of this book, is an example of what I refer to as an *irresistible image*; an image so compelling or strange or surprising that even one's ideological opponents will reproduce it—even if it undermines their own narrative (and even if only because they know that all of their competitors will be publishing it). I do not wish to overstate the value of an irresistible image; it is just one tool in the activist toolbox, and a tricky one to use, but I believe it can be a useful one in the cultural "air-war" aspect of social-movement struggle.

CIRCA's years-long tradition of stuffing our pockets with silly things to create a spectacle mocking the search-and-seizure surveillance state paid off during this carnival. A reporter for *The Scotsman* noted:

> Earlier in the day, and on a lighter note, the Rebel Clown Army had been detained while putting on their make up and red noses. Police found an arsenal of weapons including a feather duster, water pistols and soapy bubbles. About 30 of the clowns—who wore an unusual combination of army combat fatigues, neon pink wigs, colanders on their heads and other fluffy accessories—were surrounded by police in Teviot Place. Some clowns ran away giggling, but others were forced to wait while police searched them. All the clowns insisted on speaking in high-pitched voices, dancing around and making jokes . . .
>
> (Brown & Gray et al., 2005)

Page 2 Daily Mail, Tuesday, July 5, 2005

Innocent shoppers and office workers caught up in violent clashes after

The carnival that

By **Gavin Madeley, Grace Macaskill, Gordon Tait** and **Graham Grant**

RIOT police clashed with G8 protesters in a series of angry confrontations that brought chaos to Scotland's capital yesterday.

The centre of Edinburgh came to a standstill as 1,000 anarchists took to the streets in a day of violence and disruption.

Officers came under attack from activists in scenes that realised some of the worst fears of police planners.

As the fighting intensified, police asked city centre businesses to keep staff indoors and away from windows.

The violence came after an unauthorised demonstration was hijacked by protesters described by police as determined to 'inflict disruption and significant disorder'.

Among them were masked members of the notorious Black Bloc anarchist group, which caused turmoil at the G8 summit in Genoa four years ago.

Sixty arrests were made yesterday and a total of 21 people were injured, including two police officers, although nobody was thought to be seriously hurt. At least seven were admitted to hospital.

Last night, the riots reached fever pitch when protesters were joined by local thugs. In Rose Street, shopping trolleys stolen from Sainsbury's were used against police lines.

And, with more protesters arriving ahead of Bob Geldof's planned 'million-man march' on Edinburgh tomorrow, police fear that the huge numbers, combined with those intent on violence, could cause chaos today.

Yesterday's demonstrations, under the banner of The Carnival For Full Enjoyment, were said by organisers to be aimed at highlighting their anti-war and anti-wage slavery message.

Officers were attacked by protesters hurling metal bins, rocks, bottles and bin bags full of rotting rubbish.

Much of the West End of the city was closed to traffic as the protesters – many in fancy dress, with others in black with their faces masked – marched and danced to the sound of samba drums and whistles.

But the mood turned as police repeatedly prevented gangs of

Robert Hardman's view – Pages 4-5

activists from marching towards the city's financial district.

The most serious incident happened on Princes Street between the Scott Monument and The Mound, where officers confronted a group of about 200 who had been hurling rocks and missiles.

At about 2.30pm, as the clouds above Edinburgh darkened momentarily, the group's incessant chanting and taunts turned briefly to screams of panic as heavily armoured police finally moved in, their patience exhausted.

In a pincer movement, they swamped the gang, apparently concentrating their efforts on singling out ringleaders.

The sudden action caused an immediate and angry response from other protesters, who tried to block officers' way.

The melee quickly descended into a running battle as black-clad anarchists hurled waste bins and wooden staves before trading blows with baton-wielding officers dressed in riot gear and carrying full-length shields.

In a separate incident, a squad of more than 150 police officers in riot gear walked into a carefully orchestrated ambush as they pursued a gang of anarchists.

Officers were showered by missiles and rotting rubbish after being led along a dual carriageway by members of the group known as the 'Clown Army'.

Most roads in the city centre were blocked at one stage during the day and the sounds of helicopters and sirens filled the air. At about 6pm, a tense confrontation began between protesters and police.

More than 100, mostly wearing black, were channelled into Rose Street, a narrow pedestrian thoroughfare that runs parallel to Princes Street.

Chanting demonstrators began hurling bottles and tried to set up a barricade using shopping trolleys.

About a dozen mounted officers plus 30 on foot then retaliated by charging at the protesters, sparking brief but violent skirmishes.

Commemorative benches were ripped out of Princes Street Gardens, cobblestones were torn from the street and lobbed at officers and riot shields were snatched from them by demonstrators.

Police briefly advised all businesses in the city centre to close and to keep staff locked inside until further notice.

A spokesman said: 'We want staff to remain in the premises and to stay away from windows and not look out.'

Shops on Princes Street locked their doors and boarded their windows while many office workers were given the day off or were sent home early. Financial institutions were on high alert after warnings from the police and some employees were unable to get home because of roadblocks.

Kenny Ward, a 20-year-old office junior for an Edinburgh law firm, was sent out to check on the demonstrations and it was subsequently decided to close his office.

He said: 'There was a real sense of tension, as if nobody knew quite what to expect.'

David Land, of the Federation of Small Businesses, said: 'It has obviously had a major effect, but it's too early to say how much money will have been lost.'

Meanwhile, one of the ringleaders in the violent mayhem at the Genoa G8 meeting four years ago has vowed to breach police lines at the Gleneagles summit.

Francesco Caruso, leader of the Italian anarchist movement Disobbedienti, said he and his followers aimed to cause trouble in Scotland.

In Genoa, Caruso's Disobbedienti were one of the groups that caused more than £3million-worth of damage in the rioting.

He said: 'The prayers of the Pope and global concerts are not enough to convince world leaders.'

Up close: A protester in clown make-up kisses an officer's riot shield

Down and out: Riot control officers handcuff a masked female

Battle lines: Mounted officers join riot police as they prepare to advance on a crowd of demonstrators in Edinburgh's Rose Street

TODAY'S WEATHER: PAGE 6

Figure 2.4 A page from the conservative tabloid *Daily Mail.* The irresistible image of the clown kissing the riot shield provides a strange disruptive commentary on the anti-protest text of the articles including bizarre claims of a clown rubbish-ambush. Courtesy of the *Daily Mail.*

Despite very real clashes between police and citizens during the carnival, such press coverage undermined the rhetoric from the state about the threat of violent protestors. By the end of the campaign, there were some small signs of fraternization between some of the rank-and-file police and opposing clowns—an exchange of glances and

PAGE 4 DAILY MIRROR, Tuesday, July 5, 2005

G8: MAKE

RIOT POLICE... 1 ANARCHISTS.. 0

KISS AND MAKE UP: Member of the Rebel Clowns plants smacker on cop riot shield

HEAD BANGER: Protestor looks dazed after being wounded during city centre skirmishes

G-Hate aggro kicks-off as cops crush violent protesters

By RON MOORE, Chief Reporter and FIONA McGREGOR

POLICE clashed with hardcore protesters yesterday as anti-G8 extremists turned violent.

Hundreds of anarchists descended on Edinburgh to demonstrate days before the Gleneagles summit.

Some hooligans pelted police with paving stones, benches, metal bins, rocks, bottles and plants in and around Princes Street.

Officers responded by drawing their batons and charging into the crowds in front of stunned shoppers and bystanders.

One extremist group, the Rebel Clown Army, lured pursuing police into an ambush, where they were showered with rubbish.

Another rioter scaled an office building before urinating onto the cops below.

Police chiefs last night slammed the troublemakers, branding violence which marred the demonstrations as "unacceptable".

But some protesters accused the authorities of provoking trouble.

Natasha Crofton, 22, said: "I want to protest against capitalism in a non-violent way.

"The police pushed against us so we all linked arms and I got smacked twice in the face.

"We were shouting 'we are peaceful, what are you?'" The event had begun under the banner of The Carnival For Full Enjoyment.

But it was quickly hijacked by hardline anarchists from Germany, Italy, Holland and across the UK.

Groups including the Black Bloc, Dissent, Clandestine Insurgent Rebel Clown Army and Wombles led the protests.

Protesters skirmished with cops, and hurled missiles at police lines.

More than 150 officers in riot gear were ambushed as they chased a gang of clowns who had been among a crowd of over 200 protesters at the Standard Life HQ in Lothian Road.

They were showered with missiles and rotting rubbish from a bridge after being lured along the Western Approach Road.

In another flashpoint, cops were kicked and punched by a mob as they pinned an anarchist to the ground in Princes Street. They were then met with a barrage of soil and plants dug up from Princes Street Gardens.

Missiles were also hurled after protesters were hemmed in between a line of riot police and a line of mounted police near to the Scott Monument.

Officers burst into the crowd and recovered several weapons.

In a bizarre protest, one anarchist stripped off his clothes and walked naked down the street while the riot continued.

Other protesters kissed police riot shields, leaving lipstick marks. At the east end of Rose Street thugs hurled paving stones, bottles and bakery baskets from a nearby Sainsbury's store at a line of riot cops backed by mounted police.

Officers made a series of charges to push the crowd back at a point where the street was less than 40ft wide.

Police cordoned off many of the marchers in Canning Street, a lane near the city's business district, as they targeted financial institutions.

Standard Life staff were warned to stay away from windows. A wall of police also surrounded Bute House, the First Minister's official residence, and more than 1,000 police guarded the Scottish Parliament.

Some members of the public not connected to the protests were caught up within the police cordons and unable to leave the city centre.

After three hours contained between lines of police riot shields on Princes Street, protesters were allowed to leave one at a time.

But first each had to agree to give their name and date of birth to officers, while some were searched and photographed.

Lothian and Borders Assistant Chief Constable Ian Dickinson said officers had found evidence that violence was well-planned, seizing maps, radio gear and weapons.

He added: "It is clear peaceful protest was never on their agenda."

Cops, who made 60 arrests, later revealed they had targeted known ringleaders of the anarchist groups.

The "key" troublemakers had been tracked by cops across the UK and when they started marshalling the rioters, snatch squads of riot police moved in to arrest them.

r.moore@mirror.co.uk

VICTIM: Cops help injured girl

Figure 2.5 A page from the *Daily Mirror*. Again, the irresistible image of Trixie kissing the shield partially undercuts the criminalizing narrative of the text on the page. Courtesy of the *Daily Mirror*.

sympathy through the visors and makeup that covered the faces of cops and clowns. While the clowns were directing traffic at one intersection, a police van drove by and officers grinningly gave CIRCA the Clown Salute in a gesture of comradely contempt. Elsewhere, one police officer, hearing the clowns do the "Yes, let's" exercise (in which one clown says "Let's all do X!" and all other clowns in hearing range must say "YES! Let's all do X!," and then do it), said "Let's go to the park, because that's where the clowns are going and we have to follow them!" At one point, CIRCA members were once again confronted with a line of stone-faced police, and a clown began ironically thanking the police for supporting global capitalism. The heavy-handed, ironic speech went on a bit long, and another clown (activist Jennifer Verson) told the police, "If you smile, I'll tell him to be quiet." According to Verson, several of the police immediately put beaming smiles on their faces.[10]

Later, on the motorway approaching Gleneagles, a group of rebel clowns came upon four patrolmen guarding a bridge. The clowns asked them if they wanted to play a game, and they agreed. After an explanation of the rules to "Giants, Wizards and Goblins," the two sides huddled to choose a strategy, then grinningly lined up facing each other. On the count of three, both lines simultaneously aimed their outstretched arms at each other and wiggled their fingers as if casting a spell. The police and the clowns had both chosen the Wizard option. They immediately obeyed the hallowed rule of the game: if both sides choose the same creature, they have to hug. Which they dutifully did. The embrace between police-wizards and clown-wizards after days of conflict was a hopeful, if bizarre, sight (Young, 2005). While the occasional softening of relations may have been denounced by more hardcore anarchists, others, such as founding CIRCA member Jennifer Verson, saw it as a historically proven and essential element in destabilizing power, and making real social change. Activists had established a human connection with rank-and-file police, eroding anger and stereotyping, and experimenting with new methods of interaction.[11] The value of this kind of fraternization had been suggested in older sources such as the 1965 *Manual for Direct Action* (Oppenheimer & Lakey: p. 75). This is another way to creatively break cliché—in this case the cliché of automatic behavior in a confrontation that suspends thought and original, contingent action.

CIRCA confronts power by playing with it—resisting as much as possible the interpellation of conventional power relations at the immediate point of articulation of that power in public space. CIRCA attempts to create a temporary, evanescent, improvised carnival space where the rules are destabilized, and new possible relations are suggested and under experiment (Bey, 1985). CIRCA's original members have moved on to other projects, but the website with its "training manual" and videos remained until mid-2015, and the concept has

Figure 2.6 The Clown Army manifests in Rostock, Germany in a G8 protest and poses with the police, 2 June 2007. Fabian Bimmer/AP/Press Association Images.

continued to manifest around the world. A well-organized Clown Army took part in the G8 protest in Germany two years later.

In the US, when the paramilitary Minutemen were at the height of their armed patrols on the border with Mexico, a trained CIRCA-inspired gaggle calling itself the Boredom Patrol mobilized to play with, distract, and confuse them. Perhaps most inspiringly, masses of clowns mobilized to confront, mock, and deflate the atmosphere of terror and cruelty at demonstrations by neo-Nazis and Ku Klux Klansmen in Tennessee and North Carolina (Rivas, 2014; Santos, 2014; "Clowns Kicked KKK Asses," 2007).

In the San Francisco Bay Area, a short-lived CIRCA group formed in 2005, and we discovered one interesting tactical deployment: we formed a line between the riot police and the demonstration. The visual effect—clowns armed with feather dusters funhouse-mirroring the poses of police—was amusing and disarming. We thus formed a sort of clowny cushion for the protest. The police would have to hit us before beating down the other protesters, and they were aware that such a spectacle would be hard to justify. It is politically more costly to club a clown on camera than a demonstrator. Or a masked black bloc anarkid. Incidentally, CIRCA training includes how to respond to police shoving or poking with clubs: a) respond as if being tickled; b) when shoved, give way, but spin round and round like multicolored tops down the street.

These carnival-inspired power-plays can be problematic. While the experience of training and playing with CIRCA, or with carnivalesque protest in general, can be liberating for individual participants, these actions in and of themselves only hint at a better, possible world. Tactical carnival does not change the fundamental relations of production or distribution in the greater society. The liberatory spaces it creates are quickly dispersed, either by the force of the state or by the inevitable need of its participants to eventually get back to work.

Indeed, these spaces, while embracing a carnivalesque egalitarianism, are not equally open to all. The cost of participation is more easily faced by those with the resources to endure arrest. Race or class privilege lessens the risks and penalties of confrontation with the state. For an account of the community-sustaining clowning among working-class African–American youth in Los Angeles, see the movie *RIZE* (Shepard, 2005). The clowns of CIRCA wore white facepaint, but most were also white beneath the paint.

We received thoughtful critiques from several sides of the movement. A few "spiky" activists who wished to engage in street battles with police complained that the clowns were getting in the way. More conventional organizers complained that the disproportionate media we attracted made the whole movement look clownish—a claim I almost wish were true, but which I don't think is backed up by a comprehensive survey of the media coverage of events such as the Gleneagles G8. I would also repeat Hilary Ramsden's mantra, "serious but not solemn": it is possible, and desirable, to make deadly serious points in compelling and interesting ways other than with furrowed brow and clenched jaw. David Solnit, who joined CIRCA in 2005, pointed out that the CIRCA-look was still a bit ragged and strange, and that if our costumes had been more beautiful in a conventional sense we would have had more appeal outside of the protest subculture. John Jordan, who first put out the call to form CIRCA, looked back on the project and concluded that it was key that the clowns be highly skilled. When we radically increased the size of the group, we lost that quality, and it would have been better to keep the group small. Solnit and Jordan make good points; I still feel that the CIRCA concept is scalable, if strengthened with modular action concepts that are relatively easy to enact in different locations. For example, the aforementioned actions at military recruitment centers were very effective, and if reproduced in dozens of locations could have been a powerful phenomenon.

Different nations and states have different policing policies, and this radically affects the tactics and range of motion of creative protesters. Activists must adjust to their local cultural and legal terrains. For example, in Britain rebel clowns were able, at times, to interact playfully with the police; but in New York City, where the policing is more violent and militarized, it is necessary to make the fearsome context part of the shtick. CIRCA/NYC members are therefore much more likely to flee helter-skelter at the slightest hint of trouble and hide behind very small objects.

While rebel clowning is a joyful way to find courage and to play with power, there is a necessary element of sorrow or even despair mixed into these performances. It should be used sparingly as its outrageous tone does not fit every confrontation. However, no single tactic can solve the problems that the global justice movement confronts, and clowning is only one tactic among many in the ongoing experiment of resistance. Indeed, the danger of becoming predictable demands that tactical carnival creates a space for constant experimentation with new ideas and tactics.

Notes

1 Authentic rebel clown spelling of "Yay!"
2 10,000 officers had been brought up from England to police the city. For historical reasons, many local Scots resented this intrusion from the south more than they did the bizarre protests.
3 "Direct action" is a term for activist methods that directly confront and disrupt or change sociopolitical processes, as opposed to "indirect action" that seeks to lobby for change through influencing politicians or swaying public opinion.
4 For a sober and statesmanlike summary of these issues, see "All Things Considered" interview with Colonel Oftruth on NPR (13 Nov 2003).
5 See also, Colonel Oftruth's description of the action at: www.redpepper.org.uk/Keeping-alive-this-historic/
6 The ammunition was a reference to the recent incident when President Bush had choked on a pretzel. Harsh and ridiculous, the humor was in tone with the event and the tradition of the *bouffon* or grotesque clown.
7 See, for example, the mediocre clowning by the police officer in the video by Zoe Young, *Undercover Clown Cop: Lynne Watson – UK*, YouTube.
8 Our accommodations were improvised. One night, I slept with the entire Belgian Battalion, which sounds more fun than it was, since we were forced to bunk on the floor of a tiny room. However, the Belgians were brilliant clowns and their epic lullabies in eight-part harmony were enchanting.

9 Hats off to nutty protest group the Clandestine Insurgent Rebel Clown Army. They got round the no fuel situation by handing out chips to journalists last week and using the fat to power their biodiesel van to Gleneagles!

(Whelan, 2005)

10 Interview with the author, 3 July 2005.
11 Jennifer Verson, in conversation with the author, 3 July 2005.

References

Althusser, L. (1971) "Ideology and Ideological State Apparatuses (Notes Towards an Investigation." In *Lenin and Philosophy and Other Essays*. New York: Verso.

Bey, H. (1985) *TAZ Temporary Autonomous Zones*. www.hermetic.com/bey/taz_cont.html (accessed 12 Sept 2005).

Brown, A.; Gray, L.; Howie, M.; McGinty, S. (2005) "The Carnival Turns into Anarchy." *The Scotsman*, 5 July 2005.

Carnival for Full Enjoyment (2005) Flyer/pamphlet. Personal archive of the author. Also available: www.nodeal.org.uk (accessed 12 Nov 2005).

CIRCA (2005a) *G8 Briefing and Operations Information*. Pamphlet. Personal archive of the author.

CIRCA (2005b) *Radical Origami Audience Handout*. Heart-shaped flyer. Personal archive of the author.

"Clandestine Clowns and Concealed T-Shirt Brigade Lead Dissent." *The Scotsman*, 20 Nov 2003.

"Clowns to Go On Warpath." *Evening Mail*, 25 May 2005.

"Clowns Kicked KKK Asses." *Neatorama*, 3 Sept 2007. www.neatorama.com/2007/09/03/clowns-kicked-kkk-asses/ (accessed 28 Oct 2015).

"Fears of a Clown." *Daily Star*, 2 July 2005.

Fremeaux, I.; Ramsden, H. (2007) "We Disobey to Love: Rebel clowning for social change." In D. Clover and J. Stalker (eds.), *The Arts and Social Justice: Re-crafting activist adult education and community leadership* (Section 1). Leicester, UK: Niace Press.

"G8 Anarchists Planning to Send in the Clowns." *Daily Mail*, 26 May 2005.

Herbert, Dean (2005) "Militants Send in the Clowns." *The Sun*, 26 May 2005.

hooks, bell (2005) "Outlaw Culture: Resisting representation," quoted in "Radical Origami," CIRCA-published paper.

"It's Iffy Miffy, Clowns and the Wombles." *The Aberdeen Press and Journal*, 29 June 2005.

Kenney, P. (2002) *A Carnival of Revolution: Central Europe 1989*. Princeton: Princeton University Press.

Madeley, G.; Macaskill, G.; Tait, G.; Graham, G. (2005) "The Carnival that Turned Sour." *Daily Mail*, 5 July 2005.

Moore, R.; McGregor, R. (2005) "Riot Police ... 1 Anarchists ... 0: G-hate agro kicks-off as cops crush violent protestors." *Daily Mirror* 5 July 2005.

Notes From Nowhere (2003) *From ACT UP to the WTO—We Are Everywhere: The irresistible rise of global anticapitalism*. London: Verso.
Oppenheimer, M.; Lakey, G. (1965) *A Manual for Direct Action*. Chicago: Quadrangle Books.
Rabelais, François (1936, originally published 1536) *The Complete Works of Rabelais: The five books of Gargantua and Pantagruel*. Trans. Jacques Le Clercq. New York: Modern Library.
Rivas, Jorge (2014) "Neo Nazi Immigration Protest Met with Clown Counter-Protest." *Huffington Post*, 12 Dec 2014. www.huffingtonpost.com/2012/11/12/neo-nazi-protest-immigration-clown_n_2118945.html (accessed 28 Oct 2015).
Santos, Alex (2014) "Clowns Attack KKK Rally With Humor." *ColorLines*, 12 Dec 2014. http://colorlines.com/archives/2012/11/clowns_use_humor_to_protest_kkk_rally_in_charlotte_nc.html (accessed 28 Oct 2015).
Shepard, B. (2005) "The New Model Army of Clowns: From RIZE to the G8 zaps, clowning asserts a radical imagination of resistance." *Monthly Review* online: http://mrzine.monthlyreview.org/shepard160805.html (accessed 17 Sept 2005).
Swanson, Brian (2005) "Capital Braces Itself as Protestors Prepare to Bring City to a Standstill." *Daily Express*, 2 July 2005: p. 7.
Undercover Clown Cop: Lynn Watson – UK. [Digital video] Directed by Zoe Young; Distributor: Journeyman Pictures. www.youtube.com/watch?v=Kg5OlyT4bFk (accessed 18 Feb 2015).
Whelan, Charlie (2005) "G8 UNSPUN: Fry guys are no clowns." *Sunday Mail*, 3 July 2005.
Young, Z. (a.k.a. Private Individual, CIRCA) (2005) Personal video footage of CIRCA actions.

Part II

The struggle for public space

Outflanking authority, upstaging the establishment

Chapter 3

Reclaim the Streets

Tactical interaction and urban mallification/mollification in New York City

240.35 LOITERING A person is guilty of loitering when he: . . . 4. Being masked or in any manner disguised by unusual or unnatural attire or facial alteration, loiters, remains or congregates in a public place with other persons so masked or disguised or knowingly permits or aids persons so masked or disguised to congregate in a public place; except that such conduct is not unlawful when it occurs in connection with a masquerade party or like entertainment if, when such entertainment is held in a city which has promulgated regulations in connection with such affairs, permission is first obtained from the police or other appropriate authorities.

—New York Penal Code, Offenses Against Public Order

MAYDAY 2001 WRESTLING MADNESS
SUPERBARRIO MAN VS. MULTI-NEFARIOUS BOSSES
The odds may be stacked against us
The money may all be in the BossMan's Hands
But come Mayday we will collectively smack THE MAN down to the MAT
Until he cries UNCLE

—Reclaim the Streets (2001)

This chapter examines the case study of the group Reclaim the Streets New York City, and their multiyear cat-and-mouse confrontation with the NYPD and the Mayor's Office. I use this study as a way to explore the importance of the use of masks in tactical performance and the larger phenomenon of agonistic tactical interaction between movement and state, as well as to envision creative ways to evade or outflank unreasonable regulation or restrictions of oppositional performance.

May Day, 2001: Manhattan, outside 61 Fifth Avenue, March for the Rights of Immigrant Workers—Ricardo Dominguez shouts over the city noise, a booming syndicalist circus barker:[1]

> **In this corner—SUPERBARRIO! The Hero of the Neighborhood!**

About 500 UNITE Local 169 workers, Community Labor Coalition activists, and their sympathizers cheer as Superbarrio, a Mexican working-class hero in a bright red and yellow wrestling outfit and mask, acknowledges their support.

Who is Superbarrio? For the uninitiated, he is a masked Mexican wrestling hero, a *lucha libre* fighter. He battles corrupt landlords and bosses, and draws his strength from the inherent power (and cheers) of his working-class fans. Superbarrio is a *luchador* with a political, progressive emphasis; a character created by Mexican artist Marco Rascón Córdova, and played in mask and costume by multiple performers. Superbarrio even ran for the North American Presidency in 1996. Jerry Dominguez, a union organizer who is also trained in martial arts, plays our New York City incarnation of Superbarrio. He moves gracefully in his Superbarrio costume as he prepares to fight, standing in one corner of our "fighting ring," fashioned from a length of twine held at four corners by performing activists.

Ricardo Dominguez (no relation to Jerry except one of political solidarity) introduces a series of colorfully costumed Nefarious Bosses and Archvillains to fight Superbarrio. These bad guys include the Unionbusting Thug, Nike Man (a.k.a. Phil Knight the Dark Knight), the cell-phone toting Billionaire, the Demonic Dollar, ruthless credit-card wielding shoppers, and La Migra.

Two accordion players provide a dramatic score as Superbarrio battles his constantly cheating foes. The Ref, played by veteran artist–activist–author Andrew Boyd, is earnest and focused, relentlessly running around tensing his entire body, and blowing his whistle. Unfortunately, he is usually on the opposite side of the ring from the action, facing outward. As The Objective Press, I hold up a corner of the "ring," bang a gong to start each round, and denounce Superbarrio and praise his opponents in my reportage. I also hit the hero from behind with the gong when he comes close. Nike Man, a.k.a. Phil Knight the Dark Knight, dressed in sporty workout clothes, attacks with a huge Nike Swoosh emblem which he wields like a deadly scythe.[2] The shoppers pelt Superbarrio with lacerating credit cards.

Suddenly, the villains attack our hero all at once. With power drawn from the cheering crowd, Superbarrio recovers, beats his opponents back two or three at a time, and triumphs.

This performance is the work of Reclaim the Streets (RTS) activists, appearing in colorful costumes to provide political satire for demonstrators and passersby, and to perform solidarity across tensive borders of identity with immigrant workers. This activist group is dedicated to reclaiming increasingly hemmed-in, homogenized, and privatized public space for free expression and participatory protest (Duncombe, 2002).

Reclaim the Streets began in Britain as a creative action group dedicated to protecting neighborhoods from destruction by Robert Moses-style highway projects. The group also advocated for a celebratory, playful form of protest—massive, unpermitted street dance parties being the classic form. Their history of surprising, transgressive tactics inspired other chapters to spring up all over the world. In a classic action against the building of a new motorway in London, they organized a sprawling street party, complete with booming sound system and

Figure 3.1 Nike Man, a.k.a. Phil Knight the Dark Knight, has Superbarrio in a headlock as part of a Reclaim the Streets demonstration on May Day 2001 in New York City. Photo by Caroline Shepard.

partiers taking over a stretch of the road. A man on stilts wearing an enormous hoop skirt loomed over the whole affair. What turned this spectacle of defiance into a *direct action* (an action that directly addresses a problem physically, as opposed to indirect actions that take the form of petitions, lobbying, etc.) was that, underneath his hoop skirt, people were jackhammering away at the tarmac and tearing it up—the sound muffled by the loud dance music (Notes From Nowhere, 2003).

RTS has received surprising attention from select audiences. In New York City, the group became the focus of intense police activity. This attention was disproportionate for a group of its size, particularly since we were much tamer than the London group. Our actions were often unpermitted, but there was no property destruction. When I first started working and playing with RTS/NYC in 2001, I found, mixed in with the friendly camaraderie, a fair amount of reserve and suspicion. I took this as the usual concern about infiltration, but I later learned that shortly before I had met RTS, a number of its members had been hanging out on a stoop on the Lower East Side. A policeman walked by and hailed one of the members of the group, saying "Hey! I haven't seen you since the Academy, how's it going?" The RTS member blanched and said, "I don't know you." At which point the policeman walked away, embarrassed. The now-exposed police infiltrator left and was never seen again by the group. Naturally, this experience made RTS members extra-wary of new recruits.[3]

More importantly, on 11 May, ten days after this Superbarrio demonstration, and four months before the Al Qaeda 9/11 terrorist attacks on the World Trade Center and the Pentagon, the FBI issued a report calling Reclaim the Streets a terrorist threat to the United States:

> Anarchists and extremist socialist groups—many of which, such as the Workers' World Party, Reclaim the Streets, and Carnival Against Capitalism—have an international presence . . . also represent a potential threat in the United States.
>
> (FBI, 2001)

And who were Reclaim the Streets/NYC? They were a loosely affiliated group of friends and acquaintances, devoted to finding new ways to use public space for protest, and determined to use prefigurative actions to achieve a more just and sustainable urban landscape. We forged friendships and solidarity during rehearsals and actions. Graduate students, professors, civil servants and social workers, nonprofit staffers, and labor and community organizers. Situationists and *flaneurs*, white,

Latino, and black, working-class heroes, middle-class malcontents, and trust-fund troublemakers. The group was majority white and middle class. Bourgeois liberal reformers, anarchists, and generic progressives. New Yorkers, by birth or choice. Our meetings were informal, in parks or bars, and ideas were hammered out through brainstorming. (We were not yet using the hand-signals and other tools for orderly and egalitarian conversation developed by the feminist movement, and used by the Occupy movement.) Many members of the group participated simultaneously in different, overlapping projects, such as the Lower East Side Collective and Absurd Response. Responsibilities were distributed to volunteers or "assigned" according to skill. I taught a little stage combat for the Superbarrio wrestling shtick, and Bobbie Lasko used his sewing skills to add an INS (Immigration and Naturalization Service) patch onto my old army hat for his costume.[4] We came to Union Square armed with cartoonish costumes and props, to meet with the labor coalition, show solidarity, and perform radical *lucha libre* outside bodegas and businesses where immigrant workers were employed. Our goal was to embarrass and put pressure on bosses to treat their immigrant employees more fairly.

And now, on Fifth Avenue, the police are performing their own version of street theatre. There are about as many police as demonstrators, and the police, some heavily armed, form a solid ring of blue around the protesters at all times, whether marching or performing. When marching, we look like a column of prisoners under heavy guard. This wildly disproportionate police presence serves several purposes: to intimidate the demonstrators; to criminalize us to onlookers; and to block sightlines to make it difficult for spectators to see how free expression still occurs in the increasingly hemmed-in public space of New York City.[5] This is the Street Theatre of Domination, and it is as effective as it is anti-democratic and expensive to the taxpayer.

Tactical interaction and the Street Theatre of Domination

This kind of police envelopment provides unique theatrical challenges. At the Halloween Parade in the West Village on 31 October 2002, many members of Reclaim the Streets (RTS) were in the Absurd Response to an Absurd War/Perms for Permawar contingent. That contingent was the only group to be surrounded on all sides by a police motorcycle escort, making it difficult for us to give flyers to the crowds. We tried our best, keeping in character as pro-war elitists, and joking that the police were there to protect us from the hoi polloi. But the police presence was frustrating.

The Street Theatre of Domination must be acknowledged by street theatre activists and countermeasures must be developed. Indeed, activists and police departments have a history of playing cat and mouse: activists come up with a new way to transgress into bounded spaces to get their message out, and police find new ways to frustrate the new tactic. The activists create a countermeasure, and the process continues, on and on.

This process is tactical interaction, as discussed in the Introduction, in which both sides learn from each other. As stated earlier, police departments, corporations, and other state agencies have institutional memory, and are able to note and record both past mistakes and proven effective tactics. Social movements, short on archivists and archives, may seize upon old ideas without realizing they are old, repeat mistakes, and walk into well-laid traps with regularity. To guard against this, it is important to develop counter-institutional memory and to record and retell stories of successes and mistakes so that social movements can better innovate tactically.

Here are a few examples of such innovation: RTS/NYC's keystone form of action was the unpermitted street party—a street gathering suddenly manifesting into a swarm of dancers, a booming sound system, and an atmosphere of fun and loud festivity, prefiguratively performing other ways to use public space besides commuting and consuming.[6] But the challenge is: how to keep the space festive when the police arrive?

One tactic was the use of the tripod. In the Pacific Northwest, Earth First! members and other eco-activists had shown the efficacy of the tree-sit, climbing high up into ancient redwoods and creating a dilemma for the forestry agents or private logging companies: if you cut down the tree, you kill the protestor with all the attendant unpleasantness and liabilities. Some ancient trees and old-growth forests were saved this way.[7] This is a modular tactic, one that can be reproduced in other contexts and for other goals, like labor strikes and demonstrations. However, there are no trees in the middle of an urban street. So how to adapt this idea to the needs of RTS/NYC? In several street party actions, demonstrators erected a tall metal tripod, climbed up, and created the same dilemma for the police—the tripods are blocking traffic and making space for the street party, but if you simply knock them down, you kill or injure a nonviolent protestor. This tactic frustrated police efforts to stop the action and clear the streets.

However, as stated in Chapter 1, the police pay attention and learn both from their own mistakes and from a movement's good ideas. In the British city of Birmingham, when confronted with tripods, police arrived upon an effective counter-tactic. They attached wheels to the tripods and just rolled them away! At other times, cherry-pickers have been used to pluck activists right off the top of the structure.

Dear Reader, please brainstorm for a moment and use the space below to write or draw some possible countermeasures/clowntermeasures that might work against wheels and plucking tactics.

Another example of tactical interaction between RTS/NYC and the NYPD was the cat-and-mouse game of surveillance and police response. After the first few street parties, the NYPD was privy to RTS's email listserv and aware of the group's plans. They responded aggressively to a particular street party, being present in large numbers before the party even started. In response, RTS's next party gathered at a declared location, and then immediately descended into the subway, held a dance party on the train replete with music and disco lighting, and then emerged out of the train at an intersection in Brooklyn where the "real" party was set to occur. This tactic put the police off-balance enough for the party to succeed as a large and enjoyable event.

By now, the NYPD were determined to shut down the next RTS street party before it started. RTS tipped off the NYPD by phone about an upcoming action at The Cube in Astor Place in the East Village. However, this "party" took the form of half a dozen men and women in formal dress, seated at a table (complete with tablecloth and doilies) on the sidewalk:

> As Vivaldi's *Four Seasons* wafted out of a tape deck, we sat down to high tea—surrounded by more than 50 uniformed cops, a cluster of high-ranking officers, a mobile command center, and a number of arrest vans. Predicting they would respond in this fashion, we printed up flyers asking the passersby why such a heavy police presence was necessary for such "civilized" behavior.
>
> (Duncombe, 2002)

The scene echoed the provocations of the Dutch Provos in 1960s Amsterdam.[8] As Steve Duncombe said:

> We figured that since the NYPD were always showing up to our demos in massive numbers, we'd integrate them into our performances. They looked pretty silly in their riot gear surrounding an innocuous tea party—and it really underscored our point about the recent crackdown on "quality of life" offenses. And some of the cops even got into the act, accepting our offering of cake, until they were told not to by their commanding officers.[9]

Clearly, this was also an example of white activists using their privilege to mock the police state—an option not so easily available to activists of color.

What are some other ways to deal with the Street Theatre of Domination, either being surrounded or absurdly over-policed while on the street? One possible shtick that may "cool down" the emotions of confrontation while still exposing absurd policing policy could be to put some performers on stilts, dressed as cartoonish police chiefs. They would be visible from inside the police phalanx. The "chiefs" could then give orders to the police, using gestures, large-print signs, or amplified voices; ordering them to do exactly what they are doing and pretending they are doing it because of the "chief's" command:

> **All right boys: look intimidating. Good. Slap your clubs into your hands menacingly. Perfect. OK boys, follow me! To the IMF Office!**

I provide this as an example of a way to keep tension low and to comically call attention to the problem in a visually compelling and humorous way.[10]

There are moments when familiarity within agonistic conflict leads to grudging respect or mutual joshing. There is room for gibing and cross-team smart-alecking in this, though the power balance may be uneven. To protest cuts in the CUNY (university) system, Ben Shepard and I marched across a park, dressed as cartoonish students in gown costumes, chained to an enormous cardboard-and-tinfoil missile that we carried on our shoulders. Pretending to bend under the weight, we were a walking metaphor for poor policy priorities, and for Martin Luther King's quote about "guided missiles and misguided men." As we pass a police car, the officer inside vamps on the loudspeaker: "NO MISSILES IN THE PARK. NO MISSILES IN THE PARK." He gets it. Are we playing?

The next morning, we march in a massive student demonstration, a walking political cartoon, flanked by scores of motorcycle police. In character, we groan and complain "Argh! This thing is so HEAVY! We just wanted to learn something and read some books. How did we get saddled with *this* thing?"

Figure 3.2 The missile being carried by two "students," Shepard and Bogad, as a line of police ride alongside. Photo by Andrew Boyd.

One officer, hearing our groaning and not quite getting it, says good-humoredly, "You drew the shit detail today, huh?" I grinned, broke character and told him that it wasn't really heavy, only cardboard, and we were just playing up the joke. A small moment of fraternization.

Dear Reader, please use this space to brainstorm some possible other methods to counteract the Street Theatre of Domination:

Our May Day march starts with a demonstration in Union Square, and it will end outside the International Monetary Fund (IMF) building. On the way, we stop in midtown Manhattan to rally and perform outside a place of business known for unfair labor practices, including paying immigrant workers as little as $2.61 an hour. The demonstrators and spectators cheer our performances as we move on. We hope through our *lucha libre* procession to trace a connection between community history (Union Square, site of many storied labor and radical protests), the actual sweatshops, and the policy mill of macroeconomic exploitation (the IMF). This performative procession thus attempted to draw a conceptual connection by hitting *sites of commemoration* (Union Square), *sites of production* (sweatshops), and *sites of decision* (the IMF offices, where policies are formed that have caused mass displacement of Mexican workers, such as the ones on our march).[11]

Both the repurposing of urban space, and the processional connection of urban spaces, were vital to the dramaturgy of this protest (as silly as the *lucha libre* fight appeared on its surface). However, equally important to the concept of this protest was the element of *symbolically significant time*. Our demonstration occurred on 1 May, May Day, or International Workers Day. In US imagery, May Day is associated with Red Square, the Soviet Union, and endless parades of missiles and goose-stepping columns of Red Army troops passing under a reviewing stand stocked with nonagenarian Bolsheviks. In fact, the designation of 1 May as a global labor holiday, observed in almost every country besides the US, was inspired by a labor struggle that happened in the US: the Haymarket Square confrontation of 1886–87. During a national mass struggle for an eight-hour workday, and a successful and nonviolent general strike that shut down many cities, including the city of Chicago, a violent confrontation between a large contingent of heavily armed Chicago police and a small demonstration of workers led to the execution by hanging of five labor organizers for a crime they did not commit. In the global wave of protests that followed, the French Socialist Party, and eventually the workers' movements of almost all nations in the world, designated 1 May to be a labor holiday. In the US, May Day was instead celebrated as Law Day, and the history of Haymarket was deemphasized in the teaching of American history.

Demonstrating on May Day, and affirming its importance as a homegrown, all-American Labor Day of defiance and commemoration, takes on a special oppositionality in the US. It is encouraging and emotionally resonant for the activists who are aware of the history and for whom it takes on an almost sacred role—to honor the Haymarket

Martyrs and their struggle, and to trace continuity from their struggle to ours. However, demonstrating on May Day is also polarizing, causing many American onlookers to associate the demonstrators with the old Communist enemy. Nevertheless, it seems commonsensical to international participants and viewers to create a labor demonstration on May Day as that is the presumed and default labor holiday worldwide. Our choice of day thus resonated for the primarily Mexican working-class participants in the demonstration, as well as the radicals (Bogad, 2006). May Day has found a resurgence as a day of workers' demonstrations in the US, especially with Latino immigrant workers and their allies.

Just at the end of our performance on Fifth Avenue, the police arrest one of our performers—Garrett Ramirez, a.k.a. *El Dolar del Diablo*, or the Demonic Dollar. They also charge through the crowd to rough up an Associated Press photographer who took pictures of Ramirez's arrest. The arresting officer, Michael Galgano, shield 02671 of the Patrol Boro Manhattan South Task Force, invoked the Mask Law of 1845, a little-known law cited in the quote at the start of this chapter. Like many of the police officers under the Giuliani administration, he was aware of the precise phrasing of this law and used that phrasing in his police report to justify his arrest:

> (ii) amidst said gathering, the deponent observed approximately five individuals wearing masks that covered their faces; (iii) the deponent observed that said individuals with masks were congregating together in that they were in proximity to each other *and were engaged in some form of performance together*; (iv) said congregation of individuals wearing masks was not a masquerade party or like entertainment where permission was first obtained from the police; (v) the deponent observed that one of said individuals wearing a mask was a man wearing a business suit, a tie with pictures of United States currency on it, and a red mask.
>
> (The People of the State of New York vs. Garet [sic] Ramirez 2001; my italics)

In short, Ramirez was arrested for wearing a mask on the streets of New York City as part of his costume in a political performance for a legally permitted labor demonstration. We were afraid Superbarrio would also be arrested for wearing his mask, so some of us squeezed around him in the crowd, formed a human circle that concealed him, and pieced together an outfit for him from our spare clothes. He changed into our clothes in the street, and we moved on.

In Superbarrio's *lucha libre* wrestling performances in Mexico, it is only the loser of the fight who is unmasked. And if this happens, it is the worst kind of humiliation and defeat. This is the source of a great deal of drama—will the cheating, bullying villains take Superbarrio's mask this time? The choreography of the fights often centers on a moment when the hero is being held down and his mask is about to be peeled off, but he throws off his attackers just in time, and pummels them into submission. In New York City, we had to compromise this dramatic element in order to continue with the day's performances and avoid jail time for our hero. However, in effect the NYPD had demasked Superbarrio and that was symbolically discouraging.

Jerry Dominguez/Superbarrio performed at another sweatshop later in the march, without his costume and mask, but first gave a little speech out of character, acknowledging and explaining why he had removed his mask, and denouncing the police and the Mask Law. In this way, he preserved his own defiant stance and persona, both as himself and "the hero of the people" of *lucha libre* legend. The performance went smoothly, but of course without Superbarrio's costume, and lacking the Demonic Dollar, we felt the presence of the Mask Law and the state looming over the proceedings.

In all, five demonstrators were arrested that day, part of a larger pattern of unprovoked arrests at permitted demonstrations around the city, which were overturned in a series of lawsuits. As Jerry Dominguez said:

> This year they brought out hundreds of cops to arrest a few guys in tights. Apparently, they're terrified of a peaceful demonstration that brings immigrant workers and their native-born supporters together to demand the right to organize.
>
> (Wilson, 2001)

Of the few people who have heard of the Mask Law, many believe that it was passed to prevent the Klu Klux Klan from marching in New York City wearing their hoods. While the law was applied against the Klan in 1999,[12] it was originally passed in 1845 to help crush a radical farmers' revolt that had swept across upstate New York. Armed farmers, protesting the *de facto* feudal rent system of the time, which indentured them for life to a few plutocratic landowners in Albany, donned frightening masks and costumes, called themselves "Indians," and massed by the hundreds to disrupt rent collection and the auctioning of bankrupt farmers' goods (Christman, 1978; Kubik, 1997). The frightened State Legislature passed a law forbidding rebellious farmers from protecting their identities with masks—while thoughtfully providing an exception that allowed the landowning classes to enjoy their masquerade balls. The classism inherent in the wording of the law makes its own satire; it need not be enhanced or exaggerated. New York City mayors Giuliani and Bloomberg selectively enforced this law against protesters in the global justice movement at events like the May Day parades and the World Economic Forum protests.

The Anti-Rent War of 1845 was a peasant rebellion by destitute sharecroppers. Their use of masks and costumes preserved their anonymity, one of the tools that James C. Scott calls a "weapon of the weak" (1985: p. 36). Their costumes looked nothing like Native American clothing, and it is a bitter irony that they took the name of the indigenous peoples they had helped to displace. However, by thus invoking the "Indians" of the Boston Tea Party, they portrayed themselves as good patriots and brought to mind the post-Revolutionary War working-class revolts (Shay's Rebellion and the Whiskey Rebellion) that had been crushed as the new American ruling class consolidated power. As "Indians," they identified with a population on the far margins of the capitalist economy, a frightening Other with little to lose in their struggle against the system.

It is appropriate that the Mask Law, after several revisions, is now listed in the Loitering Section of the New York Legal Code. Loitering laws regulate behavior in public space, and forbid activities seen as nonproductive and disruptive—gambling, begging, peddling, sex work, and even sleeping. In the context of the corporatization of public space, often described as the replacement of Main Street by the mall, loitering laws regularly collide with free-speech rights. The original Anti-Rent rebels opposed the monopolization of arable land by the few. Modern-day protesters caught by the Mask Law oppose the mallification of public space in New York City. They partake in carnivalesque protest to attempt to reclaim the street for public dialogue—an activity that admittedly and unashamedly has no market value and may disrupt business-as-usual.

The selective enforcement of this law in practice is as blatant as the classism in the wording of the law. Can the reader imagine three costumed employees of the Disney Store, giving out coupons to passersby, being led off in handcuffs for violation of the Mask Law? Of course, the only individuals actually arrested under this law were radical protesters who annoyed the Mayor's Office by theatrically opposing gentrification, the destruction of the people's gardens of the Lower East Side, and the privatization of public space.

Ramirez spent 30 hours in jail after his arrest, and had to engage in five months of tedious legal battle to defend his First Amendment right to free expression. In an ironic twist of legal jargon, his lawyer, Edward Land, filed a successful Motion to Dismiss for Facial Insufficiency. Ramirez was arrested on May Day for showing insufficient face on the streets; that arrest was then shown to be *facially insufficient*, or farcical on the face of it; and in the end the state lost face. Ramirez's legal response in a statement to the court is eloquent in its defiance and clarity:

> It is the tradition of Mexican wrestling, especially Superbarrio, for contestants to wear masks. It is also its tradition to pit underdog working-class heroes against authoritarian villains. I portrayed one of the latter, the Demonic Dollar (*el Dolar del Diablo*), an archetype of an arrogant member of the wealthy elite, and embodiment of the pernicious influence of money and materialism in social life. . . . I'll admit that I don't have a great understanding of the law, or a record of my case yet, but I was informed by both my public defender and my judge that I committed a mere violation and should not even have been arrested, let alone booked and held for thirty hours. I feel that this was reprehensible action on the NYPD's part. I participated in a peaceful and creative protest only to be made the target of gross repression tactics. An obscure law was enforced without warning, possibly used as an excuse to harass critics of the mayor's friends and intimidate the immigrant community. . . . The anti-mask law itself is asinine and an unacceptable impediment to free expression.
>
> (Ramirez, 2002)

A key point in Land's argument was that the officer, in his own arrest report, had contradicted himself when he called our Superbarrio skit "some form of performance" while also claiming it was "not a masquerade party or like entertainment where permission was first obtained from the police" (New York vs. Ramirez, 2001). While failing to modify or overturn the Mask Law, Land was able to show that Ramirez's mask was a part of an "entertainment" and "symbolic political expression." The law's exception for masquerade balls, meant to protect the upscale diversions of antebellum landowners, was interpreted to protect free speech. It also helped that Land was able to show the Assistant District Attorney a videotape of the police beating the photographer that day without provocation. She dropped the case rather than have that video shown in court (Land, 2002).

However, the law itself was not struck down, and further Mask Law arrests of demonstrators followed at other protests, such as at the World Economic Forum protests in January and February 2002. Anarchists arrested under the Mask Law during a protest on May Day 2000 failed in their motion to dismiss because they did not show that their wearing of bandannas over their faces had been part of "a performance or like entertainment." They had "merely" been wearing bandannas to preserve their anonymity for fear of repression as anarchists, a concern made more immediate given the long-standing police practice of videotaping and photographing protestors, and the advent of facial-recognition technology that can digitally record and pick out individual faces in crowds (New York vs. Jacques Aboaf et al., 2001). Performance Studies scholars take note: fitting a police officer's definition of "some form of performance" may keep you out of jail (and you thought the *New York Times* drama critics were tough!).

While the courts have not responded favorably to attempts by progressive lawyers to overturn or modify the law, it was ruled unconstitutional in a decision concerning a group of Klansmen. However, the city appealed the ruling, claiming that the Mask Law is important for maintaining public order, and the legal battle continues (Baer, 2002: p. 35–36). The Anti-Defamation League called upon the New York State Legislature to enact a new law that would make it a misdemeanor to wear a mask in public only when the sole intent is to "threaten or intimidate" (Anti-Defamation League, 2002). However, in 2011, Occupy protesters were arrested for wearing masks, and in 2012, protesters wearing masks in solidarity with Pussy Riot were also arrested (Gardiner & Firger, 2011; Jilani, 2011; Robbins, 2012).

The willfully selective enforcement of a 150-year-old law, first passed to help crush an upstate peasants' rebellion, has raised the social cost of performative protest in the rapidly shrinking, Disneyfied public space of New York City (though things have loosened up a bit under the current DeBlasio administration). As RTS organizer Benjamin Shepard wrote:

> It was clear to everyone that the police arrests were designed to turn people away, chilling interest in future protests. Nonetheless activists around the world, aware they are making an impact, continue to link guerrilla theatre with bread-and-butter economic issues and the fight for a revitalized public sphere.
>
> (Shepard, 2003)

Shepard himself would be arrested multiple times during nonviolent creative protests in the years to come, including a protest against the

Carlysle Group on 7 April 2003. The Carlysle Group is an investment group whose major investors include the Bush family, and its main source of profit is from oil and war industries. When activists gathered outside their New York City office to protest, to raise awareness of this group and its investments and potential impact on policy, the NYPD followed the Bush Administration's policy of preemption. Before the protest could start, they sealed off the entire block, penned everyone in for hours, and then arrested every person on the block—over 100 protestors, workers, commuters, joggers, tourists, and onlookers, including Shepard and other RTS members. Years later, the arrestees received a large settlement from the City for wrongful arrest.[13]

However, the banning of the use of theatrical masks in public protest is a disaster for freedom of expression for a more fundamental reason. Masks are critical and ancient tools in the theatre arts, especially for outdoor performances. The ancient Greeks were masters of the technology of masking, and they had to be: their theatre was performed in giant outdoor amphitheaters with no electronic amplification. In addition to the perfect acoustic design of ancient stone amphitheaters, and the sound-filtering effect of their limestone seats, the masks accomplished a great deal of projection and amplification—the subtle conical opening at the mouth of the mask serving to project the orator's voice so that even those in the back row could hear his words. Then as now, a masked performer had to master great bodily gestures and postures, as the subtleties of facial expression are concealed. This is a blessing rather than a handicap since in outdoor theatre a performer must never rely on a raised eyebrow or a curled lip. Distances are too great and there is no focused lighting. Viewers are watching you from a bewildering array of distances and angles as opposed to the controlled and structured architecture of the indoor theatre. When the mask forces you to express emotion, intention, and tension with your hips, limbs, and shoulders, in broader gesture, your performance becomes more legible and powerful for an outdoor audience—especially a spontaneous street theatre audience who are on their way to work, shopping, play, or home.

In addition, the stage of the street is a challenging venue. Far from perfect acoustics in a stone ring of brilliant design, you are operating in a city full of visual and auditory chaos—honking cars, neon signs, machinery, and mayhem. You must be all the more gripping, captivating, and expressive in the postmodern city than in the ancient Greeks' seated auditoriums, and masks are a crucial tool in that effort. I propose to the reader that it would behoove tactical performers to look back to the technology of 2,500 years ago and, using modern materials that would make it more portable and manageable, adapt ancient Greek masks to our current urban environment, mask laws notwithstanding.

Masks are not only important for encouraging stronger gesture and voice. Masks are also intrinsically expressive as works of art, creating an archetypal persona on which an audience member can project empathy precisely because they are not purely realistic, but are symbolic totems of class, gender, mythic identity, and symbolic persona. The facial details of the individual performer—birthmarks, chin structure, whatever—are mercifully concealed so that they do not distract from the ideational and semiotic power of SuperBarrio, Lysistrata, El Dolar Del Diablo, and Antigone.

As already mentioned, masks have become vital in our modern era due to the advent of facial recognition technology. In a world where faces can be picked up on surveillance cameras, broken down into binary code, and connected to social security numbers, addresses, and even one's social network of friends, dissident artists and activists are understandably interested in concealing their identities. Citizens have lost jobs when employers merely found pictures of them drunk on Facebook; it is understandable that an RTS member who is a civil servant for the city might not want to be revealed as a radical street performer criticizing the mayor's real estate policies as corrupt and destructive—even if he breaks no laws in doing so.

For all of these reasons, masks are a crucial element of guerrilla theatre and tactical performance in the modern PanoptiCity. Mask laws that do not distinguish between a mask worn during a bank robbery and a mask worn during a demonstration are destructive to public discourse, and repress the arts of dissent that are crucial to a functioning republic.

Creative case study: The Masquerade Project, 2001

In order to protest at the International Monetary Fund (IMF) meeting in Washington, DC that was set for September 2001, Leslie Kauffman and other Reclaim the Streets (RTS) activists innovated a functional and artistically compelling concept using gas masks.

The problem activists faced: the state would probably tear-gas protesters. Since the First Amendment protects free expression but not one's eyes, RTS came up with a solution: wear gas masks. However, there was a corollary problem: a large mass of protesters wearing identical gas masks looks scary and alienating on television, depicting the movement as identical insectoids or paramilitary maniacs, and possibly encouraging more violent repression. The brilliant solution: decorate the gas masks in highly colorful, inventive, creative, ways—a festive feather-leatherama that would protect the eyeballs of the global justice movement while providing a media-friendly and inspiring, carnivalesque image. Masses of beautiful gas masks were prepared, each one an individual expression of beauty, creativity, and mischief.

As it happened, the IMF meeting was canceled in the wake of the 9/11 attacks. So the group defeathered the masks and donated them to the rescue/recovery effort. Nevertheless, the idea still remains for another movement to adapt and use for their specific needs.

Restrictions on public protest in New York City have extended beyond the Mask Law. On 15 February 2003, an estimated 400,000 protesters from across the US converged on New York City to protest the Bush Administration's plans for war in Iraq. However, they were legally denied the right to march in the city, a ruling that was upheld upon appeal.[14] Despite the dubious justification that the police could not control or afford a march of that size (notwithstanding the precedent of the Yankees' 1996 victory parade involving 1 million marching sports fans), it was the ban on marching itself that actually created chaos in the city. The protesters were allowed to demonstrate on First Avenue, but no approved route had been established for them to get there. Unless they could teleport, they were expected to arrive at the rally site by twos and threes, walking along the sidewalks of the city. The demonstration was massive, made up of over 70 smaller marches from all over the city that converged on First Avenue. However, many miles of First Avenue quickly filled up with protestors hemmed into cramped, restrictive "pens" or "protest cages," which was common practice in New York City.

Ultimately, there were more marchers than the sidewalk could contain, and police blocked entry to First Avenue. Huge stretches of the city, including Second and Third Avenues for dozens of blocks, were soon unavoidably and illegally filled with frustrated demonstrators who had

Figure 3.3 Disperse at Once: a policeman informs frustrated protestors on 15 February 2003 that they must move on. Photo by Fred Askew.

Figure 3.4 Breaking the Law: tens of thousands of anti-war demonstrators had no choice but to break the law by filling New York City streets on 15 February 2003, when a march permit was denied. Photo by Fred Askew.

come a long way only to be denied access to the protest assembly. They could not hear the speakers and could not move. In some places, this led to conflict with the police, who used pepper spray, batons, and horses to try to push the people back onto the sidewalk or to block them as they tried to find a way to First Avenue. In other places, it led to a carnival atmosphere as protesters created their own demonstrations on the spot, swarming neighborhoods, climbing onto parked vehicles, singing, and dancing. The NYPD was temporarily overstretched by the chaos, a clear result of the refusal to permit an orderly march.

Some RTS members, who had had no intention of entering a "cage" in the first place, wheeled their baby-carriage-cum-mobile-sound-system back across town, blasting funk music, picking up dancers and protestors along the way, and wandering the streets at will. This led to a highly cinematic moment when RTS playfully swarmed the plaza of Rockefeller Center itself, dancing and shaking their asses over the feeble protests of a single security guard. This moment would never have been possible under normal circumstances in the city. An untenable restriction of public space led to tactical opportunities for creative protest. Nevertheless, this regrettable and undemocratic refusal to issue a march permit, made possible in an atmosphere of terror alerts and permanent war, set a worrisome precedent for the regulation of public dissent in New York City.

As Alex Vitale, criminologist and Professor of Sociology at Brooklyn College, said in his Open Letter to Mayor Bloomberg:

> The decision not to grant a march permit seems difficult to defend on the grounds of deployment of police resources and concerns about public safety. Major cities all over the world were able to accommodate large marches without any major incidents. . . . One of the implications of the denial of the permit is that only marches that are large enough to potentially affect national policy can't be adequately policed. This flies in the face of the core principles of the First Amendment. . . . The decision to deny a marching permit ended up costing the city just as much or more in overtime and other expenses as a unified march would have. . . . The policing of a unified march and rally might have involved a major inconvenience to drivers, but it represents much less of a safety and security concern than having lots of angry young people marching in small groups all over Midtown in response to the denial of a march permit. . . . It is my opinion that [the protest] pens serve primarily to isolate and

> inconvenience participants and serve very little safety function. People should be able to move about the rally, come and go freely, and assemble ahead of time with their friends and co-workers. Each of these was not allowed by police on the 15th.
>
> (Vitale, 2003)

As elsewhere, protesters and performers in New York City are often ringed by walls of police, crammed into "protest cages," and otherwise restricted in their access to audiences, both live and mediated. Another classic and instructive example was the Puppetistas. During the Republican National Convention (RNC) in Philadelphia in 2000, a group of artist–activists, loosely identified as the Puppetistas, gathered in a warehouse to build puppets for a demonstration. Their group was infiltrated by police, and then raided. Seventy-five artists were arrested preemptively, and some remained in jail for several weeks. The police claimed that the Puppetistas were making firebombs and slingshots, referring to paint thinner and wooden sticks found in the warehouse. They then destroyed all the puppets rather than preserving the evidence, which would have backed the activists' claims. Every Puppetista arrested was eventually exonerated, but they suffered a loss of legal fees and wrongful imprisonment, and perhaps worst of all were prevented from making an eye-catching, media-friendly, and Constitutionally protected political statement on the streets outside the RNC (www.R2Kphilly.org, 2003; MacPhee & Reuland, 2007). The City of Philadelphia wanted the RNC to be a success, not out of political loyalty but from a desire for their new Convention Center to develop a reputation as a favorable site for major clients.

The use of colorful masks and puppets is a tactic to overcome restrictions in a creative, nonviolent manner, and to communicate more effectively through entertainment. It also makes protest more joyous for participants facing intimidation. The state's inventive application of the Mask Law, and the prospect of jail time and legal troubles, may deter some carnivalesque protesters, but others will find innovative, artful responses.

Improvisation and tactical interaction will continue as social movements and the state contend the uses and regulation of public space. Complaining about the problem is not enough. What are creative ways to outflank restrictions, spatially, conceptually, and/or performatively?

Masks: a thought experiment

Perhaps in localities where Mask Laws are in effect, protestors could call attention to the absurdity of the law by wearing masks that are identical to their own faces. Comic moments could ensue as they take off their masks on command to reveal the same bemused faces. Another possibility could be the wearing of masks of playful or pointed figures such as Mickey Mouse, Bambi, or Foucault while distributing flyers about the Mask Law to passersby and the police themselves. Foucault masks could

Figure 3.5 The author violates the Mask Law at a New York City anti-war protest on 26 October 2002. Photo by Fred Askew.

have cartoon speech-bubbles attached to them with succinct quotes about the panopticon. Perhaps protestors could wear mirrors over their face, reflecting the face of the arresting officer at the moment of protest. (I would recommend a non-glass reflective surface to avoid shattering and injury). In fact, this technique was recently used in the Ukraine with protesters holding mirrors rather than protest signs in their hands ("Kiev Protestors Hold Mirrors," 2014). And of course the red nose of the clown is the smallest mask in the world: clowns could arrive wearing little round red noses, and then produce from their pockets bigger and bigger noses, testing the police to see at what point the nose becomes "too big for the law," and then moving back and forth across that arbitrary line. In all of these cases, the protestors would be trying to put the police into a *decision dilemma.*[15] If they arrest clowns, they and the law look ridiculous. If they do not arrest, the law is weakened through a publicly performed precedent of defiance and transgression. Decision dilemmas are a classic tactic of social movements and they serve as a conceptual crowbar or lever, a force multiplier where a weaker movement can potentially gain outsized reforms or advances or at least greater creative space for future action.

Dear Reader, please use the space below to brainstorm new ideas for creative mask actions to subvert the Mask Law.

The next chapter examines the phenomenon of the major convention, such as the World Trade Organization and the Republican or Democratic National Conventions. What are the pros and cons of movements reactively protesting at these massive and massively guarded events, benefitting from the global media coverage these events receive, as opposed to proactively creating their own events and interventions on their own schedule and chosen terrain?

Suggestions: to be tested in pratice

1 Coalitions across boundaries of race, class, and identity can be strengthened, affirmed, and tested through live performance under pressure.
2 Tactical interaction is unavoidable: respect your opponents as you would a dance partner—study their moves (such as infiltration, envelopment, criminalization, etc), and take them seriously enough to develop countermoves.
3 Traveling protest processions can link symbolic spaces, times, and institutions to a unifying critique (for example, the IMF and the sweatshops on May Day), as can performed allusions to past struggles.
4 Sometimes a light touch and disarming affect is the perfect way to set up a decision dilemma.

Notes

1 Dominguez has continued his distinguished career in artistic activism as a tenured professor at the University of California. He was at the center of a national controversy as the innovator of the Transborder Immigrant Tool. (More on this in Chapter 7.)
2 Nike Man was played by Matthew Roth, a photographer–activist who bears an uncanny resemblance to Nike co-founder and chairman, Phil Knight.
3 Of course, infiltrators and agent provocateurs are not always this ham-handed. See Chapter 2 for examples of police infiltration in the Clown Army, and the group's clownter-measures.
4 Bobbie Lasko was later beatified as a Saint of the Church of Stop Shopping in recognition of decades of service to the movement. Such rituals were an important way for individuals to be recognized and acknowledged by the resistance community.
5 A friend from Chicago (and originally from Iran), who arrived to the demonstration late, wondered if the police union was marching for May Day until he spotted protesters through the solid wall of blue uniforms.
6 Of course, the domination of city streets by cars is not a natural phenomenon; it was the end result of a protracted political, social, and cultural

battle between drivers and non-drivers between the 1910s and 1930s as documented in Peter Norton's book *Fighting Traffic* (2011). The autofication of city streets in America was analogous to the privatization of US radio and television airwaves—now accepted as the natural order, but actually the result of a specific conflict lost not long ago; a result that could be revisited and revised.

7 Tripods and lockdowns were also used to block logging roads as part of this campaign.

8 For more on the Provos, see Chapter 1 of *Electoral Guerrilla Theatre: Radical ridicule and social movements*, 2nd edition (Bogad, 2016).

9 Interview with the author, 5 July 2015.

10 In Chapters 2 and 4, we look at different ways in which members of the Clown Army refused Althusserian interpellation in their relationship with the British and New York City police, and instead found other surprising, disarming, and cliché-breaking ways of engaging with them.

11 *Beautiful Trouble* (Boyd & Mitchell, 2012) categorizes sites of action in terms of production, destruction, decision, and assumption: the latter being more metaphysical—actions that impact the cultural assumptions and ideologies of the viewer. I have added the idea of sites of commemoration to this list to emphasize the importance of social-movement memory. *Beautiful Trouble* also recommends performing at "sites of destruction"—forest clear-cuts, toxic waste dumps, etc.

12 While the Klan have hidden behind their infamous masks to commit atrocities with impunity, they now claim they need their masks to protect themselves from popular reprisal as a despised, weak group ("Court Rules," 1999). They also claim the masks are part of their political message.

13 For more on this pattern of preemptive arrests of activists in New York City, see Lee (2003).

14 In the next chapter, we will see how the Billionaires for Bush and other groups responded creatively to unconstitutional bans of protests in New York City during the 2004 Republican National Convention.

15 With thanks to Philippe Duhamel.

References

Anti-Defamation League (2002) "ADL Calls on New York State Legislature to Re-Draft Anti-Mask Law." *Anti-Defamation League*, 20 Nov 2002. www.adl.org/PresRele/CvlRt_32/4196_32.asp (accessed 23 June 2003).

Baer, Harold Jr. (2002) "Judge Baer: Decision of interest." *New York Law Journal*, 25 Nov 2002: p. 35–36.

Bogad, L.M. (2006) "Monumental Dialectics: Staging Haymarket confrontation." *Fifth Estate*, Issue 372: p. 9–11, 16.

Bogad, L.M. (2016) *Electoral Guerrilla Theatre: Radical ridicule and social movements*, 2nd edition. London: Routledge.

Boyd, A.; Mitchell, D.O. (2012) *Beautiful Trouble: A toolbox for revolution*. New York: OR Books.

Christman, Henry (1978) *Tin Horns and Calico: The thrilling unsung story of an American revolt against serfdom*. Cornwallville, NY: Hope Farm Press.

Court Rules KKK Must Unmask to Rally in New York. *CNN* [TV News]. 23 June 1999. www.cnn.com/US/9910/22/klan.03/ (accessed 25 July 2003).

Duncombe, Stephen (2002) "Stepping Off the Sidewalk: Reclaim the Streets/NYC." In R. Hayduk and B. Shepard (eds.), *From ACT UP to the WTO: Urban protest and community building in the era of globalization*. London: Verso.

FBI (2001) Statement for the record, Louis J. Freeh, Director, Federal Bureau of Investigation, on the threat of terrorism to the United States before the United States Senate Committees on Appropriations, Armed Services, and Select Committee on Intelligence. Retrieved from: www.fbi.gov/congress/congress01/freeh051001.htm (accessed 23 June 2003).

Gardiner, Sean; Firger, Jessica (2011) "Rare Charge Unmasked," *Wall Street Journal* online, 20 Sept 2011. www.wsj.com/articles/SB100014240531119 04194604576581171443151568 (accessed 15 Aug 2015).

Jilani, Zaid (2011) "New York City Police Use 150-Year-Old Law Against Wearing Masks To Arrest Wall Street Demonstrators." http://thinkprogress.org/economy/2011/09/21/325014/new-york-150-years-wall-street-protest/ (accessed 11 Aug 2015).

"Kiev Protestors Hold Mirrors to Police." *CS Monitor*, 17 Jan 2014. www.csmonitor.com/World/Europe/2014/0117/Kiev-protesters-hold-mirrors-to-police-literally-as-new-confrontation-looms (accessed 22 Feb 2015).

Kubik, Dorothy (1997) *A Free Soil—A Free People: The anti-rent war in Delaware County, New York*. New York: Purple Mountain Press.

Land, Edward (2002) Phone interview with the author. 15 Sept 2002.

Lee, Chisun (2003) "Rescuing Protest before Bush '04: Activists push back at NYPD," *Village Voice*, 48, 27 (July 2–8): p. 28–32. www.villagevoice.com/news/activists-push-back-at-nypd-6410048 (accessed 28 Oct 2015).

MacPhee, J.; Reuland, E. (2007) "When Magic Confronts Authority." In J. MacPhee and E. Ruin (eds.), *Realizing The Impossible: Art against authority*. Oakland: AK Press.

New York vs. Ramirez (2001) Docket No. 2001NY038641: People of the State of New York against Garet [sic] Ramirez. Reply Affirmation in Further Support of Motion to Dismiss for Facial Insufficiency.

New York vs. Jacques Aboaf et al. (2001) 721 N.Y.S.2d 725, N.Y. City Criminal Court, 23 Jan 2001.

Norton, Peter (2011) *Fighting Traffic: The dawn of the motor age in the American city*. Cambridge, MA: MIT Press.

Notes From Nowhere (2003) *From ACT UP to the WTO—We Are Everywhere: The irresistible rise of global anticapitalism*. London: Verso.

Ramirez, Garrett (2002) "Legal Statement." Email to lawyer, forwarded to author, 31 July 2002.

Reclaim the Streets (2001) "MAYDAY WRESTLING MADNESS!! SUPERBARRIO MAN!!" Email to author, 19 Apr 2001.

Robbins, Christopher (2012) "City Dodges Legal Challenge to 1845 Anti-Mask Law." *Gothamist*, 12 Dec 2012. http://gothamist.com/2012/12/12/city_dodges_challenge_to_anti-mask.php (accessed 11 Aug 2015).
Scott, James C. (1985) *The Moral Economy of the Peasant: Rebellion and subsistence in Southeast Asia*. New Haven: Yale University Press.
Shepard, Benjamin (2003) Email to author. 13 Apr 2003.
Vitale, Alex (2003) "Open Letter to Mayor Bloomberg." Email to author. 13 Apr 2003.
Wilson, David L. (2001) "Superbarrio Eludes NYC Police on May Day." *Independent*, 5 May 2001.
www.R2Kphilly.org. (2003) "Remaining RNC Puppet Warehouse Defendants Cleared of All Charges." 23 June 2003. http://r2klegal.protestarchive.org/r2klegal/press/pr-121300.html (accessed 25 June 2003).

Chapter 4

Breaking conventions, breaking into conventions (from the WTO to WTF?)

This chapter begins with a tactical examination of the vast and diverse protests around the Republican National Convention (RNC) in New York City in 2004, to advance a larger conversation about the pros and cons of protesting at large corporate or state events such as the RNC, DNC, G20, WTO, IMF, and other acronymic gatherings of the powerful. The "Counter-Convention" against the RNC was a massive, varied, creative local social-movement campaign that fostered many ties between groups for future actions, even though it did not yield tangible results in terms of the national election. This chapter discusses the performative strategies of the Republican Party as well as those of the various groups that made up the chaotic Counter-Convention, and discusses and evaluates which actions on both sides were successful and which failed in terms of media impact, policy impact, or other goals. Ultimately, the reactive nature of convention protest is examined in a larger, global sense. While many groups are examined in this chapter, the Billionaires for Bush and the New York version of the Clown Army are the primary case studies—unified by their common satirical bent, but distinct enough to make different contributions to the Counter-Convention—as this moment was the heyday of their arcs as street theatre/media intervention entities. Since these events in 2004, significant expansions in the instant connectivity of the internet—the advent and massive popularization of YouTube, Facebook, Twitter, and ownership of smartphones in general, just to name a few—have changed many aspects of organizing. However, the fundamentals in the contestation of public space, the creation of irresistible images, and rhetorical deployment in performance remain relevant from this case to the present day.

It has become increasingly challenging in the US to exercise one's First Amendment rights. Many demonstrations have been banished to the confines of Orwellian "Free Speech Zones": out-of-the-way lots and streets ringed by fences, with police-controlled access and egress. Creative dissidents have resisted being "put in their place" by defying permit bans, using art, direct action, and diverse tactics to project their objections over the fences and out of the margins, and to disrupt the dramaturgy of state, corporate, and political events.

This struggle over protest-place was particularly intense in New York City—where real estate is always at a premium—during the RNC of 2004. The RNC, backed by massive state power, demarcated, occupied, and fortified a heavily mediated space from which they could project to the nation a hegemonic monologue that would elevate their candidate to saviour status while overwriting any inconvenient facts or ongoing wars of choice. The anti-Bush Counter-Convention contradicted the RNC in both content and form; this was a multivocal, dialogical, free-flowing, and many-faced mass entity, which moved throughout the city, enacting the global justice movement's slogan "We Are Everywhere." The Counter-Convention infiltrated and engulfed RNC events, and contested space in the streets and in the local media. Even though it lacked the RNC's power and resources, the Counter-Convention nevertheless attempted to disrupt Republican symbolism and dramaturgy with oppositional imagery, while building and deepening intra-movement coalitions and connections for future action.

The convention's delicate dance

There are compelling reasons for social movements to stage mass protests at summits and conventions. It is a clear, visual way to perform opposition to the policies of the elite for a global audience. The conventions are already being covered by the media due to the prestige of their attendants and the high-stakes decisions being made. Party conventions have their own rigid and predictable dramaturgy—smarmy biographical videos of the candidate, and the inevitable dropping of the balloons. The parties want these images broadcast to hundreds of millions of viewers, and they do not want them disrupted. Economic conclaves such as the World Trade Organization (WTO) prefer more discretion, so calling attention to their agenda through dramatic disruption is a common goal of activists. The organizers of major US political party conventions face an impressive dramatic challenge: they have to achieve the following goals in the same high-budget, live-broadcast event.

1. *Fire up the base while appealing to the center.* The event must be exciting to the party militants who will vote, donate money, and devote countless hours of volunteer labor to the electoral campaign. Their concerns, agenda, fears, and hopes must be addressed specifically and zealously, but without terrifying centrist voters needed for nationwide electoral victories. This strategy explains why some conventions are filled with subcultural "dog whistles"—quotes and references that only extreme followers will understand. To the rest of the country these messages are mere nonsense or innocuous phrases. These phrases often allude semi-obscurely to worldviews not shared by the majority of the electorate (for example, expressing that the millennium is nigh, and the unfaithful will be destroyed, by quoting lesser-known phrases from the Bible). The nation as a whole must be celebrated while the party's identity remains firm enough to work as a "brand" in corporate terms.
2. *Use strategic ambiguity and multivalence to hold the megaloparty together.* This is similar to the point above, but is a more internal concern. Due to legal and extralegal restrictions that limit the avenues for the participation of minor and third parties in the US electoral system, there are only two parties acting in duopoly. (The US is one of the most restrictive democracies in the world on this point). This system is relatively stable, but that stability is achieved by submerging the interests and concerns of many groups—usually the ones with the least political pull and capital. The sprawling Democratic and Republican parties are in effect what I refer to as *megaloparties*—parties stretched over feuding voting blocs in a barely tenable, tensive sprawl—containing multitudes and contradicting themselves without Whitman's gentle acceptance of internal diversity. So as the party plays a delicate game of presentation to undecided and centrist voters, it must also address the concerns of its various and conflicting factions—libertarian billionaires and xenoglossic xenophobes, downsized workers and the technological innovators who eliminated their jobs, etc.
3. *Make the candidate a hero for our time.* The candidate is the culmination and personification of the party itself. His or her life story must be told in enough detail to be compelling, and to flatter the "exceptional nature" of the US and the candidate. Nation myth and hero myth must intertwine in the glossy biographical videos and hagiographic speeches by defeated rivals. This occurs in a national context where the body of the candidate is hyper-regulated and

> restricted by heteronormativity and class hegemony (Bogad, 2016). The candidate-body must appear poised and expressive (not too stiff), but not flamboyant or vulnerable. Admitted or known flaws must be acknowledged and forgiven, or overwritten and erased from the public memory. Most of all, the hero's mythic journey to this culminating moment must also show why the candidate is *the* needed leader for this country at this specific moment. The candidate has been *created* to address the crisis of our times.

The actual uniqueness of the human individual must actually shine through all of these lenses. This is a tall order, and sometimes it falls flat. Rivals go rogue and almost "forget" to endorse the candidate in their speech (for example, Governor Chris Christie, RNC 2012); or subcultural dog whistles come front-and-center to the befuddlement of the mass of the country (for example, Clint Eastwood mocking and berating an empty chair, RNC 2012). To script a convention that walks all of these thin lines, while actually making concrete, but not too specific, claims for a policy agenda, would give a veteran Hollywood screenwriter a headache.

The delicacy of this task makes the convention a tempting target for creative protest in an attempt to nudge the well-heeled players off their rhetorical tightrope. The 1968 Democratic Convention in Chicago, with images of police beating protesters and Mayor Daley silencing the microphone when a delegate tried to discuss it, helped tip the national election to Nixon. Tactical performers have to calculate not only the vector and velocity of their interventions, but also whether or not a convention is a timely and worthwhile target in the first place.

To convene or not to convene? The pros and cons of crashing the party

If a mass protest at a convention is visually stunning, performatively dynamic, and succeeds in disrupting the operations of the summit or convention, it can force a grudging, distorted acknowledgement in the global media of the existence of the movement and its critique. This is the mass, radical equivalent of someone jumping in front of a television camera covering a sports event and yelling "Hi Mom!" The cameras are already there, already rolling—you just need to leap in front with something fascinating, attractive, disturbing, and disruptive. These are the factors that led to the now mythologized success of the anti-WTO protest in Seattle in 1999—a complex, heterogeneous mass creative disruption that brought many different social movements into coalition, and introduced the global justice movement and its urgent agenda to the Global North. Labor unions and environmentalists, direct action street-blockers, puppeteers, and priests all united with a diverse set of tactics to disrupt the meeting of the WTO. Though demonized by the corporate media for a few broken windows, the movement taught the American public about the WTO and its unelected power.

In short, these major conventions can serve as *pressure points on the body politic*. In a type of *political aikido*, results can be achieved by pressing on these points with relatively little force—ideal for resource-poor social movements.

On the other hand, half a generation after the Seattle success, convention protests are far more problematic. The enterprise is, by its very nature, reactive rather than proactive. Conventions take place on the terrain and time of the opponents' choosing: Sun Tzu teaches us that this is a very, very, bad way to enter a conflict. To summarize, the problems with convention protests include:

1 *They know you are coming.* Like you, your opponent will learn from mistakes as well as successes. The state, Exxon, the WTO, et al., are *also* engaged in praxis. In fact, corporations, states, and police agencies have a far greater institutional memory than social movements, and are less likely to make the same mistake twice. Seattle was a defeat for the image of global capitalism, and an embarrassment for the state, and those entities have learned from those mistakes and have taken appropriate action.

   At the moment, every major international corporate and political party convention attracts mass protest. The element of surprise so crucial for effective dramaturgy is already lost. Also, police resources devoted to these events are staggering. Protest groups are surveilled and infiltrated by police agents for months before the event itself. And the onus of state violence is applied most brutally to people of color who dare to dissent.

   The convention area itself will either be in a remote, hard-to-reach area such as the resort of Gleneagles (G8 2005), or in a heavily fortified and aggressively garrisoned urban area. At the G20 in Pittsburgh in 2009, more money was spent on convention security in a few days than the entire annual arts budget of the whole state of Pennsylvania. The entire downtown was fenced off with checkpoints manned by actual Federal Border Patrol Agents—enforcing not a national border, but the border between inside and outside the power elite. Phalanxes of police and armored cars amassed to block Liberty Street, unaware of any irony. At one point, I walked alone down an empty street, wearing a puppet mask on my head, and was followed by a marching phalanx of 80 riot police who simply had nothing else to do. I felt like Buster Keaton in his film *Cops*, in which there are so many police in an empty cityscape that they flow into the street like water, inundating everything, and then flow away, only to rush back again in the next constabulary flash flood.

Actions against these conventions face a higher and higher bar of ingenuity to be successfully disruptive. Why move against an opponent at their strongest and most prepared point of defense?

2 *The spectre of cliché haunts this practice.* One of the challenges faced by social movements is to keep the actions interesting, dramatic, pointed, and unpredictable. This is not only to evade state agents, but also to engage the interest of a national or global audience and create that "man bites dog" factor that attracts the mass media. As stated in the Introduction, cliché is the bane of any art

Figure 4.1 Border Patrol Agents manning the border between the G20 and the rest of the world in Pittsburgh. Photo by L.M. Bogad.

Figure 4.2 Blocking Liberty/No Turn on Red: police block Liberty Avenue in Pittsburgh as part of the general fortification and shutdown of downtown. Photo by L.M. Bogad.

Figure 4.3 Police assemble underneath a movie theatre whose owner has composed and posted a protest haiku. Photo by L.M. Bogad.

form—protest included. After the high point of Seattle, the notion of mass protests at conventions has become an expected and uninteresting phenomenon, unless the actions are very creative and innovative.

3 *It is resource-intensive as a practice.* Typically many protesters travel across the world or the country to join actions at these events; a great expense of money and time. It is worth asking the question: could airfare, carbon, and other costs be better spent on a series of local, proactive, and thematically unified actions that are coordinated globally for free on the internet? This has been done effectively with the Carnival Against Capital, the Lysistrata Project, and more recently the wave of Black Lives Matter protests across the US, which was held in scores of locations, but unified in theme and slogans through social media.

Nevertheless, conventions remain a popular target for protest and, despite pitfalls, can be valuable for a movement. Participation in these spectacles of dissent and the attendant repression builds a culture of personal and collective storytelling; socially connective webs of story ("You were there too?") that is morale building. And yes: interventions are still effective from time to time. At the Democratic National Convention (DNC) in Boston, authorities designated an Orwellian "Free Speech Zone" for legal protest—a fenced-in cage under a highway overpass. Most protest groups refused to accept such an inhospitable and prison-like sanctioned space for protest. But a pro-Palestinian group innovatively used the repressive cage as a stage:

> The cyclone fencing and barbed wire provide an ideal visual backdrop to their message of opposition to the Israeli occupation of the West Bank. "We want to draw attention to what Palestinians have been subjected to for years," said Marilyn Levin of the group, United for Justice With Peace. "We can leave our cage, but Palestinians cannot leave theirs."
>
> (Kifner, 2004)

But more often, such restricted spaces do not provide symbolic backdrops that illustrate one's issue. They are obstacles for activists to outflank, literally, rhetorically, and performatively.

The RNC'S dramaturgy: revenge and the savior–warrior

This chapter focuses on the 2004 RNC, five years and myriad convention protests after the Seattle WTO shutdown, as a test case. It focuses on a few of the many creative approaches that were used to protest against this fortified and massively policed convention. What was the Republican strategy for telling a story to the US public that would enhance Bush's chances for re-election? Why did they choose the liberal bastion of New York City as the site for their convention, and why hold the convention so late in the electoral season (30 August–2 September)? Why was Madison Square Garden chosen as the venue? Did it have such great acoustics and sightlines to justify jumping into the belly of the beast—one of the few cities in America with a relatively large and organized progressive activist community that was hostile to the neoconservative agenda?

New York City is not only the home of the Mets, the Met, a large labor movement, and a host of theatrically trained leftists. It is also the site of the 9/11 World Trade Center terrorist attacks. And this was the memorial site that the GOP hoped to activate for their revanchist narrative of Bush as a savior and protector in the War on Terror. They needed to associate their party with that history. Not as the people in charge when the attacks happened, but as the party that could be trusted to execute global revenge and protect the US from further attacks.

For this to work dramaturgically, the GOP needed a clean platform on which to perform. New York City was such a backdrop. It was a site of bereavement, solemn commemoration of terrorism, and the *casus belli* of the wars that the Bush Administration had chosen to pursue in Iraq and Afghanistan.

From the RNC's perspective, disruptive protests were not completely unwelcome. If actions could not be prevented, the RNC would use them as fuel for the culture war; the conflict needed to be depicted as "un-Americans" versus "real Americans"—protesters serving as traitorous foils to the angelic hosts of GOP delegates serving their country as protectors. The city had to be massively policed to prevent effective or convincing protest that actually undermined the GOP narrative. Protests had to be marginalized geographically, in the media, and in the public imaginary. There is a long history of protests at big-party conventions being repressed, such as the famous 1968 DNC police riot that crushed the anti-war protesters in Chicago; and the wrongful arrest of 75 puppeteer activists during the 2000 RNC in Philadelphia, which was described in Chapter 3.

The space of Manhattan had to be policed and controlled for the RNC to be successful dramatically. Not only space, but also timing and the use of symbolic sites were key to the impact of the event. One of the culminating planned events of the RNC was President Bush's visit to the site of the World Trade Center to make a speech there, locking in his role as the avenger for the US public of the crimes of Al Qaeda. This act would symbolically overwrite his failed promise to pay for improved security, the rehabilitation of victims and injured first-responders, and the rebuilding of the devastated economy of New York City post-9/11.

Naturally, all sides in this sort of confrontation can make mistakes and mis-steps, as well as exploit the mistakes of opponents. When the RNC realized the scope of the protests that were being prepared in New York City, it floated the idea that delegates should not be harassed by staying in hotels in Manhattan, but should stay on a cruise ship docked on the West Side, and ride back and forth in limos to Madison Square Garden every day (Slackman, 2003). While many New Yorkers complained of the hotel and concession revenue this would cost the city, many of us in the social movements were praying that the RNC would go forward with this idea. Such a decision would be fodder for endless class-critique and satire, and would be the visual and performative equivalent of Bush's famous quote to campaign donors at the Waldorf-Astoria in 2000, when he called them the "haves and have-mores," and told them "some people call you the elite. I call you my base." Sadly, the RNC thought a second time about the elitist symbolism and nixed the cruise ship idea.

The Counter-Convention's disruptive dramaturgy

The Counter-Convention was a fundamentally antithetical entity to the RNC it was gathering to protest—radically different in both ideology and structure. As opposed to the RNC's top–down and monolithic, hierarchical party structure, the Counter-Convention was a heteroglossic and horizontalist hydra—a beast with many bodies as well as many heads. It operated with a diversity of ideologies, tactics, and even goals.

While the Republicans had federal, city, and state governments and their massive strategic power to occupy and hold space, social movements had one tactical advantage. They were working in familiar home territory among a mostly supportive population, and its members boasted a wide diversity of skill sets, identities, and modes of performance and protest. The Counter-Convention staged meetings, councils, conferences, cultural events, and many kinds of street actions all over Manhattan and Brooklyn; the Republicans found that they had a more limited range of motion outside of the cordon of police protection at scheduled events. Some RNC delegates may even have experienced a sense of being out-of-place that perhaps they never felt before as white, privileged, and entitled Americans. Republican delegates were taunted as they went to Broadway shows and dined at Tavern on the Green.

Republican delegates attending an auction of Johnny Cash memorabilia at Sotheby's were confronted by 400 Johnny Cash lookalikes[1] who denounced this cooptation of this musician of the people by strumming and singing Cash songs that advocated for the poor and the imprisoned. The pseudo-right-wing Missile Dick Chicks, described in faux-phallic detail in Chapter 1, infiltrated a Republican private party as the "entertainment"; it took a while for the partiers to realize they were being lampooned by their hired "showgirls," and it took even longer to throw the Chicks out. Indeed, there was so much varied protest in New York City during the RNC that the local media, and even the neoconservative press, who normally dismissed such protest, gave it major coverage. It would have been too eerily Orwellian for the media *not* to acknowledge protest that everyone could see happening around them.

This was the kind of action the Counter-Convention generated—oppositional, multivariate, and semi-improvised. The challenge was how to keep the momentum going for actions as disparate as banner-hangs, party-crashings, guerrilla theatre, and enormous marches of hundreds of thousands of people from all over the country in the face of the city's bans and hyper-regulation of protests. The RNC had Madison Square Garden and access to all the luxury that Manhattan could offer. The Counter-Convention did not even have permission to peaceably assemble. This problem of permission had to be confronted creatively.

Place, protest, and permission

Frisbees and grass. In the lead-in to the RNC that summer, the Republicans made it clear that both of these things were more important than the First Amendment to the Constitution. The United for Peace and Justice (UFPJ) coalition wanted to stage a massive rally on the Great Lawn in Central Park, a space big enough to accommodate the hundreds of thousands of demonstrators expected to gather to protest the Bush agenda. However, New York City's Republican Mayor, Michael Bloomberg, bending to pressure by the Bush Administration, insisted that so many people in the park would kill the grass. Bloomberg further claimed that such an enormous protest would violate the rights of people who wanted to play frisbee in the park, despite the precedent of many concerts and baseball World Series celebrations held in the Park, attended by hundreds of thousands of people. During one activist spokescouncil, a gathering of Counter-Convention affinity groups for brainstorming, collective communication, and planning, I proposed we simply show up in the park, each carrying a frisbee—all 500,000 of us. Frisbees could be decorated with individual political slogans, and the outbreak of a massive game of anti-authoritarian frisbee football could be a fitting answer to this unjust refusal of a permit. Any resultant mass arrests would simply dramatize the absurdity of a permit ban. Mercifully, this idea was not implemented.

Dear Reader, you're about to read how several groups responded creatively to the protest ban in Central Park. Use this space to brainstorm two or three possible ideas of your own. (Oh, and by the way, what would be the rules of anti-authoritarian frisbee?)

As already discussed, like all political conventions, the RNC is a tightly coordinated ritual designed to overwrite the differences between the factions of the host megaloparty (for example, between the fiscal and the social conservatives), and to present compellingly emotional and strategically vague symbols and personas to the nation through television. To make all of this cohere, the convention needed a powerful event-narrative, and perhaps this was why the RNC was scheduled later than any other RNC. It would take place close to the 9/11 anniversary. By occupying this hallowed time and space, the Republicans hoped to stage a pageant with the following storyline: a grateful New York City embracing their President–protector–avenger as he coopts the memory of that tragedy for his re-election campaign.

To oppose this storyline, the battle for the right of peaceable assembly was key. A massive, peaceful, festive, creative, public rejection of Bush at a historic, picturesque site in the city would certainly speak against the event-narrative. Beyond the Great Lawn, protestors intended to stage a Counter-Convention all over the city that would express a wide range of voices in dissent against the monolithic monologue of the RNC. Thus the pressure on Bloomberg to marginalize the protestors as much as possible, claiming it was for their safety in the post-9/11 era, or for the sake of the grass. Without a legal permit, many people, fearing arrest, would be intimidated and stay at home. If the protestors were denied a viable permit, some frustrated protestors might engage in civil disorder, confirming the "culture war" for the viewers at home and mobilizing the law-and-order Bush base.

The protestors were told that they could exercise their constitutional right to peaceable assembly in the borough of Queens, several miles away across the East River from Madison Square Garden where the RNC was to be held. When protestors refused, they were told they could gather on the West Side Highway. Although this location was deemed inhospitable (the lack of shade put protestors in danger of sunstroke), and too far from Madison Square Garden, the UFPJ gave in to the city's hardball negotiating tactics and accepted this protest venue. However, UFPJ's outraged grassroots members threatened to drop out of the coalition and march *en masse* in Central Park, permit or not, rather than stand on the Highway. Finally, the city and UFPJ agreed to a march, without a rally, that would gather west of Union Square, pass Madison Square Garden, and double back to disperse at Union Square. This was hardly ideal, but UFPJ decided to make it work, all the while resenting the fact that the people were not allowed to meet in their own park.

The movement staged many responses to the government's restrictions on peaceable assembly, and to the over-regulation of dissent in public space in general. Massive anti-Bush banners were illegally hung from hotel roofs—the most famous one being a huge banner strung from the windows of the Plaza Hotel, with an arrow labeled "TRUTH" pointing in one direction and an arrow labeled "BUSH" pointing in the opposite direction. This was a powerful and easily readable image, and also an inside activist joke, a reference to a 1999 Seattle protest banner where the arrows were labeled "WTO" and "DEMOCRACY." Some groups rented billboard space, while others creatively altered commercial postings ("subvertisement"), to make them anti-RNC (Adler, 2004).

ACT-UP activists stripped naked outside Madison Square Garden, their stenciled skin screaming, "STOP AIDS DROP THE DEBT"—a reference to the crushing debt of African nations that made it impossible for them to effectively combat the AIDS epidemic. This last action was a classic example of ACT-UP at their best—an elegant, eloquent, resource-cheap, and courage-intensive action. Naked bodies starkly proclaiming their defiance, calling for an actionable, specific policy objective in the face of heavily armored riot police, barricades, and the hard urban environment. They were aware that, once again, their naked queerness would make them a novelty item in mainstream culture, and this titillating nudity could not be shown without also showing the words on the exposed flesh. They made the front pages of several major newspapers, and even the conservative, pseudo-populist *New York Post* put them on the front page with the headline: "WELL, IT *IS* THE NAKED CITY." This was simple and effective body politics in action. This act was reflective of ACT-UP's consistent strength—an awareness of the value of the *frisson* of savvy transgression—for political leverage, personal and collective empowerment, and injecting alternative values into the mainstream.

Times Up!, the bicyclist group, staged the largest Critical Mass bike ride in the history of New York City, which clogged the avenues of Manhattan for hours. An estimated 8,000 bicyclists participated in the ride, which stretched on for blocks and shut down auto traffic. The author can attest that there was some magic to coasting silently through a car-less Times Square as part of a carbon-free fleet of bicyclists stretching endlessly in either direction. The police, frustrated with the size of the mass of riders, threw orange nets on entire groups of bicyclists, knocking them to the ground so they could be arrested. About 10% of the ride or 800 bikers were arrested that night. This included the Billionaires for Bush's media team, resulting in the group's decision to draft me as a replacement for a last-minute appearance in character on a satellite radio station the next day.

Members of Code Pink managed to infiltrate the RNC itself, standing up at key moments during Republican leaders' speeches to hold anti-war banners. They were quickly apprehended by security and dragged away, but the brief interruptions were televised. Of course, such action is polarizing—it encouraged the RNC's opponents but raised the righteous hackles of RNC supporters who resented the disruption. Yet this duality is a necessary aspect of this kind of action.

For 40 weeks, Reverend Billy and his Church of the First Amendment (his Church of Stop Shopping's name changed to fit the current conflict) staged a recurring action in the recently reopened World Trade Center subway/PATH station. Every Tuesday evening during rush hour, anonymous performers would join the swarms of commuters, scuttling around and talking on their cell phones; however, as they did so, instead of chatting to their spouses or giving orders to subordinates back at the office, they recited over and over the First Amendment to the United States Constitution:

> **Congress shall make no law respecting an establishment of religion, or prohibiting the free exercise thereof; or abridging the freedom of speech, or of the press; or the right of the people peaceably to assemble, and to petition the government for a redress of grievances.**

This mass recitation would gradually escalate from invisible theatre to a crescendo of screaming glorious First Amendment worshippers, and police found it understandably hard to arrest them as they chanted those sacred words. Billy's director, Savitri D, was released just as a police officer was cuffing her wrists: he just couldn't go through with it. I found the escalators to be one of the best places to recite the First Amendment—the other escalator riders were close by, and were a captive audience for the 30-second journey either up or down. One could then ride the other way and recite it for the people going up, and so on.

Big shoes in the Big Apple

The Clandestine Insurgent Rebel Clown Army (CIRCA) ran pell-mell through the streets without a permit, alternating between clownarchic swarming, strict military formation marching, cowardly fleeing, "sneaking" in plain sight, and hiding behind very small objects. These all sound like familiar maneuvers for the reader of Chapter 2, but the newly recruited and mobilized New York gaggle of CIRCA had many differences. When I returned from the UK, the Reclaim the Streets/Lower East Side Collective crew wanted to work with the Clown Army concept to protest the RNC, and in a warehouse that was probably bugged, the brainstorming and mutual co-training began.

I introduced our UK training techniques to the group—a combination of traditional clowning and *bouffon* performance chops, collective improvisation, nonviolent civil disobedience, and Theatre of the Oppressed exercises. RTS members such as Monica Hunken and Chuck Reinhardt quickly added their own training in proper clowning to the mix, while Ben Shepard created a constantly cursing, paranoid Nixon-clown character that shook up the paradigm as a sort of anti-authoritarian non sequitur. Jason Grote, Mark Read, and Ludmila Svoboda jumped into the clown collective, and Stephen Duncombe started working on satirical symbolism. We quickly realized that we would have to adjust CIRCA methods to the local terrain—a more militarized and aggressive police force than in the UK and a rigidly restricted protest space. Whereas the original Clown Army engaged the local constabulary with kisses, tickles, and pseudo-groveling over-compliance, such behavior in New York City would simply result in a speedy clown beat-down and lots of red noses in the lock-up. We also posted *plainclothes clowns* in a perimeter around our group, who served as scouts to warn us by phone if, for example, the police were coming our way with handfuls of plastic handcuffs.

More than the original CIRCA, CIRCA/NYC was highly interested in using old-fashioned street theatre to create a political meme, image, or living cartoon that ridiculed Bush and the GOP, and undermined the RNC's narrative and the hero myth of the President as constructed by the GOP.[2] What shtick could we devise that would be incisive and readable in a few seconds of television, easily described on radio or in print, and the least likely to trigger bludgeoning by the NYPD? If the shtick could provide us with a method for getting off the sidewalk and out into the streets from time to time with some modicum of freedom, all the better. We went with the idea of Bush clowns. CIRCA/NYC decided to remind spectators of Bush's now-infamous jetfighter landing on an aircraft carrier, costumed in a flight suit, putting his thumbs up, and announcing the end of major combat operations in Iraq under a "MISSION ACCOMPLISHED" banner. That intrepid appearance had been stunning in its crafted, mediated lack-of-place; in fact, the carrier Bush landed on had been just offshore of San Diego, not in the Gulf. Normal conveyance for such an executive visit would have been a quick shuttle on a helicopter. However, the jetfighter looked much more daring and exciting. The supersonic warplane and the aircraft carrier were commandeered as the set and backdrop for Bush the hero figure. The entire carrier group sailed in circles as it stayed out of port for Bush's dramatic visit, cameras aimed out to sea so that the California coast would not be in the frame. The crew, who by the rules of military discipline, had to cheer their Commander-in-Chief, served as adoring extras in this high-seas adventure. This image had been devised by Bush's aides to be a lasting triumphalist image of presidential war heroism. And, briefly, it was a great success. However, that success soon became a liability as the war escalated and, contrary to the predictions of the Administration, thousands of American troops were killed by the insurgency in Iraq. In time, the image of a flight-suited, grinning, thumbs-up Bush in front of that Mission Accomplished sign became a great liability, and something the GOP wanted voters to forget. We knew that we had to do everything we could to press down hard on this symbolic pressure point, to refer to that image and remind the public. We were also aware of a tragic miscalculation of the Administration when, as part of a comic video for the annual White House Correspondents Dinner, Bush was seen jokingly searching around the White House for the never-found weapons of mass destruction that were the stated rationale for the invasion of Iraq in the first place. Some found this joke troubling, to say the least.

CIRCA clowns Harpo-Marxed on this image, wearing flight suits labeled "MISSION ACCOMPLICATED" on the back. With costumes finalized, we still needed a central motivating dramatic premise for our days of marching. What was the story? Why were the clowns mobilizing? This guiding principle would be the spine upon which the rest of our prepared and improvised antics would hang. We decided that we would be both looking for weapons of mass destruction, and trying to get into the RNC as delegates. I wrote a ridiculous communiqué to that effect and read it on Air America. Thanks to a graphic artist in our midst, by the time the RNC started, we sported official looking ID cards as delegates to the RNCC (Republican National Clown Convention) around our necks. The NYPD were not impressed with our credentials, but several journalists were, including Amy Goodman of the radio program *Democracy Now*, who we encountered and briefly alarmed in the subway.

Our city marches consisted of searches for weapons of mass destruction in restaurants, mailboxes, and the body cavities of passersby, playfully referring to those moments on the aircraft carrier and the Correspondents Dinner gaffe. Our central goal was to remind the public about the moment that the GOP wanted everyone to forget. Sure enough, in many media outlets we were referred to as a "flight suit-wearing 'Mission Accomplicated' troupe."

We marched with long white cardboard tubes instead of parade rifles. This gave us more of a mock-martial look, and we used the tubes for various parade maneuvers. From time to time I would yell the infamous neoconservative tax cut slogan, "Stimulus Package!" At this point, we would all jump into the street and begin using these giant straws to snort the painted white lines in the streets and crosswalks. Thusly "stimulated" we became more wired and joyfully manic for a few minutes. This was to remind the viewer of the President's narcotic habit of times past. It also provided us with a theatrical motivation and rationale to jump into the street and block traffic briefly without a permit.

Figure 4.4 The Clown Army crossing the street in stealth mode. Photo by Fred Askew.

We also periodically played a game called Golf War, using the white tubes as clubs, a clownish reference to Bush's many golfing vacations. We puffed ourselves up as macho and brave, with warlike slogans, and indeed both male and female clowns packed their crotches to create provocative bulges. However, at the slightest hostile gesture by police, we would run away in abject terror and hide behind very small objects such as a fire hydrant, a toddler, or a ballpoint pen. This was done to avoid being beaten, create spectacle, lampoon the chickenhawk biographies of Bush and his core of advisors, and for fun.

CIRCA/NYC used the pirate model of democracy to avoid long discussions in the middle of the fray when quick decisions had to be made. (This had been a problem with the 150 clowns amassed in Scotland during the G8: the BBC noted the lengthy and constant meetings we would have in the middle of an action day to decide our next step.) On many pirate ships of the seventeenth and eighteenth centuries, the crew would generally make decisions democratically—where to sail, how to divide duties and booty, etc. However, in the thick of battle, the pirate captain gave orders, as there was no time to debate or vote when the shrapnel was flying. Along the same lines, while in the street, we would rotate play-calling and decision-making authority to different clowns.

I asked the group to experiment with envisioning a dial that goes from 1 to 10; at moments, either after a number had been called out or collectively imagined, the group would tune the frenetic energy of its clowning up or down between 1 (tiny movements, almost still, silent) and 10 (clownarchic mayhem, screeching and bouncing and careening off the walls). We had fun practicing this, and it introduced to the mix a collective theatrical dynamic—an aesthetic variation that keeps things interesting and unpredictable. Sound and fury is for selected special moments; if you're always at "10" as a performer, especially as a radical street clown, pretty soon you will lose your audience's attention and patience. This rehearsed principle is useful on a stage, but it came in particularly handy throughout long days of clownfrontational maneuvers between police, passersby, fellow protestors, violently angry rightist counter-protesters, and journalists.

At one point, the clowns ran into a Starbucks in search of weapons of mass destruction. There was giggling from the customers, eye-rolling from the staff, and aggravation from the manager as we looked under tables and up noses with our bad Bush accents. Encouraged by this, we ran outside, and charged into the McDonalds next door with the same mission. As we burst in, we encountered an entire squad of police sitting at tables near the front door having their lunch. The police turned and stared intently. I recognized them making that unconscious, tiny pelvic move that prepares a body for leaping out of a chair. If we ran, they would charge after us. Immediately and by silent, instant consensus, the entire clown squad turned it down from 10 to 1. We silently and almost contemplatively began to lift napkins just a hair, and slowly look under them. With tantalizing precision I inspected the tiny pepper packets, holding one to my ear and shaking it with great care as if afraid it would explode. The police relaxed. We relaxed. A few customers chuckled at what we were doing. After a minute or two, we silently finished our search and sashayed out onto the street.

When we arrived at Central Park, after a long day of clowning all over downtown Manhattan, the media was waiting for us. Well, not specifically for us, but they had been lying in wait to see which protesters would demonstrate in the Park without a permit and what would happen to them. They swarmed us, and at one point there were more television cameras aimed at us than there were clowns. Reverend Billy was holding a mass wedding to the First Amendment in the park, and the Bush clowns stumbled onto this sincere and beautiful pro-Free Speech ritual. In shaky improvisation, we crashed the party as our rude, entitled neoconservative clown personae. The banter with Billy was fun, but there was some dissonance between his earnest and sincere style and our radical ridiculousness. Just as we were beginning to worry that we were distracting from the event and should extricate ourselves, the Reverend called on the Spirit to exorcise us. We fled helter-skelter to safer grounds.

While CIRCA/NYC hardly changed the course of history, we made a joyous noise, adding another note to the dissonant/dissident cacophony that was the Counter-Convention. With just a few dollars for costumes and a hefty helping of donated playtime from a dozen individuals, we had a great deal of defiant joy and performed, in a concise, clear, media-friendly and ridiculous way, an oppositional image of the hero–savior elevated by the RNC (Power & Russakoff, 2004; Wheeler, 2004).

A host of bells, triumphant

As the Convention's crown piece, the RNC scheduled a ceremonial visit by Bush to the site of the World Trade Centre. This offended many New Yorkers who felt that Bush had never delivered the economic or security aid that he had promised to the city after 9/11. But how

The Chuck factor

One clown who stood out from the rest was the recently departed Chuck Reinhardt (1943–2013), a longtime peace activist who was the only one among us who included big clown shoes in his costume. Chuck had many years and beers under his belt, and he had done peace work with youths in Bosnia for a dozen summers. He brought a different sensibility to the group. When I spoke to him later, Stephen Duncombe summed it up best:

> At first I was getting aggravated by Chuck, he was always lagging behind, messing up, falling over himself and generally not working well with the group—or that's what I thought. Then for a moment I found myself a block away from the group, and I was able to look at the whole picture, and I saw how perfect Chuck was in what he was doing in relation to the whole, and it all made sense.

Chuck's clown—older, stockier, clumsier, and always rushing to catch up, falling over, and out of step. He embodied the horn blast at the end of the joke, the squawk in the aria. He was the special ingredient that made the troupe *work*. Immaculate and holy. More than an inspiration, Chuck Reinhardt was a tactical necessity. If you don't have a Chuck in your troupe, go out and recruit one. Rest in Peace. Honk honk.

to protest it? The police were prepared to keep all protesters far from the event. In response, activists planned a mass bell ringing all over the neighborhood to non-verbally signal a protest to Bush's presence (Archibold, 2004).

Even the NYPD could not stop sound waves and the symbolism of thousands of "liberty bells" ringing out against the President. The protest would be resonant literally and figuratively. The rap singer and producer P. Diddy, whose office looked down on the site, put up anti-war posters on all of his many windows, a visual that clashed with the event's solemn obeisance and obedience to Bush. The RNC chose to cancel the event, keeping their dramaturgy within the more manageable and hermetically sealed venue of Madison Square Garden. This was no small victory for the Counter-Convention movement; disrupting a planned ritual at the site of those horrific terror attacks made the Republican cooptation of 9/11 less explicit, and thus less powerful. As Rebecca Solnit points out in *Hope in the Dark* (2005), many victories have invisible outcomes, simply because they prevent something worse from happening. This cancellation of a state event through the threat of a simple, nonviolent, inventive, mass action stands as just such a victory.

The Billionaires for Bush

There is one voice that the author has shamefully neglected in this tract: that of the elites. Their response to all of these provocations was crucial to understanding the civic dialogue taking place in the streets of New York City. On Sunday 29 August 2004, the day of the big march, about a dozen people arrived on the Great Lawn dressed in lovely opera gowns and tuxedos, and festooned with blinding jewelry. These were the Billionaires for Bush (B4B), and they archly informed the amassed media that, in fact, the real reason one million "hoi polloi" were denied access to the Great Lawn on that day was because they, as members of the upper 0.00001 per cent of society, had already reserved the space to play lawn games. They pointed out that this was part of their agenda to "Privatize Everything"—from the Park to the City Library, to the electoral process itself: "one dollar, one vote!" (Haugerud, 2013a & 2013b).

The dazzling gaggle of haute-reactionaries then spread out over the massive lawn, playing croquet and badminton (Conan, 2004). The sight of a few well-to-do cartoon characters having their elitist way on that massive green space sharply evoked the absence of the million protestors. This was a typical B4B action: riffing on reality; using satire to surprise, amuse, and engage; and straight-arming the "red-state/blue-state" culture-war binary by trying to get Americans to once again think about *class*. This was their unique (and no doubt tax-deductible) contribution to the Counter-Convention. Through ironic adoration they disrupted Bush's constructed persona as a straight-talking, dirt-under-his-nails everyman, redefining him as the upper-class wastrel-turned-warmonger that billionaires loved so much. Of course, class was a key component of the irony of the project. Assuming character names such as "Noah Countability" and "Lucinda Regulations," B4B represented a collective, conscious attempt to bring a progressive analysis of economic class back into the national conversation in Bush's America. The sight of plutocrats marching in the streets with signs underscored the reality that street protest is not something to which elites need resort. B4B manifested themselves as a funhouse-mirror image of the very elites whose globalized "liquidity" is one of the foundations of their power. Since real oligarchs would never demonstrate in the streets, the Billionaires for Bush provided the punchlines, playing both sides of the debate with joyously heavy-handed mockery.

B4B had approximately 2,000 members in 100 local chapters across the US at its height during the 2004 presidential election campaign. This group of merry pseudo-oligarchs greeted President Bush and his inner circle on the campaign trail, carrying signs such as "FOUR MORE WARS," "CORPORATIONS ARE PEOPLE TOO," "FREE THE FORBES 400," and "DICK CHENEY IS INNOCENT."

Like public protest in general, the very concept of socioeconomic class, or the identity of a ruling class, has been denied a place in mainstream American discourse. "Class warfare" has become a term used by pundits and politicians to denounce not the elites, but anyone who critiques the elites, or even acknowledges that they exist as a class. Commentators on all sides do flips in order not to utter the phrase "working class," resulting in such terms as "the working poor" and "working families." The Billionaires for Bush used cartoonish irony to bring class back to the forefront of discussion, and to mock the exploitive policies of the Bush Administration. They also added an element of tactical ambiguity to street confrontations where tensions can run high. Their relentless cartoonish depiction of the corrupting effects of oligarchy on the American republic foreshadowed the mass class-consciousness of the Occupy movement and its differentiation between "the 99%" and the "1%."[3]

One key aspect of the Billionaires for Bush concept was its own name as a meme. The three-word name succinctly contained the critique and point of the whole group. If B4B was discussed at all in the media, no matter how hostile the commentary was, as long as the group's name was mentioned, a concise argument about the President's elitism was unavoidably included in the coverage. This is a tactic well worth considering for current and future groups.

Billionaires for Bush spread their ironic message on radio, television, and the internet; this multimedia approach added layers to the campaign, and B4B's performative irony allowed them to play both sides of the debate. As my Billionaire character, "Ollie Gark," I found that doing a radio interview on a progressive radio show that usually emphasized issues of gender equality enabled me to draw connections between class and gender oppression with a smarmy, condescending tone. The affable, self-satisfied demeanors and a repertoire of one-line jokes led to a great deal of media and press attention for B4B.

The website www.billionairesforbush.com, designed to present both the satirical group-persona and an earnest political critique, helped spread the concept. People looking to start a chapter in their hometown could download well-produced graphics, slogans, performance ideas, and even original songs in karaoke version so they could sing them with a boom box back-up. These resources helped ensure the consistency of costume, graphics, and "branding" of the group across the country, while allowing for flexibility, creativity, and idea-sharing among and between the local groups. The website also provided a virtual place to coordinate far-flung actions.

B4B bird-dogged Bush on the swing-state campaign trail, setting up their red-white-and-blue piggybank banner and cheering him on with "Two Million Jobs Lost: A Good Start!" In fact, in York, Pennsylvania, Bush gave us the double thumbs-up as his motorcade whooshed by. The Billionaires for Bush also swung through the swing states during their Get On the Limo tours, spreading the gospel of greed and seeding new chapters as they went. Their Block the Vote tour in Florida, a reference to the Rock the Vote youth voter registration campaign, addressed the tradition of Republican disenfranchisement of African–Americans, and was enhanced by the soundtrack of rapper 50 Billion:

> **"The Billionaires are in the house**
> **The Billionaires are in the WHITE House . . .**
> **Buying access**
> **Seeing progress**
> **And making a mess**
> **Of the political process**
> **Oh yes!"**

Irony can always be misinterpreted, especially when a group uses the same shtick on multiple audiences simultaneously. The police tended to treat Billionaires for Bush members more politely, perhaps because of their generally genteel, entitled demeanor, or perhaps they activated some ingrained instinct to protect the propertied. There were incidents when police mistakenly sequestered B4B members with pro-Bush demonstrators, and at least one time when those Bushites took the group seriously, joining in on chants such as "Four More Wars!" in earnest—a chilling example of the complexities of irony as a tactic. Still, these moments demonstrated how effective irony could be for engaging people who would otherwise tune out a message, by creating momentary confusion and a pleasing "Aha!" moment.

During my own participation in the group, I noted that B4B members often discussed the value of the "Aha!" moment, when passersby would stop, listen, and then decode the satire for themselves. Even if they disagreed, at least they had engaged for a few seconds instead of instantly dismissing the group's critique. Often the response would be positive and playful. A performance that opens public space rather than simply occupying it can offer playful surprises. Surprise can create personal connections and break up stereotypes, clichés, and other mind-deadening habits of thought. Only a stimulated imagination can break paradigms and conceive of better worlds. Moreover, it is a show of respect to passersby when the performance's pitch is not obvious. In this sense, space-opening performance calls on the *polis* to co-create both the event and its importance.

Reflecting back on B4B practices, Marco Ceglie, one of the group's central organizers and performers, noted that the group was at its best when it used humor and an ironic approach to surprise and "get around ideological walls . . . as soon as they have you pegged, you're done . . . but if you make them laugh once, they'll think twice" (Ceglie, 2009). For Ceglie, predictable or dogmatic forms of protest simply turn off people when they're not already on your side, making it easier to stereotype and dismiss activist–actors. Even if participants weren't going in full Billionaire regalia, Ceglie advised members to "wear polo shirts and slacks" as opposed to stereotypical "activist" gear. Indeed, if the purpose of a tactical performance is to infiltrate both spatially and ideologically neutral, contested, or enemy territory, then social camouflage is essential—but of course social camouflage is easier to achieve for people with race and class privilege.

Ceglie preferred the more subtle Billionaires' actions to their heavy-handed ones. He recounted an appearance in Iowa in which the B4B parody "was so thick that there was no room for dialogue." A conservative man ended up punching their documentarian's video camera in anger. However, at the PGA golf tournament in Wisconsin that same year, the Billionaires for Bush arrived early in "nice" clothes, set up a table to give out literature, and didn't lay it on too thick. As a result, they engaged people far more effectively. Ceglie explained:

> "Is this real? Is it not?" Let *them* figure it out. It's not so good when it's ugly parody. It doesn't work; it just devolves into hack humor and obvious jokes. Sometimes demonstrations seem to only speak to our own subculture, like it's a big party. That has its place, but it's important to reach beyond.
>
> (Ceglie, 2009)

Ceglie also noted that because working with B4B was creative and fun, it attracted new people to the struggle, who were nonactivists and not part of the protest subculture. He went on to make a key point about the group's appeal:

> Positive energy is key, in order to reach beyond our subculture . . . [The] jokes resonate because they come from the truth. When I appeared on the radio, in character, against Laura Ingram or Ann Coulter, I never got mad—be as pleasant as possible; let *them* get upset. Agree with everything they say, and then turn it around with Billionaire logic.
>
> (Ceglie, 2009)

And if this provokes the reactionaries to revert to their rage and rhetoric?

> It's like chum to the lions. Because you're not talking to the reporter or the GOP hack or Ann Coulter—you're talking to the audience at home. Let *them* [Coulter, et al.] get angry and alienate the audience . . . We also need to learn from neoconservatives like Rush [Limbaugh]. They're brilliant at couching the most outrageous, extreme positions as if they were common sense, "Of course, everyone knows . . ." That assumption of truth.
>
> (Ceglie, 2009)

Ceglie is arguing here for a kind of rhetorical bullfight—provoking the hate mongers into a froth, letting them charge, then using light and deft irony like a skilled matador, making graceful moves to elude goring and score a point. The Billionaires for Bush were rarely so subtle, but it is a horizon of excellence to strive towards.

B4B flash mobbed the city in actions planned and spread by the internet and mobile phones, such as waltzing *en masse* in Grand Central Station. They disrupted a Karl Rove speaking event in New York City by getting there first with a Karl Rove lookalike, who got out of his limo with a young woman on his arm and immediately went over to the Billionaires for Bush to hail them as his most devoted "supporters" (Paster, 2004). Earlier, on 15 April 2004, the deadline for the filing of income tax returns, B4B had chosen the ultimate captive audience for their street theatre: the throngs of people lined up at the main Post Office on 34th Street in Midtown Manhattan to pay their taxes. Garbed in cartoonish bling, the Billionaires held signs saying

Figure 4.5 Billionaires for Bush on Tax Day at the New York City Central Post Office. Photo by Fred Askew.

Figure 4.6 A Billionaire for Bush on Tax Day at the New York City Central Post Office. Photo by Fred Askew.

"THANK YOU FOR PAYING OUR FAIR SHARE" and quoting Leona Helmsley's infamous "TAXES ARE FOR LITTLE PEOPLE." They proceeded to improvise and schmooze with the taxpayers in character, making snide comments that showed their gratitude to the GOP for tax policies that let them off the hook at the expense of the generous working stiffs assembled before them. Unlike most street theatre audiences, these folks were stuck there and had to listen. The venue was well chosen because the location, timing, and theme of the action were so perfectly matched. A nonpolitically oriented friend of mine was standing in line there to file her taxes, and had no idea what to expect. She called me later and said: "Well, the circus was in town today and it was pretty funny."

Picket line on the basketball court

In a bit of intra-social movement theatre, the Billionaires for Bush accepted a challenge to a smackdown game of basketball in Roosevelt Park on 25 August 2004, against the organizers of the Poor People's Economic Human Rights Campaign, a sincere and authentic working-class organization focused on bread-and-butter issues such as the minimum wage and rent control. On the surface, they were the polar opposites of B4B (Heller, 2004). The game was to raise money for the travel costs of poor and homeless families coming to New York City from across the country in order to protest.

As the highly corrupt referee, I can report that at one point in the game B4B were losing to the Campaign by around 96 to 2.[4] (I was chosen to be the referee for two reasons: I was considered to be pretty good on my feet as a street-theatre ham and could call some "plays" from that position with the whistle, and I was no good on the court.[5]) B4B tried to change the game to polo so they'd have a chance of winning, knowing the Campaign members didn't own horses. Or a yacht race—but we were landlocked. Fortunately, in the course of the game, B4B made a few phone calls, and were able to privatize the city basketball court, purchase it, and evict the Campaign from the grounds.

Actually, a lot more happened during that basketball game, and it was a teachable moment about the limits of irony as a form of engagement, and the *differences that make a difference* in socioeconomic class and artistic activism. The event was the result of a conversation between organizers of both groups, during which the Campaign challenged B4B to a game. There were a few Billionaires who thought they could play well enough. Both groups were aware of the bonds that can form from low-stakes and playful team sports, and we both wanted to do something that would be fun symbolically and literally. It was also a fundraiser for a worthy cause. A few media outfits came to cover the game, including an Italian television crew. Hence, the event served several purposes—to boost the morale of the participants, to build social connections for future coalition, and to reach a remote audience via broadcast (the game lacked a big live audience, as there was no local publicity). There was no planning made ahead of time in terms of theatre shtick or intentions. What was going to happen when a group of mostly middle-class people pretending to be rich played against poor people playing themselves?

Was the event pure street theatre, or a real collegial game with a little bit of in-character joshing? The problem was: no one had decided. Both teams brought cheerleaders—the Billionaires for Bush were regrettably gender-normative with blinged-out females as cheerleaders and males as players. The Campaign did the same, with women and kids on the sideline to cheer them on in their battle against the bosses. However, as I blew the whistle and unfairly passed the ball from the Campaign to B4B while counting my bribe money or receiving stock tips, it was irksome to those people on both sides who just wanted to play. Some people were really annoyed by the in-character "cheating" of B4B—and it turns out that even some of the Billionaires were hoping for less shtick and more game. Clearly, we did not communicate enough with each other before the event.

Nevertheless, the most brilliant, poignant, and savvy moments during the game came from the other side. While B4B performed their usual shtick without much fresh material, the Campaign found characters by being their own heroic selves and responding openly to what was happening. The Billionaires had brought a few extra T-shirts with our red-white-and-blue piggy bank logo, in a bid to extract some comedy from trying to steal players from the other side. When one Campaign player decided to play along and put the Billionaire T-shirt on, his friends howled in protest. He shrugged, grinned a huge broken-tooth smile, and said: "Hey, they said they'd give me dental!" This was tragicomic, savvy, and was better than anything scripted—a man was corrupted, not by gold or a yacht, but by dental treatment because this is the only way a poor man can get his damn teeth fixed in contemporary America.

Eventually, there were twice as many Billionaires on the court as Campaign players—the result of cheating, corruption, and a terrible referee. This was moderately interesting as it was an absurd though simple metaphor for the rich stacking the deck and changing the rules for their own benefit. The Campaign massively improved this imagery with another creative reaction. Swarms of Billionaires ran amok over the court and the referee continued to blow the whistle at inappropriate times. The Campaign could take it no longer. Its cheerleaders—a dozen women and children—stormed the court with their economic-justice themed signs, and formed a picket line in front of their basket. This was both practically effective—the Billionaires could not get close enough to the basket to score, given their limited skills—and visually poignant. Working-class women and children used that old tactic—the picket line—in a strange and new context that effectively stopped the cheating of the 1%. It was a beautiful sight. For a change, B4B did not have the last laugh—the other side was delivering the best and smartest punchlines. Finally, a few Campaign women came up and offered me one of their T-shirts. Following the improvisation rule of always saying, "Yes and," I put the T-shirt on and declared my allegiance to their cause. The game ended shortly after that with friendly conversations and farewells.

B4B were at their best when doing surprising, media-friendly, "air-war" actions, riffing on reality and providing a punchline to the oppressive joke setups provided by the real neoconservatives. The Great Lawn action, the Karl Rove prank—these proved to be some of the best examples of the potential of B4B. Occasionally, the Billionaires would descend into simple and obvious sarcasm that didn't appeal. For example, B4B activists showed up at a demonstration of the unemployed where they made their point by taunting the protestors in character. This action was fine, but not particularly compelling. A group should not attempt to do everything; nevertheless there was sometimes something missing from B4B operations due to a partial disconnect from the "ground war." Operating off the cuff, activists with the Poor People's Economic Human Rights Campaign came up with some of the best visuals and riffs, simply by acting sincerely and cleverly from their class position. Who knows what great shtick and results might have come had B4B enjoyed more direct liaison with working-class progressive activists?

The movements move on

Limited communication with other organizations and their rank and file members diminished the payoff of some other B4B actions. This is a problem that I experienced as a performer several times when B4B performed at labor rallies. The union organizers who invited us were always in on the joke. However, they and we sometimes failed to communicate the joke to union members, which resulted in ironic dissonance and misfire—many members simply not getting it. Some thought the Billionaires were real elitist counter-protesters, and grew riled up until the irony was explained to them (Haugerud, 2013a: p. 148). This was the mirror image of the misfire when B4B protested in front of conservatives who expressed admiration for them and joined in with their ironic chants. Such confusion at labor events defeated the purpose of appearing—which was not to aggravate, but to entertain, encourage, and create bonds by all "getting the joke" together. More sensitivity and effort could have been put into not just mass media relations but also grassroots communication—and tweaking our act to improve the out-of-character "wink" during the first moment of contact, learning to recognize when the interaction was going off the rails, and being savvy enough to jump out of character to share a comradely moment when confusion had clearly set in. All these tactics would have easily circumvented this recurring problem.

Bush was re-elected in 2004. Thanks to wartime incumbency, targeted voter suppression and intimidation, an insufficiency of voting machines in minority districts, and the well-coordinated character assassination of Democratic Party candidate John Kerry, the day ended in victory for the real billionaires. While refusing allegiance or devotion to the corporate-captured Democratic Party either, B4B had hoped that electoral defeat would rein in the worst excesses of the Right. When this didn't happen and activists were confronted with the devastating consequences of the Bush victory, the cadres of B4B faltered as the joke began to wear thin. The class warriors of the radical Right continued their drive to further privatize everything—from human genes to prisons to national forests—while striving to overwhelm discussions of class with calls for culture war at home and wars of choice abroad. They moved to dominate further all branches of the government, sectors of civil society, and farther-flung corners of the world.

Remaining in character, the B4B website immediately hailed the results, noting that the group had "paid for eight years," and celebrated "the disappearance of over 1 million votes." As an extended multimedia subvertisement, B4B had to evaluate how to retain momentum after the election, and fit into a more long-term strategy. The purpose of the Counter-Convention was not only to protest the RNC, but also to build lasting activist groups and coalitions for future action—and this was true for the Billionaires as well. The same group of seasoned satirists continued to be active in slightly altered versions, including Lobbyists for McCain (2008), Billionaires for Wealthcare (2009), and Republicorp (2010), along with their earnest collective alter ego, the progressive group The Other 98%.

And the New York Clown Army? When the RNC was over, the activists of CIRCA/NYC wanted to move from reactive to proactive modes. Now that there was no longer a political convention to protest reactively, what local issue did the group want to champion? They came up with the Bike Lane Liberation Clowns (BLLC). This group did highly visible and media-friendly patrols of bike lanes to call attention to the need for more and safer lanes in New York City. They also wanted to show that the rules to preserve bike lanes were not being enforced, causing dangerous situations for bikers when people were allowed to double-park and block those lanes. This was an ecological issue as much as it was a public safety issue—the movement asserting that cities need to consume less fossil fuels, and that bikes are an important part of the solution to that problem.

As the reader probably knows, clowns do not have brakes. So when the BLLC came upon a big SUV blocking the bike lane, they simply could not stop and one after the other, smacked into the car and rolled all over each other and the car itself, sweetly inquiring: "Wow! What kind of bike is this?! It's got 4 wheels! But it must be a bike, it's in the bike lane!" They would continue to fall over the car and clown around until the driver agreed to leave. This was playful and mediagenic and the BLLC, who still ride from time to time, were thus able to publicize the overall movement for more and safe lanes in the City, which has found a great deal of success in recent years. The New York Clown Army proved that the move from reactive to proactive—from a one-off response to a long-term positive campaign—could be both sustainable and impactful.

Clearly, the performance CIRCA gave at the G8 and the RNC represented only one tool in the repertoire of the global justice movement—only one approach of many, and not to be relied upon exclusively or inflexibly. Groups like Billionaires for Bush continue to experiment with techniques that are not purely reactive, and help to create a culture of shared meanings that can in turn sustain an oppositional movement even in the darkest of times. The satirical struggle continues.

Creating a place for protest necessitates building a joyous, dialogical space that can attract and include the voices of many diverse counterpublics. The movement of movements contains differences not only in beliefs, but also about how to act on those beliefs. Some feel that an oppositional movement should not even ask for a permit from the state, or that only direct action is effective and not mass demonstrations. Places for protest should look and feel different from those created and occupied by governments or political parties, which—in the infamous words of one Republican advisor—"create their own reality" in fortified, hegemonological, and placeless spaces where the waters off San Diego stand in dramatically for the Persian Gulf, where Madison Square Garden is the Central HQ of the culture war, where war is peace and ignorance is strength. The movements do not have the power to create such places. All the better. They are rooted in localities while reaching out to each other, coordinating virtually, and gathering on the street and in closely surveilled meeting places.

Election protests are not only about pandering to the "swing states" (in the parlance of the day). Movements perform not only against what they oppose. They also embody and enact visions of the world we want to see—to invest our places with our own cultures. These places, created and sustained through performance, are not merely reactive encampments outside the fortified institution or convention hall. They are the beginnings of a new place to live.

Oppositional places need to be constructed not only in response to events such as the RNC, but also, as the Counter-Convention taught, they must deepen intra-movement connections and coalitions across boundaries of geography, identity, and privilege, through cooperation, performance, and praxis under pressure.

Suggestions: to be tested in pratice

1. In performative coalitions, mix the insights and creativity of groups with different levels of privilege—middle class and working class, for example—not only because you achieve deeper insight into your issues and create a complex coalition, but also because the jokes are better. These links are complicated because the stakes of the groups are different, and care must be taken to ensure that frontline communities and their agendas and needs are respected.
2. Irony can be a sharp tool, but it can also misfire or backfire. When using an ironic approach it's important that all participants in a complex coalition are up to speed on what the joke is and who the target is. It's equally important, however, that the jokes are written well enough that these elements are clear.
3. Before rising to the challenge and targeting a convention or similar conference, the pros and cons should be weighed carefully. Will

there be a reasonable chance for a meaningful intervention? If so, an analysis of the opponent's story, and respect for the power of that story, will help to develop a compelling counter-narrative. If not, it might be best to use your resources to create a tactical performance in an unexpected context elsewhere.

4 Activist energy doesn't have to simply dissipate when the convention is over; groups that have bonded and developed skills while creating a Counter-Convention can channel those assets and momentum into proactive and sustainable campaigns on local issues.

Notes

1 Also known as the Defend the Man In Black Bloc, a play on the name of the anarchist Black Bloc.

2 This difference in style between CIRCA/NYC and the original CIRCA/UK reflected both the needs of the moment in this electoral intervention, and the personal styles and preferences of the individual members in this affinity group. I was the only member of both CIRCAs; the local New York City members, who had been in RTS/NYC and other local groups, were simply less interested in the personal-liberation and paradigm-shifting aspects of rebel clowning and more interested in its power to create mediagenic oppositional images and moments.

3 The Billionaires for Bush started in the 1980s and 1990s among progressive organizers for economic justice in Massachusetts, where "Fat Cats" in the western part of the state and "Class Acts" street performers in the eastern part experimented with playing the elite satirically for protest purposes. From the character name of the leader, "Phil T. Rich," to the very name of the group, many core elements of what would later become a famous meme were developed there. For more on this history, see Haugerud (2013a & 2013b).

4
> Although the Billionaires were eventually able to purchase a few players from PPEHRC the final score was: PPEHRC—A LOT . . . Billionaires—a little.
>
> (Heller, 2004)

5 Despite my own father's basketball prowess, crafted in the South Bronx at an early age, I couldn't dribble without hurting myself. It was better to trust me with the whistle.

References

Adler, Margot (2004) "Activists Take to NYC Streets." *NPR Morning Edition*, 30 Aug 2004, 10am EST. www.npr.org/programs/morning-edition/2004/08/30/13095180/ (accessed 28 Oct 2015).

Archibold, Randal (2004) "Hey Hey, Ho Ho, Those Old Protest Tactics Have to Go." *New York Times*, 13 June 2004. www.nytimes.com/2004/06/

13/nyregion/hey-hey-ho-ho-those-old-protest-tactics-have-to-go.html (accessed 28 Oct 2015).

Bogad, L.M. (2016) *Electoral Guerrilla Theatre: Radical ridicule and social movements*, 2nd edition. London: Routledge.

Ceglie, Marco (2009) Personal interview with the author, 20 March 2009.

Conan, Neal (2004) Protest at the Republican National Convention. *NPR Talk of the Nation*. 26 Aug 2004, 3pm EST. www.npr.org/templates/story/story.php?storyId=3872727 (accessed 12 Aug 2015).

Haugerud, Angelique (2013a) *No Billionaire Left Behind: Satirical activism in America*. Stanford: Stanford University Press.

Haugerud, Angelique (2013b) *No Billionaire Left Behind*. Documentary Film. Directed by A. Haugerud. http://vimeopro.com/user22454323/no-billionaire-left-behind (accessed 3 Nov 2015).

Heller, Samantha (2004) "Poor People's Economic Human Rights Campaign vs. Billionaires for Bush in Basketball Fundraiser." *New York City Independent Media Center*, 20 Aug 2004. http://publish.nyc.indymedia.org/es/2004/08/40763.html (accessed 5 Jan 2015).

Kifner, John (2004) "Demonstrators Steer Clear of Their Designated Space." *New York Times*, 26 July 2004. www.nytimes.com/2004/07/26/politics/campaign/26street.html (accessed 28 Oct 2015).

Paster, Heather (2004) "Irony and Politics do Mix for Street-theater Group." *The Villager*, Vol. 73, No. 54, 12–18 May 2004. http://thevillager.com/villager_54/ironyandpolticsdomix.html (accessed 28 Oct 2015).

Power, Michael; Russakoff, Dale (2004) "200,000 in N.Y. Protest Bush: President and GOP Convention unwelcome, demonstrators say." *Washington Post*, 30 Aug 2004: p. A01.

Solnit, Rebecca (2005) *Hope in the Dark: Untold histories, wild possibilities*. New York: Nation Books.

Wheeler, Jacob (2004) "United for Peace and Justice, Today's Protestors are Mature, Artful, and Productive: Peaceful protest precedes opening of Republican National Convention." *Utne Reader*, Aug. www.utne.com/community/unitedforpeaceandjusticetodaysprotestorsarematureartfuland-productive.aspx (accessed 28 Oct 2015).

Part III

Eschew cliché!

On the value of surprise

Chapter 5

Critical simulacra and tricknology

Oil Enforcement Agents, Yes Men, and Survivaballs

This chapter examines several examples concerning the use of fantasia and simulacra in the service of creative direct action on the issue of climate change. The creation of new symbols, and the repurposing of old symbols, as well as the use of an opponent's hypocrisy or dishonesty as a play space, are all explored. What are the ways in which a movement can playfully surprise the public, the media, and one's powerful targets to generate pressure for practical policy change?

Pulling into the Ford dealership where you work, you stop short. A man dressed in black, with a baseball hat and shades covering his eyes, brandishes a badge and grimly signals you to stop. As you step out of the car, the authority figure briskly hands you some official papers, explaining that your dealership is under investigation by the Oil Enforcement Agency (OEA). You have been subjected to an energy audit by the OEA's expert field agents, and they have found you in gross violation of the Agency's standards. The average fuel efficiency of Ford vehicles is 19 miles per gallon, and you have some SUVs on the lot that get a mere twelve. By comparison, the Ford Model T, back in 1923, ran at 25 miles a gallon. Clearly this is unacceptable. The polar ice caps are melting. The oceans are rising. You as a dealer have a responsibility to pressure the Ford Motor Company to start designing and making more fuel-efficient cars for you to sell.

You ask when the Oil Enforcement Agency was created, as you hadn't heard of it. The agent tells you that, in his most recent State of the Union address, President Bush stated that "America is addicted to oil," and that we must "move beyond a petroleum-based economy"

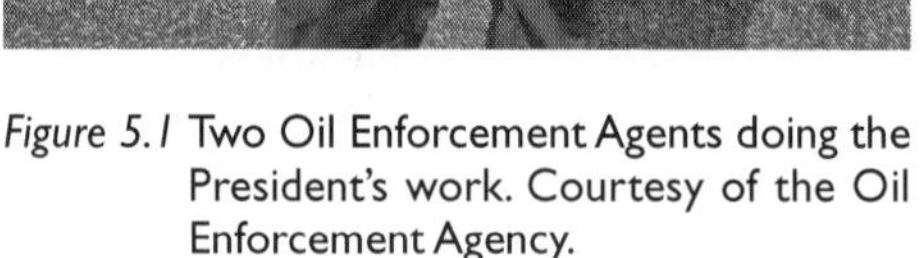

Figure 5.1 Two Oil Enforcement Agents doing the President's work. Courtesy of the Oil Enforcement Agency.

Figure 5.2 The OEA Seal. Courtesy of the Oil Enforcement Agency.

(President's State of the Union address, 2006; Bumiller & Nagourney, 2006). The Agency is carrying out the President's agenda to save the economy and the environment from collapse. Don't you support the President?

His badge and papers bear the OEA seal: a skull and crossed gas pumps.

At what point do you realize this is an act? A prank? No—more than a prank—a radical, performative simulacrum?[1]

Perhaps immediately. But maybe you read the pamphlet and consider the argument before the "Aha!" moment strikes. Regardless, you are not the only audience for this grassroots simulacrum of a regulatory agency. While the OEA may not have any actual regulatory power, it uses radical performance to ask: "Why not? Shouldn't the government be doing something proactive to save the planet from global eco-collapse?"

The OEA was conceived in 2006 as part of Jumpstart Ford,[2] a campaign launched three years earlier by a coalition of the activist organizations Global Exchange, Rainforest Action Network, and the Ruckus Society. The goal of the campaign was to put pressure on Ford to use its technological capabilities to make more fuel-efficient cars—a goal that would be better for the environment, citizens, consumers, and even Ford itself, as less wasteful cars would be much more competitive in the global market.

Why pick on Ford, especially at a time when that corporation was in such bad shape?[3] Creative activist Andrew Boyd, co-founder of Billionaires for Bush and other campaigns, pointed out that yes, Ford had the most fuel-inefficient fleet, but it also had a classically American history of industrial ingenuity and innovation; a history that could be invoked in the name of fuel efficiency. Jumpstart Ford had created other mock-organizations such as OAA (Oil Addicts Anonymous), but after three years of fairly effective actions, the campaign was running out of steam, and its organizers hoped that a mass radical performance could re-energize and publicize the effort. In essence, the Oil Enforcement Agency was intended to jump-start Jumpstart Ford, and help spread its critique into a wider campaign against the major automakers—a campaign for freedom from oil.

Boyd and James Levy were hired to make the concept a reality . . . well, a convincing simulacrum of a reality at least. They became the co-creators of the Oil Enforcement Agency. They shaped its brand, look, "training manual," and its first creative component, a mockumentary film that pretended to "uncover" and dramatize the controversy around this shadowy organization. This film was made available on YouTube and similar sites in a bid to get as much viewership as possible and to build the myth of the OEA.

I had the pleasure of acting in this film, playing a quirky academic who had been studying the OEA "for years." It was an enjoyable challenge to improvise in an interview format, voicing my actual analysis of the group, filtered through a more objective character than myself. The film was soon edited into a two-minute teaser video that would attract people to the (now defunct) website, on which they could watch the full film, download the "top secret" OEA training manual, and access other informational resources.

The training manual was both humorous and practical. The front page of the document made it clear that this was a symphony tuned in the key of clown. The manual called something freely downloadable on the internet "Top Secret," and made the following sardonic disclaimer:

> **Legal Note: This guide is for entertainment purposes only. No one involved in this publication endorses or engages in any of the activities described in this guide. As middle-class beneficiaries of capitalist inequity, we have no incentive to contest the structures that guarantee our special privileges, nor do we ever do so.[4]**

The manual described the history of American volunteerism, depicting the OEA as a proud part of that heritage. It also made the argument for ending oil addiction, presented statistics and information about climate change, and revealed the role of the major automakers in that ongoing disaster. The manual laid out the agenda of the OEA, and the specific changes in policy for which it was fighting. It then explained how to create an OEA character, train other agents, and ramp up pressure on a group's local car dealer with increasingly theatrical and intense OEA tactics. The goal was to convince dealers to lobby auto companies to make more fuel-efficient cars—producing models averaging at least 40 miles per gallon (mpg) of gasoline with a long-term plan to introduce electric cars. Finally, the manual provided a guide on protest tactics to use at major auto shows, and included an appendix that gave OEA agents the technical knowledge to argue for a 40 mpg consumption standard. The manual was an omnibus document—offering history, motivation, techniques, and talking points for interactions with media, "civilians," and opponents. It was filled with plenty of creative action ideas.

Within the bigger picture of performance activism, the OEA is in a different category than satirical groups like Billionaires for Bush, the open-hearted radical ridicule of the Clandestine Insurgent Rebel Clown Army, or even the stark, visually confrontational images of One Thousand Coffins. The OEA is sincere in its pranksterism. Part of the joy of the OEA is that the concept is positive, proactive, and a vision of the world as it should be. It is an example of prefigurative politics, an experimental performance of a better role for government, and a modeling of a more creative and participatory mode of citizenship.

The performative utterance, the visionary gesture that sparked the OEA's theatrical premise, came from the President himself in his plea against oil addiction in his 2006 State of the Union address. The Bush Administration composed these words and then did less than nothing on the issue of fuel efficiency and oil dependence. This was shameful—but the Administration's neglect also provided an opportunity. The greater the gap between an authority's rhetoric and reality, the more space there is for a satirist to play. Because President Bush's actions were so far from his words, he provided a special opportunity to *perform that gap*—to embody and enact that vast discrepancy and hypocrisy. By taking him at his word, and creating a performance which takes seriously, respectfully, and enthusiastically the insincere words of the leader, the OEA pointed out not only how dishonest Bush was, but also how desirable such a policy would be, and to depict a better world where the President means and acts upon the things he says. As Boyd explained:

> Instead of attacking the target, it's taking the target up on its best rhetoric and saying, "live up to it!" Saul Alinsky would say Bush is being hoisted on his own petard. Bush said "America is addicted to oil, we must move beyond a petroleum-based economy," so we say, "All right, let's do it! Hmm . . . you don't seem to have set up much programmatic infrastructure or enforcement, so we're going to step into the breach." I love that positioning. You can be sort of poking fun, chiding without being mean-spirited . . . just taking the President at his word! Giving him the benefit of the doubt . . . as the Billionaires, we were inhabiting the voice of our class enemy, of our target, amping that up and caricaturing it, a very effective rhetorical device, that was great and it allowed for a new way to message. But you get tired of that after a while, and what's really nice about the OEA is, we're inhabiting an almost superheroic role.
>
> (Boyd, 2007)

The OEA is also more tactically flexible than Billionaires for Bush because the theatrical premise allows for it. Having performed with the Billionaires for Bush and understanding how they work, I can agree with Boyd when he declares:

> Unlike the Billionaires, the OEA is able, *within the theatrical conceit,* to engage in a whole escalating range of actions, in more confrontational and serious direct action . . . the Billionaires couldn't really do a sit-in or civil disobedience, *that wouldn't really work with our character/conceit* . . . but in this case we can! All sorts of different interventions. We can't do a sit-in but we can do an occupation, where we're acting as agents. We can give "tickets," regulate traffic, do various kinds of direct action—showing badges and stopping vehicles, taking over offices, staking them out, checking people's ID . . .
>
> (Boyd, 2007; my italics)

The parameters of the fictional conceit *matter*. This is *whimsy with consequence* and must be designed carefully. While the Billionaires for Bush ruling-class appearance and demeanor insulated them from police harassment, it also made all but the most basic media intervention a bit out of character: billionaires would never get their hands dirty with a blockade or a banner-hanging. (Although it might have been fun to break that boundary of ironic pseudo-plausibility, Billionaires for Bush never did.) On the other hand, the OEA could disrupt public spaces in a more tangible way: their very reason for existence called for it. After all, they were posing as a regulatory agency enforcing the will of the chief executive.

This doesn't mean that OEA activists couldn't be arrested. It was this aspect of the simulacrum that was put to the test during actions. How could the OEA operate without being found guilty of impersonating law enforcement officers? How could they make clear that their authority was desired rather than actual? This pinpoints the issue of audience interpretation: the Billionaires for Bush often enjoyed an "Aha!" moment—that is, the instant when an audience member realized that the Billionaires were being ironic, and that their group was in fact a troupe of merry pranksters making a point. With the OEA, there was also an "Aha!" moment, but one with a hopeful, indignant twist. "They're not real," an onlooker realizes. "But wait a minute! Why aren't they real? Shouldn't they be real?"

As central organizer Matt Leonard, a long-time activist and veteran of Greenpeace and 350.org stated:

> Sometimes theatre is so goofy you lose impact. It's easily read and dismissed by people. The OEA was satirical but just serious enough. You couldn't just glance at it and dismiss it as a joke. It took those extra few crucial seconds of attention. It was also a highly accessible and replicable idea—you just needed a T-shirt, a hat, and to jump in.[5]

In the midterm elections of 2006, the Democrats gained control of the House of Representatives and the Senate, as well as a large number of state-level positions. This did not affect the work or relevance of the OEA. In fact, the Democratic victory was an opportunity. Bush was still President, and now more than ever grassroots pressure was needed to make Democrats act effectively on global warming and environmental regulation.

The OEA launched its first direct action in December 2006 at the Los Angeles Auto Show, which featured green, ecologically friendly cars of the future. The huge digital displays in the front of the lobby of the L.A. Convention Center showed images of concept cars that got tremendous gas mileage with low carbon emissions. Even though these were not the cars being mass-produced for the consumer market, the local Los Angeles media was largely supportive of the Auto Show's marketing image, uncritically celebrating its claims of championing green technology, despite the fact that the cars on display were the same sorry collection of massive and wasteful SUVs and trucks. The Toyota Tundra was there, an enormous pickup with a name that brought to mind threatened habitats. (The model's Monsoon sound system also aptly evoked environmental destruction and climate chaos.) US manufacturers Ford, GM, and Chrysler were equally guilty, rolling SUVs off their production lines since, at the time, these gas-guzzlers boasted a higher profit margin than sedans or hybrids. The ecological concept cars looked great, but as Sarah Connolly of Rainforest Action Network put it: "You can't drive a concept car"[6] (Abuelsamid, 2007).

As I have already mentioned, the greater the gap between rhetoric and reality, the more space there is for artivists to dance. The gap between the Auto Show's self-presentation and reality was a crack into which we could insert the crowbar of the OEA, prying it open for the public to scrutinize. Auto shows had already been identified as great sites for environmental protest—a venue with clear symbolism and plenty of media in attendance—and continue to be to this day.[7]

The timing of this event also made it a desirable site for the OEA's first intervention. The L.A. Auto Show had previously been held concurrently with the much larger Detroit Auto Show, but had decided to move a month earlier to December in order to step out of Detroit's media shadow, to realign itself as a hip, innovative show, and to "land more automotive debuts and international coverage" (Nauman, 2006). This suited the OEA and its partner group Freedom from Oil, as they wanted to use the L.A. Auto Show as a dress rehearsal and a place to experiment with creative actions, in preparation for the big Detroit show in January 2007.

On the morning of the action, OEA agents assembled in full uniform—black shirts and hats emblazoned with the Agency logo—outside the entrance of the L.A. Convention Center. Wearing dark glasses and smiles, they held clipboards and asked convention-goers if they were willing to answer a survey. Some agreed and were asked the following questions that I had frantically written in a café the day before:

1. Are you aware that President Bush has said that the United States is addicted to oil, and that we need to move beyond a petroleum-based economy? Yes or No?
2. Do you support the President? Yes or No?
3. Do you love America? Yes or No?
4. Are you aware that unless our policies change, including the fuel efficiency of the cars we mass produce, climate disaster will result in a 6.5 foot rise in sea levels by 2100? Yes or No?[8]
5. Do you agree that all Americans have the constitutional right to be submerged under water *only when they choose to be*? Yes or No?

The survey was designed to appear serious at first, and only gradually reveal both the OEA's political critique of the Auto Show and that the exercise was a joke that the interviewee could laugh at while arriving at our point. Ideally, by the last question people would grin and play along, and they would have our critique and ecological perspective freshly in mind as they entered the Convention Hall.

The survey seemed to draw more participants than a conventional group of activists would have attracted. People were interested in the uniforms, and curious as to what was going on. As rehearsed (see the box below), when participants asked if the agents worked for the government, they stated simply: "We support President Bush in his efforts to rid America of its oil addiction." Some people laughed, others rolled their eyes, and still others were briefly confused. But no one yelled or was hostile; a far cry from the usual mixed response to an ecological picket line. However, this survey action was only the beginning of the day's events.

The rehearsal process

Before a performative action like this, it is important to rehearse, develop characters, and role-play different scenarios and interactions, especially if members of your group are not experienced. For the action at the L.A. Auto Show, I was enlisted to run the rehearsal process.

Many in the group were veteran activists who had never performed in this way. They were more accustomed to defying death or imprisonment while locking down in front of a bulldozer, or delivering a complex policy speech before a mass audience.

Nevertheless, some of them were nervous or unclear about what to do. I began by asking them to stand, pose, move about, and speak in the character of a benevolent authority figure—we were trying to be Officer Friendly after all—and project the type of authority we wanted to see in the world. We wanted to create not a negative stereotype of a federal agent, but of someone approachable, knowledgeable, confident, and helpful: someone to whom passersby would want to talk. I paired up the activists so that they could interact, tackling various scenarios, such as:

1 An OEA agent and a confused or interested bystander asking what was going on.
2 An OEA agent and an LAPD officer asserting authority.
3 An OEA agent and a television reporter asking questions.

At first, a few of the activists were surprised at how difficult they found this role-play. They wondered: "When do I break out of character, if ever?" and "How do I deflect anger or handle heckling while keeping the upper hand and getting my message across?" With a few intense sessions of role-play, they developed a repertoire of soundbites, made mistakes they would not make later in real interactions, and became more confident and better able to stay focused and improvise under pressure. This simple exercise was vital to instill discipline and build skills for a solid creative action.

And as already stated, since impersonating a federal agent is a felony, activists rehearsed the accepted response in the event that they were asked if they are federal agents, the response being: "We support the President's statement that America is addicted to oil and we must move beyond a petroleum-based economy."

After an hour of conducting surveys, 30 OEA agents donned plainclothes, entered the Convention Hall, and infiltrated the Toyota and Ford display floors. Once in position, they quickly removed their civvies, revealing their black uniforms. The agents surrounded the largest and least fuel-efficient vehicles, taping them off with yellow tape emblazoned with the words: "CLIMATE CHAOS CRIME SCENE." The activities of the agents mixed the serious and absurd. While some agents gave out literature about the environmental dangers of SUVs and megatrucks (cautioning show attendees, "People, please step away from these vehicles; these cars hurt America; thank you for your cooperation"), other agents lay down under the cars "measuring" the emissions coming from tailpipes with measuring tape. These Brechtian "winks" were included in the repertoire to give spectators the hint that this was play. Our goal was not to deceive, but to create just enough of a simulacrum of a "police raid" to draw interest, surprise, and then satisfaction once they realized what was actually going on (Barthes, 1975).

Agents were careful to also make "crime scenes" of foreign-made megalocars to preempt accusations that the group was picking on American cars only. This paid off when an older gentleman shouted: "Why are you just going after American cars?" and other customers replied: "No, they're doing it by the Tundra too." As mentioned in the Introduction, it is vital to anticipate and prepare for hostile responses.

The OEA agents unfurled their large banner, while those of us who remained in plainclothes quickly took out cameras to record the event for YouTube. We had expected that we would only have a few seconds to enact and video the stunt before corporate security shut us down. But much to our delight, we achieved that rarest of prizes—*tactical surprise*. The management of the Auto Show did not expect this action, and the private security force was slow to respond. It is possible the alarm was not raised for a while because we might have looked like yet another group in silly costumes doing guerrilla marketing, which corporations often stage at events like this.[9] When two security people finally did arrive, I heard them say into a walkie-talkie: "There's 30 of them and they have a banner, we're going to need backup."

In the meantime, the cheesy Auto Show announcer, who was in the process of announcing that a basketball star would be signing autographs at a certain booth, declared over the sound system: "Everyone, pay no attention to those crazy people in the black outfits by the Tundra." Immediately, a throng of people streamed over to us to see what the "crazy people in the black outfits" were doing. Our audience was larger and our action lasted longer than expected: some of our head agents improvised in-character speeches, warning the general public about the dangers of these cars and how alternatives had to be sought by policymakers.

After several long minutes of improvised oratory and spirited discussion with a growing crowd of consumers, the bulk of the security force and a contingent of the LAPD arrived. I saw at this moment an image I will never forget: a private security guard, an LAPD sergeant, and an Oil Enforcement agent standing in a huddle, discussing exactly what was happening and what should be done. Here they were: representatives of corporate power, state power, and an imaginary progressive pseudo-power, ruminating and negotiating.

The OEA quickly followed its prepared exit plan. Saluting the LAPD, we said things like: "OK men, our brother officers are here to take over this crime scene. Thanks guys, this is your jurisdiction now, we're moving out." Then we saluted and marched away in formation with dignity intact, and bodies untasered, unbeaten, and unshackled. It was my favorite exit ever.

Jumpstart Ford took other actions during the Auto Show. The day before, as a way to introduce the term "greenwashing" into the media dialogue, a Greenwash Car Wash was set up in front of the Convention Hall with scantily clad men and women, some on roller skates, washing a giant white Hummer to the tune of the old seventies song, "Car Wash." Using this eye candy to attract attention, activists then swathed the huge white car in green suds, making a spectacle while explaining to media and passersby that the L.A. Auto Show and the major car companies were trying to greenwash their image—pretending to be ecologically concerned while actually following the same old oil-addicted policies and production models (*Jumpstart Ford Greenwashing*, 2006).

Inside the hall, immediately after a speech by General Motors (GM)'s CEO Rick Wagoner, activists Matt Leonard and Mike Hudema, dressed in crisp suits, took the microphone, thanked Wagoner for pledging to move his company in the direction of higher gas mileage and lower emissions, and then asked him to sign a pledge, which they produced on a large placard, in order to make it a specific policy target rather than a vague utterance. Wagoner declined and had the Jumpstart Ford activists taken off the stage where they were surrounded and questioned by curious reporters[10] (Neff, 2006; Phelan, 2006).

This mixture of different styles of actions began to have an impact on the way in which the Auto Show was being covered by the local and national media, and the term "greenwashing" began to be used.[11] In one article, *Newsday* stated:

> A consumer group called Jumpstart Ford protested at the show, saying that the vehicles on display provide too little, too late. "While the public is being shown eco-demonstration vehicles at the auto show, the automakers' efforts sadly fall far short of the response needed in order to effectively break America's oil addiction," the group said in a prepared statement.
>
> (Gentile, 2006)

As activist-organizer Matt Leonard said:

> We changed the L.A. conversation. If it was just one day of action, they can shrug it off. It was having sustained action for most of a week, which was part of an ongoing campaign we'd been doing for a long time—so it wasn't a new issue to the reporters. This barrage of actions with a common theme—that's how we managed to create a circus that changed the conversation.
>
> (Leonard, 2015)

GM does praxis too: the price of predictability

The Detroit Auto Show, held the next month, was a different story. Having learned from the embarrassment inflicted in Los Angeles, corporate management hired private detectives to keep the activists under surveillance and track their activities. They provided the police with photos of the activists, and in Detroit the OEA was quickly shut down, its agents arrested or driven off. As Matt Leonard put it:

> We underestimated how much of a company town Detroit is. The experience was totally surreal. On a night several nights before the Auto Show, we were scouting out a V.I.P. party. Mike [Hudema] and I were in suits, with Jodie van Horn and Sarah Connolly in nice dresses, just walking in the neighborhood of the event, several blocks away—and we realized we were being followed by plainclothes. We split up, walked a hundred feet, and a couple of police cars pulled up to us. Then police got out and detained us. In a few minutes, there were 30 to 40 cops, from multiple jurisdictions, all around us. We were detained for 30 minutes, and we saw they were flipping through printouts of our Facebook profiles, social media information, and bios: they weren't even trying to hide those documents from us. We kept asking "Are we free to go?" and they would just say in a threatening manner, "We know who you are, if you think you're getting away with anything . . ." They let us go, but a cop car followed us. We ducked away, but every door we went out of, another officer would be there, following 50 feet behind. We went into the huge Greektown Casino, split up, went into different rooms, but no matter what door we exited from, there were police. They devoted so much manpower to following us. The companies must have hired a pretty decent PI firm. This was private

> security feeding our information to the Detroit police. That was the most robust investigation I've ever been under. And that says something. That level of response was huge.
>
> (Leonard, 2015)

Was there consolation in knowing that at least the OEA was effective enough in LA to elicit a major response from auto companies and the police in Detroit?

> . . . We should have understood that, because we were so successful in L.A., being sneaky was not going to work twice. We should have done a mass rally, something totally public. We actually got a couple of people into the Auto Show, but because they were known, they were immediately detained and one was even turned over to the Department of National Security, though no charges were ultimately filed.
>
> (Leonard, 2015)

I asked Matt if, even with this level of security, would we have had a few moments inside the Auto Show to make a playful scene if we had simply done an OEA "raid" with different, new, and unknown people? He said this tactic would have worked, but just for a few moments. Matt went on to make an important distinction between action types and security culture:

> I don't want to foster paranoia about security. But I believe actions should either be secret, in which case you work in small tight groups, or totally open mass public events in which you assume everything you do is known and it's all above board. I think you get in trouble when you're somewhere in the middle.
>
> (Leonard, 2015)

As discussed in the Introduction, both sides learn from tactical interaction. The creative actions in Los Angeles were a major success, even to the point of personally annoying the CEO of General Motors. Although Jumpstart Ford saw Los Angeles as a rehearsal for Detroit, the playbook had to be changed. Trying to do the same thing with the same crew to the same opponents in Detroit one month later resulted in running headfirst into countermeasures. A costly lesson was learned, and that is the nature of tactical interaction—both sides improve their game in an ongoing, interactive, hybrid, and agonistic/antagonistic relationship.

A pause for praxis

Dear Reader, please use this space to brainstorm what the Oil Enforcement Agency could have done to avoid walking into obvious countermeasures in Detroit.

Here are a few examples:

1 Do similar actions, but with different "agents." Using the same faces was asking for quick and easy identification and preemptive arrest.
2 Change the game plan. Go to the Auto Show with a radically different idea: for example, using a guerrilla sound system to make announcements, etc.
3 Don't show up. If they know you're coming, don't go. Find a separate, but equally valid and evocative site for creative action.

With organizations such as the OEA, the global justice movement can use serious play to create its own stories and myths that hopefully cross over from countercultural in-jokes to widespread, compelling, and progressive actions. By embodying and performing these "fantasies," we hoped to make them irresistible and self-fulfilling. The OEA continued its mass prefigurative gestures for several years all over the US, including at the New York Auto Show and outside a Portland, Oregon city council meeting where plans for expansion of a major highway were being considered. OEA agents collaborated in this action with an "oil-worshipping cult" that assembled to bow before a 12 foot derrick they erected on site. The OEA agents strung "Global Warming Crime Scene" tape in front of Portland's City Hall, established a checkpoint, and wrote tickets for members of the Portland Business Alliance who were entering to testify in favor of the highway expansion. OEA performed a mock arrest of the cult members as part of the street theatre, and were driven away by an "oil-worshipping dominatrix" ("Oil Enforcement Agency Busts," *Earth First Journal*).

The OEA did not enjoy the mass participation of groups such as Billionaires for Bush, but they used some of the same strategies to enlist volunteers; professional graphics, and a website that equipped local groups with start-up materials and tactics. The OEA's great range of action raised the bar: any ham could don a top hat and jump into some Billionaires for Bush street theatre, but risking arrest in a direct action at a car dealership or auto show demanded more from activists.

While the OEA did not single-handedly remove SUVs from American highways, the group remained a colorful part of an overall movement that has had some impact on the major car companies—along with rising gas prices and economic recession. On the cultural front, they evoked a hopeful vision of a government and a social movement that takes responsibility for the environment and holds corporations accountable. It was an earnest vision that good-humoredly pierced the cynicism of the moment.

Survivaballs: a darkly prefigurative, shape-shifting Swiftian symbol of climate disaster/climate heroism

Survivaballs first appeared in the world as a Yes Men stunt against Halliburton and major oil and auto companies. Claiming that Halliburton had invented a solution for climate change, the Yes Men shared with the media the Survivaball™—a bizarre costume in the shape of a huge one-person bouncy sphere. Only the wearer's face is visible, and there are tiny flaps for hands (the Survivaball has an inner fan to keep it inflated and round). The costume is funny looking and inherently amusing, but has a darkly Swiftian meaning: it is touted as a $4 million one-person biosphere, which will keep the wealthy owner alive when all the earth's biosphere has collapsed due to climate change (Deans, 2009). "It's a gated community for one," crowed its public spokesman.

Over time, several dozen Survivaballs were constructed with volunteer labor at the House of Yes in New York City. They were so round and big that they could theoretically be used to block office doors, and the Yes Men began to playfully threaten exactly that. During the 2009 United Nations Climate Summit, Survivaball-clad activists waddled into the East River and threatened to swim upstream and block the doors of the UN building until delegates came up with a binding agreement on climate change. There was no fear of this actually happening: Survivaballs, alas, do not float (*New York Post Not Laughing*, 2009). Police on foot, boat, and helicopter responded briefly to the Survivaballs, resulting in good-natured coverage of the incident on CNN. Part of the behind-the-scenes story: at first, the police did not respond, so a member of the crew called the authorities and

Figure 5.3 Survivaballs wallow in the East River, threatening to wobble upstream to the United Nations Climate Summit, and block the doors until a binding treaty on climate change is signed. Note the police boat approaching to investigate. Photo by L.M. Bogad.

said "not an emergency, but there are some people in costumes down here and you might want to check it out." This brought the police into view. Also, Yes Man activist Andy Bichlbaum was arrested at the event, which made the action look all the more transgressive in the news (he was actually arrested for an outstanding cycling-related ticket) (Millman, 2009).

After serving as a grinning spokesman for the Survivaball corporation at the event, I was scheduled to speak at a Billionaires for Bush action across town at a labor rally. Using my unfair advantage as a white man in a suit, I walked through the assembled police who were checking IDs, caught the crosstown bus, and headed for the Billionaire rally. This was convenient for me, but also serves as a good example of how racial bias and social camouflage can influence the response of law enforcement during an action.

Shortly thereafter, Survivaballs marched on the US Congress in a scene that evoked both the 1920 Soviet "mass spectacle" *The Storming of the Winter Palace* and the Woody Allen movie *Sleeper*. Dressed in wobbly, bubbly Survivaballs, activists waddled up to the steps of Congress. After activist Mike Bonnano was pushed by a security guard, he rolled back all the way down the stairs, where, obviously in pain, he stayed in character and declared: "I'm fine, no matter what comes as a result of climate change; Survivaball will protect us against anything that might happen . . . Ow . . ." (*Survivaball Plunges*, 2009).

Symbols shift in valence over time, and in this case the Survivaballs did exactly that (Kertzer, 1988). These personal biospheres morphed in meaning from a simple Swiftian satire of corporate ruthlessness to a cartoonish, tragicomic, and heroic tool for direct action. In either interpretation, Survivaball's eye-catching absurdity told its story compellingly.

Suggestions: to be tested in practice

1 When constructing a radical simulacrum with a familiar image and parody, aim for complicity with the audience, not deception. Facilitate the joy of discovery and creative interpretation. Know what you're imitating and the better possible future you are whimsically aiming for. What is it you want?

2 The premise or theatrical conceit matters. Like science fiction or fantasy, it doesn't have to be completely faithful to the world as it is, but the premise should have its own internal logic and consistency. The clowns of CIRCA perform in a certain way, the Billionaires for Bush in another, and the OEA agents in yet another. If you drop the conceit, or if you break character, it should be deliberate. Why are you breaking character and to what end?
3 The gap between a target's rhetoric and the reality of their actions is the play-space for your radical performance.
4 Even when you achieve tactical surprise and score a success—especially when you do—assume your opponent will quickly develop countermeasures. You must adjust and innovate new tactics, anticipating those countermeasures and more.

Notes

1 By this I mean something that does not represent reality, nor attempts to deceive by misrepresenting reality, but is a creative act that becomes its own reality (Baudrillard, 1995; Boyd & Duncombe, n.d.).
2 Now called Freedom from Oil.
3 Ford is doing much better at the time of this writing, and was the only one of the Big Three automakers (Ford, GM, and Chrysler) not to take federal bailout money during the economic crisis.
4 *Oil Enforcement Agency (OEA) Top Secret Training Manual.* Author's personal copy.
5 Interview with the author, 7 January 2015.
6 Abuelsamid quotes Connolly's colleague, Mike Hudema (campaign director at Global Exchange), who linked fuel efficiency with the problem of domestic unemployment:

> The average fuel-economy of new vehicles today is worse than it was 10 years ago . . . We are in Detroit to ask the automakers which one of them is going to commit to leading the industry in fuel economy and greenhouse gas reductions, which one of them is going to commit to bringing jobs back to Detroit?
>
> (Abuelsamid, 2007)

7 Examples include: Critical Mass bicyclists, polar bears, Santa Claus, a Car Alarm Symphony, and muffler and snow tire jugglers protesting the Chicago Auto Show (Rowe, 2006; "Bicyclists Protest," 2007); a massive banner hung over the entrance to the Javitz Center in New York City, at which police used a cherry-picker to apprehend activists (Faherty, 2007; Schembari, 2007); an anti-Hummer protest using body bags to connect US oil dependence to wars in the Middle East (Vigil, 2004); PETA members protesting the use of animals in crash testing ("Activists Protest," 1993); and

guerrilla videographers and pickets focusing attention on Toyota's lawsuit against California's emission laws (Durbin, 2007).
8 Source: "Sea Level Rise," www.nationalgeographic.com.
9 As noted in the Introduction, our opponents borrow ideas from us, and vice versa.
10 See Neff (2006) and Phelan (2006) for a conservative perspective that flatters Wagoner's handling of the situation. One Vice President of GM was so enraged that he threatened physical harm to the activists.
11 Contrast, for example, the positive coverage in Nauman (2006) with those of Gentile (2006), Vigil (2004), and Durbin (2007).

References

Abuelsamid, Sam (2007) "Freedom from Oil Campaign to Protest at Detroit Auto Show," *Autoblog*, 5 Jan 2007. www.autobloggreen.com/2007/01/05/freedom-from-oil-campaign-to-protest-at-detroit-auto-show/ (accessed 31 May 2009).

"Activists Protest at Auto Show." *The Buffalo News*, 14 Feb 1993.

Barthes, Roland (1975) *S/Z: An essay*. New York: Hill and Wang.

Baudrillard, Jean (1995) *Simulacra and Simulation*. Trans. Sheila Faria Glaser. Ann Arbor: University of Michigan Press.

"Bicyclists Protest Chicago Auto Show." *Chicago Tribune RedEye Edition*, 12 Feb 2007: p. 9.

Boyd, Andrew (2007) Interview with the author, 17 Mar 2007.

Boyd, Andrew; Duncombe, Stephen (n.d.) "Manufacturing Dissent: What the Left can learn from Las Vegas" *Journal of Aesthetics and Protest* online. www.joaap.org/new3/duncombeboyd.html (accessed 28 Oct 2015).

Bumiller, Elisabeth; Nagourney, Adam (2006) "Bush: America is addicted to oil." *New York Times*, 1 Feb 2006. www.nytimes.com/2006/02/01/world/americas/01iht-state.html (accessed 8 June 2011).

Deans, Zev (2009) *My Survivaballs Infomercial for the Yes Men*. [Digital video] YouTube. 23 Sept 2009. www.youtube.com/watch?v=H6wWOvU-Mf0 (accessed 28 Oct 2015).

Durbin, D. (2007) "Auto Show Protesters Put Toyota in Hot Seat: Company resists state law calling for stricter fuel economy rules." *Long Beach Press–Telegram*, 15 Nov 2007: p. 3B.

Faherty, Christopher (2007) "Security Officials Shift into High Gear for Auto Show." *The New York Sun*, 5 Apr 2007: p. 2.

Gentile, Gary (2006) "Los Angeles Auto Show Critics, Tired of Concepts, Want Greener Choices Now." *Newsday*, 24 Dec 2006: p. E12.

Jumpstart Ford Greenwashing Action at the December 2006 LA Auto Show. [Digital video] YouTube. 30 Nov 2006. www.youtube.com/watch?v=hlXRkFTv-L0 and www.youtube.com/watch?v=hUSiYClnn3o (accessed 6 Jan 2015).

Kertzer, D.I. (1988) *Ritual, Politics and Power*. New Haven, CT: Yale University Press.

Leonard, M. (2015) Interview with the author, 12 Mar 2015.
Millman, Jennifer (2009) "Cops Arrest 'Yes Man' Co-Founder in Latest Prank." *NBC News New York*. 24 Sept 2009. www.nbcnewyork.com/news/local/Fake-Post-Guys-Pull-Another-One-Yes-Man-Arrested-60700217.html
Nauman, Matt (2006) "Clean Fuel's the Story at the L.A. Auto Show." *San Jose Mercury News*, 30 Nov 2006.
Neff, John (2006) "Environmental Protesters Crash Rick Wagoner's Keynote." *Autoblog*, 29 Nov 2006. www.autoblog.com/2006/11/29/environmental-protesters-crash-rick-wagoners-keynote/ (accessed 28 Oct 2015).
New York Post Not Laughing at Climate Change Spoof. [Digital video] CNN. 23 Sept 2009. http://edition.cnn.com/2009/US/09/22/new.york.fake.newspaper/index.html?eref=ib_us#cnnSTCVideo (accessed 28 Oct 2015).
"Oil Enforcement Agency Busts Oil-worshiping Cult." *Earth First Journal*. www.earthfirstjournal.org/article.php?id=403 (accessed 31 May 2009).
Phelan, Mark (2006) "Wagoner Defuses a Protest with Sill Behind the Wheel." *Detroit Free Press*, 10 Dec 2006: p. 2C.
President's State of the Union address (2006). 31 Jan 2006.
Rowe, Anita (2006) "Running Down a Dream – Shutdown Fest protests auto show." *The Wicker Park Booster*, 8 Feb 2006: p. 1.
"Sea Level Rise: Ocean levels are getting higher." *www.nationalgeographic.com*. http://ocean.nationalgeographic.com/ocean/critical-issues-sea-level-rise/ (accessed 3 Nov 2015).
Schembari, James (2007) "Protesting From the Rafters." *New York Times Blog-Wheels: The nuts and bolts of whatever moves you*, 4 Apr 2007. http://wheels.blogs.nytimes.com/tag/new-york-auto-show/page/3/?scp=10&sq=New+York+Auto+Show+protesters&st=cse (accessed 10April 2007).
Survivaball Plunges Down Capitol Steps – See it to believe it. [Digital video] YouTube. 20 Oct 2009. www.youtube.com/watch?v=SZuyiAFTtb8 (accessed 28 Oct 2015).
Vigil, Delfin (2004) "Hummer Foes Take Message to Auto Show – Protesters see link between war, Americans driving gas guzzlers." *San Francisco Chronicle*, 22 Nov 2004.

Chapter 6

All the news we hope to print

The creation and mass distribution of progressive prank papers

This chapter provides a behind-the-scenes look at the secret creation and surprise mass distribution of three different radical prank newspapers. In 2008 and 2009, progressive fantasy-versions of the *New York Times*, *International Herald Tribune*, and *New York Post* were distributed for free in the US and Europe. Although they looked the same on the surface, these three art–activist projects had different political goals, resulting in key differences in aesthetics and narrative strategy. I draw on my experience as a contributing writer and strategist for the first newspaper, and a co-Editor-in-(Mis)Chief and lead writer on the second and third, for which I wrote about half the articles. This chapter looks at the different aims and techniques for each iteration of this spectacular, mildly transgressive prank.

Spring 2008: A group of artist–activists are meeting in a bar in downtown New York, trying to think of ways to protest the upcoming Democratic National Convention in Colorado. None of us is excited about reactively protesting at conventions anymore. If we do so, it should be something interesting and provocative. We'd like to create a vision of the world we want to see—something we had tried with Reclaim the Streets' urban street parties and other prefigurative actions.

The questions: How to do something that is prefigurative and proactive in the context of a convention protest? Should we have clown parachutists descend from the heavens, landing on the roofs of the city with festive and joyful slogans on their canopies? Maybe we could thank the Democrats for doing all the things that in fact they had failed to do—thank you for stopping the wars, thank you for promoting alternative energy, etc. We could make a grand utopian gesture that pretends the Democrats have done what we wanted, echoing Yoko Ono and John Lennon's "WAR IS OVER (if you want it)" posters. But none of these ideas were very compelling.

I suggested sidestepping the conventions altogether, and just going to individual strategic sites, such as global bank headquarters, with performers who would festively pretend we'd already won victories, and thank those powerbrokers for finally giving in and following our specific, innovative and progressive policies to make the world more livable. ("We're so happy Citibank figured out a way to make some profit without blowing up all the mountains in West Virginia.") We would avoid the fortified convention spaces altogether, and open up imaginative spaces to present an image of the world that we could aspire to or work towards. But of course this would require a lot of performers, writing, rehearsal, and it would be tough to pull off logistically.

Finally, Steve Lambert and Jacques Servin came up with the idea to make a fake *New York Times* with all the news we wanted to see in the world. Every news item, whether funny or serious in tone, would tell the story of a progressive policy victory being implemented, thanks to mass popular pressure and activism.

I was drafted in as a writer/editor. Dozens of volunteers contributed their services as writers, layout artists, graphic designers, etc. For about seven months, a voluntary collective secretly put the project together. We worked on wiki documents, and our team, whose members boasted a variety of different skillsets, collaborated over long distances. The project served to build personal connections between activists for future projects, as well as the present one.[1]

This was a project of larger than usual scope—ultimately 100,000 copies of the newspaper would be printed and distributed for free on the streets of New York City and elsewhere. Our plan was transgressive and slightly risky, which was part of its appeal and its spectacular nature. This was not *The Onion*, which has its own masthead and no legal problems. We were stepping into the guise and voice of a global newspaper. We knew it had to be kept secret so that there would be no preemptive "cease and desist" measures coming from the *Times*. We also knew that this project would be interesting to the media because of its boldness and potential scandal—"You can't really do that with the *New York Times*' masthead, can you?"

The masthead

Legally, we would have a strong case in the event of a lawsuit. It would be obvious that the newspaper was a parody, and it would not be sold but rather produced and distributed for free at a loss. Therefore, it appeared to fit into the "fair use" category. It was an act of radical simulacrum, a progressive fantasy of what would be possible, not if those in power suddenly did the right thing, but if masses of people mobilized and pressured them to do so. We didn't expect anyone to be fooled for more than a few seconds. We didn't want them to be. Let the neoconservative pundits of the world leave lies in the public consciousness. Our job was to provoke with a playful prank, an illusion that exposed itself within just a few magical moments. We wanted to create a fleeting and wondrous feeling of "what if?" We wanted to create a moment that suspends disbelief in the same way as powerful theatre. We wanted to deliver this moment straight to people on the street.

The newspaper's masthead was both the most prominent part of the illusion, and the mechanism by which that illusion would melt away within a second or two. It used the *New York Times*' famous font, recognizable all over the world. On the other hand, there were three huge clues, or Brechtian winks, on the top of the front page, which let the reader know that this was a prank. Firstly, our "special edition" was *free*. Secondly, instead of their famous slogan, "All the News That's Fit To Print," our paper's slogan read, "All the News We Hope to Print." Thirdly, in a dead giveaway of our satirical intentions, the date of the paper was Independence Day, 4 July 2009, about 8 months after its actual release in November 2008, right after Election Day. This date would combine American patriotism with an imaginative twist—could we become truly independent and truly free by the next Independence Day? This newspaper was an artifact from the future—a message about how much better the world could be, not from elite largesse or *noblesse oblige*, but if social movements could make it so. This design of the masthead was crucial. It was the most prominent and attention-demanding part of the paper, and obviously false. This was a Baudrillardian simulacrum with a radical turn. The entire paper made no pretense to be real, but had its own elements of the real, or as Stephen Colbert would say, "truthiness" to it, although its pages were chock full of radical critique.

Ideally, we hoped the reader would pick up our *Times*, look it over, skim the headlines and gasp, flip through the pages, scan it a bit more, and experience a lovely moment of suspension of disbelief, a synaptic disruption, an opening of the imagination, and the inevitable questions—"What if these things were true?" and "What if we all got together, became active, and made them happen?" Then that moment would fade as it became quickly obvious that the paper was a playful prank. But it could leave radical residue in the mind, and the thought—"Wait, can we make those things happen?" Is another world possible, as the global justice movement's slogan suggests? The whole newspaper was essentially an artful and poetic articulation of that slogan, on newsprint in *Times* font.

As for the fear of a lawsuit, someone on our team came up with a brilliant idea. The name of the company set up to receive the many small donations to fund the project would be titled, The Spirit of Free Speech in America, LLC. Thus, if the *Times* did choose to sue, the title of the legal case, as would be reported in the media and in legal history books forever, would be: "The *New York Times* versus The Spirit of Free Speech in America, LLC"—not a prospect the *Times* would relish. This is another example of the value of thinking a step ahead, and raising the costs of a repressive response. As we've discussed earlier, it's more costly to club a clown (see Chapter 2). And if there were a lawsuit, it would be a wild ride that would increase exponentially the importance, prominence, and relevance of the prank.[2]

The faux-*Times* was an attempt to open up a brief imaginative space in the mind of the reader for the possibility of positive, collective action and change. Its articles were a combination of wishful thinking and cutting satire. The main headline, written at a time when the war was at a ferocious peak, declared: "IRAQ WAR ENDS." This headline was supported with a simple photo of a helicopter flying—perhaps, homeward bound. The reader could project his or her own meaning upon it. Other articles showed American evangelists taking the New Testament to heart, and agreeing to accept war refugees from Iraq into their own homes; the implementation of a Maximum Wage Law; and free tuition for public universities. Fake adverts in the newspaper included: a recall announcement for all automobiles; a plan to use the profits from blood diamonds to pay for the prosthetic limbs of victims of those conflicts; and a declaration from GM that they would bring back the EV1 electric car that they had invented and then destroyed in the 1990s. There was even an advert from McDonald's in which they try to fit into the new zeitgeist by coopting the images of radical icons such as Che Guevara and Rosie the Riveter.

I wrote a piece, "Military Recruiter Goes from Marketing the Military to Marketing Himself," which was used as an example of tone and style for volunteer writers. In this article, a military recruiter loses his job because the war is over. As he hunts for work, facts about the realities of military recruitment techniques are revealed. The reader learns that recruiters are allowed to make any kind of false promise when recruiting young people to the armed forces. Nothing they say is legally binding. The ex-recruiter interviews for a job in advertising, then real estate. Rejected and dejected, he sits in a church and contemplates joining the priesthood ("I'd rather sell Heaven and Hell than Iraq and Afghanistan!"), but is finally offered a job on a used-car lot owned by the father of one of the young men he recruited to fight in Iraq, who lost an arm but holds no grudges. The tone of the piece was pointed but brisk—I tried to make it obviously fictional, but fun to read.

The "special edition" of the *Times* was printed and distributed (after a last-minute panic in which the printer got scared and refused to print it, and another printer had to be found), on 12 November 2008, and posted online. The faux-*Times* received worldwide coverage due to the transgressive nature of the prank, the prestige of the actual *New York Times*, and the wealth of material inside (it was 14 pages) to report about and quote from. From Germany to China to South Africa, and across the US, the media commented on or discussed our paper and its contents at length. The *Times* stated that they would look into the incident, but ultimately decided to take the high road and released a statement in their own pages acknowledging the prank and placing it in the context of a history of such pranks. As a spectacular cultural act ("air war," as I describe in the Introduction) that is unconnected to a specific social-movement campaign ("ground war"), the project was limited in some ways, but it was still wildly successful on its own desired terms.[3]

The *International Herald Tribune*

The next such project was a "special edition" of the *International Herald Tribune* (*IHT*).[4] This was also created in secret, and was also filled with happy "news" about activist victories. It looked a lot like the *Times* but was different in several key ways, which affected the project.

Firstly, this prank newspaper was not a general expression of radical desire. It was aimed specifically at a key event—the EU Climate Summit in Belgium in June 2009, which was a preparatory meeting for the UN Climate Change Conference scheduled for December 2009, to which so many hopes for a binding resolution on climate justice had

"All the News We Hope to Print"

The New York Times

Special Edition

VOL. CLVIV . . No. 54,631 NEW YORK, SATURDAY, JULY 4, 2009 FREE

IRAQ WAR ENDS

Nation Sets Its Sights on Building Sane Economy

True Cost Tax, Salary Caps, Trust-Busting Top List

By T. VEBLEN

Troops to Return Immediately

U.S. Army helicopters begin moving troops and equipment from Saddam Hussein's former Baghdad palace.

Maximum Wage Law Succeeds

Salary Caps Will Help Stabilize Economy

By J.K. MALONE

TREASURY ANNOUNCES "TRUE COST" TAX PLAN

By MARCUS S. DRIGGS

Recruiters Train for New Life

USA Patriot Act Repealed

Last to Die

Evangelicals Open Homes to Refugees

Public Relations Industry Starts to Shut Down

Ex-Secretary Apologizes for W.M.D. Scare

300,000 Troops Never Faced Risk of Instant Obliteration

By FRANK LARIMORE

Popular Pressure Ushers Recent Progressive Tilt

Study Cites Movements for Massive Shift in DC

By SAMUEL FIELDEN

Protests organized by Witness Against Torture helped pave the way for the close of the Guantánamo facility.

Nationalized Oil To Fund Climate Change Efforts

By MARION K. HUBBERT

Continued on Page A6

Continued on Page A5

Continued on Page A5

Gitmo, Other Centers Closed

Iraqi Refugees Worldwide Celebrate Withdrawal

Conflict of Interest Law Will Stop Revolving Door

Health Insurance Act Clears House

Bush to Face Charges

Corporate Personhood Gets Real

Bicycle Lanes Inaugurated

A Lobbyist Defends Lobbying

Thomas L. Friedman

A Baboon Troop's Experience

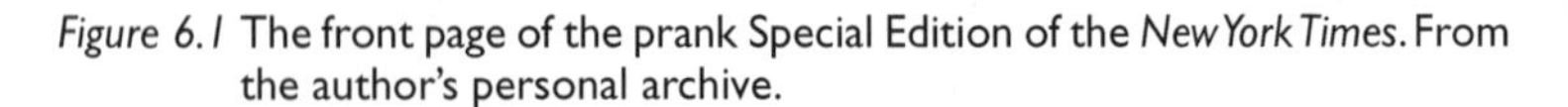

Figure 6.1 The front page of the prank Special Edition of the *New York Times*. From the author's personal archive.

been tied. With the headline "Heads of State Agree Historic Climate-Saving Deal," this paper was meant to both call attention to the specific issues at stake at that summit and perhaps to influence the media and delegates in attendance. It was a more focused intervention at a pressure point, centered on one major issue. About 50,000 of these newspapers were printed—35,000 distributed at the conference, and 15,000 were spread around the world, from China and India to Mexico and the US and across Europe.

Secondly, the faux-*Tribune* was not funded by many small donations accumulated over time, but was sponsored by Greenpeace International from its headquarters in Amsterdam. They saw the value in such cultural–artistic activism, being veterans and innovators of artistic and direct-action campaigns themselves. They contributed both technical and creative skills and the money the project required. Because they were not over-controlling or censorious, this was the best of both worlds—not always the case when there is a sponsoring organization.

Thirdly, and most importantly, this prank paper attempted to serve as a connector between air-war and ground-war efforts. The paper was released on 18 June 2009, but like the *Times*, bore a future date—19 December 2009, the day after the big conference in Copenhagen would end. In the fantasy narrative told by the newspaper's articles, the delegates at Copenhagen, under tremendous pressure from the mass nonviolent civil disobedience of their citizenries, had come to a binding climate-saving deal. So far, this sounds very much like the radical fantasia of the fake *Times*. However, the *IHT*'s articles also sang the praises of an actual website, built to help people coordinate direct actions and civil disobedience. We used the radical simulacrum of the newspaper to promote this real device for direct action, and then pretended in its pages that the direct action had already been successful, which we hoped would further encourage participation. We hoped to spark a virtuous cycle of life imitating art imitating life. As our press release said:

> The paper describes in detail a powerful (and entirely possible) new treaty to bring carbon levels down below 350 parts per million—the level climate scientists say we need to achieve to avoid climate catastrophe. One article describes how a website, http://BeyondTalk.net, mobilized thousands of people to put their bodies on the line to confront climate change policies—ever since way back in June, 2009.
>
> (Bogad & Servin, 2009)

The ideology of our prank *Tribune* insisted on the importance of change coming from the grassroots up, from direct democracy and social movements, rather than from some sudden benevolence of the elites. We were sure to make clear in the press release that the newspaper was fake—we were not attempting a lasting deception. The importance of nonviolent direct action was emphasized both in the press release and the newspaper.

> Leading American environmentalist Bill McKibben was enthusiastic about the newspaper's message and the methods BeyondTalk.net calls for. "We need a political solution grounded in reality—grounded in physics and chemistry. That will only come if we can muster a wide variety of political tactics, including civil disobedience." . . . The fake newspaper also has an ad for "Action Offsets," whereby those who aren't willing to risk arrest can help those who are.
>
> (Bogad & Servin, 2009)

At eight pages, this project was smaller than the *Times*. Referring to the quote above, I still believe in the idea of "Action Offsets," although I wrote that article with a good-natured and whimsical tone. The piece was meant both to satirize "carbon offsets," which are a fraudulent dodge from the actual solution of a carbon tax, and to advocate for the idea that movements should be open to any form of contribution—not everyone can afford to get arrested, but some can afford to pay the bail of those who do.

An advert for "Action Offsets"

. . . Yes, we're all grateful to those who put their lives and livelihoods on the line in the streets, shutting down offices, power plants, docks, highways, etc. But humanity also owes a debt to an unsung group of people.

The people who didn't get up off their couches.

The people who sat back and watched it all happen on their TVs.

The only finger they lifted was to push a button on their remote, or to click their mouse, yet they proved vital to the mass movement.

Thanks to the concept of "action offsets," people who were unable or unwilling to risk arrest themselves were able to log on to websites like Beyond-Talk.net and donate vital funds to the movement to make up for their own inaction. These donations provided money for food, transportation, shelter, and bail money for those willing to participate more directly.

"It's like 'carbon offsets,' where you pay to plant a tree to make up for flying on an airplane . . . Except in this case, it's not bullshit. Your money actually does fund direct action in a clear and useful way. Maybe not everyone can get in the streets, but lots of people have a few extra bucks. Every successful movement has to meet people where they are, and accept support in whatever form people are able to give it."

Indeed, thousands of "eco-couch potatoes" signed up to financially offset their inaction, and help the active, on BeyondTalk.net.

"I was thrilled to be able to participate," said Meryl McIntyre, 47, an accountant in Fargo, North Dakota. "Since I'm the sole breadwinner, my husband didn't want me to go raise a ruckus. But I could put a bit of that 'bread' into something I believe in."

"Honestly, I just really hate the smell of tear gas," said Bruno Schmidt, 24, a car salesman in Bonn. "I'm very sensitive to that, and I also have a neurotic fear of being dragged over asphalt by burly men. But I've had a good year, sold a lot of hybrids. And I knew it was time to give something back. I logged on to BeyondTalk.net, and for just a few hundred euros, I paid for the train tickets and food money for an entire affinity group of climate activists. They sent me a thank you email with photos of their arrest. It's a warm feeling."

Source: Special Edition of the *IHT*

HISTORIC WIN FOR AMAZON PROTECTION
PAGE 4 | WORLD

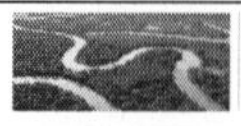

CELEB CLIMATE DENIER RECANTS POSITION
PAGE 5 | VIEWS

RENEWABLE BOON ON TRADING FLOOR
PAGE 6 | BUSINESS

GREEN DIRECTOR FACES HITCH
PAGE 7 | CULTURE

International Herald Tribune

SATURDAY, DECEMBER 19, 2009 — A SPECIAL EDITION OF THE INTERNATIONAL HERALD TRIBUNE

Markets soar on news of Copenhagen climate deal

LONDON

Germany, Denmark and Spain are winners of the new energy economy

BY JIM MADDOX

A TURNING POINT FOR THE PLANET French President Nicolas Sarkozy, German Chancellor Angela Merkel and European Commission President Jose Manuel Barroso congratulate each other following the Copenhagen Climate Summit, where world leaders agreed to massive reductions in greenhouse gas emissions. The new policy came about in response to public protests around the globe demanding that world leaders do the right thing for the planet.

Mass activism just clicks for more people than ever

COPENHAGEN

Websites and networking help thousands to save climate, make change

BY PETER BAUMANN

Heads of state agree historic climate-saving deal

COPENHAGEN

European leaders instrumental in driving the agenda

BY MICHAEL COUNTRY

Sarkozy: Nuclear is dead

PARIS

France revolutionizes the climate summit, stuns delegates and leaders

Sarkozy announces an end to reliance on nuclear energy in France.

WE, THE LEADERS OF THE EU, WOULD LIKE TO THANK YOU, THE EUROPEAN PUBLIC.

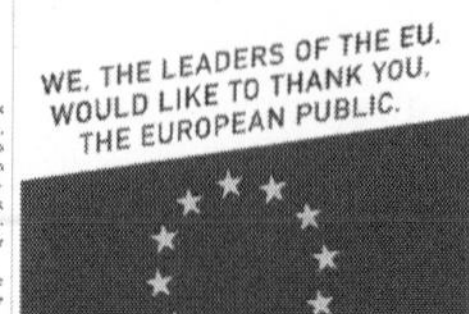

YOU FORCED OUR HANDS.
YOU SAVED OUR LIVES.

Thanks to your non-violent direct action, our civilization stands a chance at survival!

BEYOND TALK.

Global Warming Skeptics Switch Positions

'Clean Coal' Prank Gone Wrong

Climate Activists Worry

From the Publishers

Figure 6.2 The front page of the prank Special Edition of the *International Herald Tribune*. From the author's personal archive.

The prank *Tribune* told many more stories from our fantastic future where people's movements won victories to save the environment from climate disaster. Other adverts and articles included:

1. "Militias Turn Green in the USA," in which the militia movements realize their freedoms and liberties are directly threatened, not by black UN helicopters, but by the perpetrators of climate chaos. To call attention to the dangers of rising waters, and to publicly shame CEOs, they begin to take direct "dunking and dousing" actions against climate criminals.
2. An article debunking "sequestration" schemes for CO_2: "According to experts, any kind of underground sequestration is merely a temporary solution. Eventually, CO_2 will escape back into the atmosphere. 'It's like trying to hold in a fart for all eternity; It just doesn't work,' said Nobel Laureate Herman Hebdige, tipsy from celebrating the success of the Copenhagen Climate Summit . . . The coal industry is scrambling for new technologies to make coal plants ecologically sustainable. The latest proposals include a *Star Trek*-style matter transfer system to send carbon gases to the moon, and, according to one coal-industry CEO, time travel: 'We're going to send carbon to a more advanced future version of our civilization that will be better equipped to deal with it.'"
3. Two whimsical articles concerning the elites reverting to social-movement protest tactics: in one, nuclear-energy CEOs chain themselves to a Belgian reactor set to be decommissioned. In a movement in-joke, "Police Captain Herbert Marcuse" proves tolerant to their protest. In the other article, top CEOs take to the streets to protest the abolition of "carbon offsets:" "'We tried to get our interns and lackeys to do this stupid street protesting for us, but they told us to go f*** ourselves,' said one CEO. 'The creation of all these green jobs means you just can't find servile help anymore.'"
4. An advert for an Ikea Wind Farm, which can be constructed from the ground up with just one little wrench.
5. A proclamation from British Petroleum in which, having just greenwashed their name to stand for "Beyond Petroleum," they are changing it yet again to "Beholden to the People." They admit that they have had to capitulate under mass pressure and are now *really* changing their corporation into a renewable-energy company.
6. An announcement from the leaders of the EU, thanking the European public for their direct action that resulted in a climate change treaty. "You forced our hand. You saved our lives."

The "special edition" of the *IHT* upped the ante by linking to a website serving as an action-planning switchboard. It was also a specific intervention at an important convention rather than a more general air-war cultural action. This intervention was unusual—we sought not to block the doors to the convention, but to infiltrate the meeting with provocative ideas by handing free newspapers to the delegates as they went into the building. In fact, during the convention, several progressive and Green delegates held up the newspaper and said things like, "I know this is a prank, but look at these headlines! We need to make this kind of news here today!" We had provided sympathetic politicians with a prop for their speeches at the summit meeting. The website had limited success and is now defunct, but it did draw some participation and has since been replaced by more successful websites with the same concept, such as https://actionswitchboard.net/.

In the end, we wanted to convert dream energy into real action—giving people a fun but sincere vision of a better possible world, and promoting a website so that people could sign up for actual nonviolent civil disobedience in their area, or simply take a climate pledge of resistance.

The real *IHT* did request that Greenpeace remove the website. Their statement, as reported by the *Huffington Post*, claimed that "To have our name and image (misused) as a politically motivated publicity stunt is wholly contrary to our values of independence and accuracy" (Letchford, 2009). Fair enough.

The *New York Post*: playing right into Murdoch's hands, literally (and literarily)

> We were fooled—for a moment.
>
> The blaring headline makes you think you're just picking up the same ol' rag that's always shouting about something.
>
> (Gittens, 2009)

Finally, there was the "special edition" of the *New York Post*. This project was also designed to target a specific event—the 2009 Summit on Climate Change at the UN Headquarters in New York City. Scheduled for September, this summit was another preparatory meeting for Copenhagen. We wished to draw the attention of New Yorkers to this summit in their city, and to raise awareness among New Yorkers specifically, and the world in general, of the threat of total climate calamity. The Yes Men also planned to use the prank *Post* to help promote their upcoming movie, *The Yes Men Fix The World*. This project diverged from the other two fake newspaper actions in the following ways:

1 It would be set in the present. This made the action more transgressive as the newspaper bore the actual date of its release—21 September 2009—and was thus less obviously fake.
2 The news inside was entirely accurate. This was not an upbeat fantasy of future victories, but rather a "special issue" of the *New York Post* devoted entirely to climate disaster, how it would affect New York City, and what New Yorkers were doing about it. All facts were checked; all science was peer-reviewed.

In fact, as I grew fond of saying, the only lie in our paper was that the *New York Post* would tell the truth about climate change. The actual *Post*, part of Rupert Murdoch's media empire, was a denier of climate science, and the conclusions and consensus of the global scientific community. In their coverage of the September 2014 Climate Change march, which with 400,000 participants was the largest demonstration in world history on the issue, the *Post* gave as much space to climate science deniers as they did to the actual event. We wanted to draw on the *Post*'s local popularity—though not prominent worldwide like the *Times*, it has a larger circulation in New York City due to its low price and tabloid format. We also wanted the transgression and *frisson* of copying the *Post*'s masthead and tabloid tone, but reversing its ideology.

The *Post* is infamous for its outrageous headlines and faux-populist tone. It reads like *Fox News* on newsprint. There is a lot of macho posturing, surprisingly old-fashioned redbaiting, and wannabe-Damon Runyon tough-guy talk. Its headlines are the best part, with beauties like "Headless Body Found in Topless Bar." After much debate, our headline sacrificed the *Post*'s usual brutal poetry for the stark-and-simple:

> **WE'RE SCREWED**
>
> **(What you're not being told: Official City report predicts massive climate catastrophes, public health disasters.) NEW YORK FIGHTS BACK!**

I grew up with the *Post* and was always amazed and amused by its absurdity—a fun read with juicy propaganda packed in every page. The style, or persona, of the paper is strong: an anti-intellectual, suspicious,

NEW YORK POST

Page Six

MONDAY, SEPT. 21, 2009 / Sunny, 72° / Weather: P. 26 ★★ EARLY CITY SPECIAL www.nypost-se.com FREE

WORLD LEADERS SLIP ON UN SUMMIT SLOPE

PAGE 6

WE'RE SCREWED

NEW YORK FIGHTS BACK!

What you're not being told: Official City report predicts massive climate catastrophes, public health disasters.

SEE PAGE 3

Figure 6.3 The front page of the prank Special Edition of the *New York Post*. From the author's personal archive.

and aggrieved voice, cynical in all the wrong ways. What if we could inhabit that persona, detour it, and make it resentful and self-righteous about an actual ecological threat to our survival? It was key to get the tone right: the pseudo-populism and sense of patriotism-as-grievance, turned towards the cause of climate justice.

This was a vision, not of the world we'd like to see, but the *Post* we'd like to read; one that was honest and concerned about the impact of climate change on all New Yorkers. We chose to draw on real stories from sources that *Post* readers would be more sympathetic towards, like the report from the Pentagon that climate change was not only real but a serious national security threat, or the NYPD's recognition of the dangers to the city of climate change and their need to prepare for it.

We also appealed to patriotism by including articles about how China was being allowed to outproduce the US in solar panels and capture that global market to the detriment of our economy.

On the positive side, we had many articles about what people and organizations were doing proactively to combat climate change. I included a piece promoting the activist Reverend Billy's run for Mayor of New York City, and an article about the Bike Lane Liberation Clowns (see Chapter 4). The "Around the Boroughs" section included a score of true examples of successful local eco-activist projects. In the celebrity-gossip section, we reported on eco-gestures made by celebs. Even the sports page was eco-themed.

The adverts, designed by Kelly Anderson, made the prank clear (Noor, 2009). One was a full-page advert for tap water as a product, to discourage the use of plastic bottles. ("It literally comes right out of your faucet!™") This fantastic product had qualities such as "Free," "Necessary for Life," "Easily turned into Ice," and "Not yet owned by Coca-Cola." Another full-page advert, a swipe at the carbon-intensive tourism industry, featured a romantic couple on an island getaway, but it was actually an advert for "SEX. Why travel? You just wanted to get laid anyway, right? . . . Sex™. Awesome. No carbon emissions." This was funny, but also politically in tune with the overall message of the project. As Anderson said:

> All these advertisements for these exotic locations are very sex heavy. It's basically what they're selling anyway. So instead of selling something that involves a lot of money and a lot of emissions, we say why not just stay at home and order a pizza and hang out with your partner?
>
> (Noor, 2009)

On the day of distribution, when we were giving out our *Post* for free, its being free was less of a clue that it was a prank than with the *Times* and the *Tribune*. The *Post* is much cheaper than the *New York Times*, and is occasionally given away for free as a promotion. This, and the fact that it was dated in the present and not the future, made the satire a little more believable, but only for a few additional seconds. That every single article reported on climate chaos made it clear to readers that this wasn't the real *Post*.

Hundreds of volunteers gave out 85,000 copies of our *Post* that day. I led the Grand Central Station crew, and we gave out thousands of newspapers to bleary-eyed commuters getting off the trains at dawn.

Some refused to take the paper because they hate the *Post*, but reconsidered when one of us explained: "Well, if you hate the *Post*, you'll like this *Post*."

A few of my crew ran up to me excitedly. They had handed a copy of the fake *Post* to Rupert Murdoch, the *Post*'s owner. He had walked by surrounded by bodyguards. Someone held a copy out for him: "Paper, Mr. Murdoch?" and to their surprise he took it. The crew were ecstatic and wanted to take a stack of papers to the main door of the *Post*'s nearby offices, and give them to *Post* employees on their way in to work. This sounded like a nice escalation of the concept so I agreed and gave them a few hundred copies. As more and more *Post* reporters kept arriving in their office with fake *Posts* in hand, the police were called and the three intrepid "paperboys" were brought into the building by NYPD to be questioned by private security—a legally questionable move. In answer to "Who are you? What is this? Who are you working for?" came the very apt response "Um . . . it's an art project?" Eventually they were let go, but the NYPD made off with about a hundred of our newspapers, which we would like returned (Del Signore, 2009a & 2009b; Bercovici, 2009).

As *NBC News New York* reported:

> . . . Perhaps the police were still riled from the Yes Men's stunt on Monday, when volunteers distributed a million copies of the fake "We're Screwed" edition of the *New York Post*, including to News Corp. Chairman Rupert Murdoch, who owns the paper. It was after Murdoch got hold of the bogus paper, decidedly not written in his style, that cops were called and detained three volunteers for questioning . . . A day after the hoax, the *New York Post* published an editorial claiming they were flattered by the Yes Men's hijinks. We're not so sure we believe them.
>
> (Millman, 2009)

And the *Daily Finance* added:

> The *New York Post* does not have a sense of humor about itself, it would seem. Early this morning, some 2,000 activists affiliated with a group called The Yes Men handed out copies of a 32-page parody issue calling attention to climate change. But when volunteers tried to distribute copies outside the *Post*'s offices, they were detained by police and their papers were confiscated, says an eyewitness.
>
> (Bercovici, 2009)

The fake *Post* received a fair amount of coverage, which spiked during the day due to the confrontation and police intervention at the *Post*'s office. But it did not have as much impact on public conversation as the first two newspaper actions.[5] There are a few reasons for this, as Jacques Servin, Andrew Boyd and I discussed in an interview (Jahn & Ünsal, 2011). First of all, this was the third time this crew had conducted an action like this, and surprise and interest always wears off with repetition. Secondly, hitting the *Post* was not going to attract global attention in the same way as the prestigious and globally recognized *Times* and *IHT*. The *Post* is the most widely read single newspaper in New York City, but is not read much outside the larger metropolitan area. Thirdly, a deeper reason may be that our intention on playing it straight, on being factual and earnest in our message, limited the poetry of the project and may have undercut its effectiveness. In the interview, Andrew Boyd made several salient points, connecting this problem with a condition that affects radical artists who infiltrate electoral systems rather than newspapers:

> . . . this is an issue you are dealing with all the time when you are investigating electoral guerrilla interventions (see the book *Electoral Guerrilla Theatre*). The ridiculous and provocative art form, when it becomes real, loses something. It's like shaving off the edges to make it fit into a very prosaic form of an election. It's the difference marking the two kinds of performance—a vote-getting performance, and an artistic performance . . . Bogad's point that [the *Post* is] a self-parody is an interesting one. How do you parody something that's already a self-parody? We took their ridiculous language and voice, and made one very important content shift. But . . . they were already in the gutter . . . we were trying to raise them up, and that's a hard move to do—to raise something up rather than knock it down. For the *Post*, the effect we had was more of a poke in the eye rather than a knock down.
>
> (Jahn & Ünsal, 2011)

In addition, we were funded by a local climate change oriented group who, unlike Greenpeace with the *IHT*, became involved in every editorial decision, including rewriting copy. Sadly, their involvement leached much of the humor and whimsy from the project. It is risky to take money from one single donor for a project of this kind.

All three of these projects were logistically complicated and involved secret mass production and distribution of an art piece that infiltrated the brand, logo, and format of an established newspaper. These were acts of *detournement*—we took something widely known and turned it around for progressive purposes. However, when examined more closely, it becomes clear that they were related, but divergent projects that required varied tactics and aesthetics. The results were mixed, but activists have continued to create prank newspapers to surprise people in everyday life—whether by just printing a false front page and putting that in the newspaper box on the street, or by going to the outrageous trouble of making a whole original paper. This is a very labor-intensive type of project and not one to be taken on lightly. The design, tone, and content of the project should match the goals of the activist organization, and the clearer the group is on those goals at the beginning of the project, the better.[6]

Suggestions: to be tested in practice

1. The resources necessary for an action should be calculated at least roughly, before deciding if it is worth the intended effect.
2. "Air-war" actions are more compelling when produced in conjunction with "ground-war" campaigns (see the Introduction).
3. Some actions are as much about building skills and networks for the future as they are about the impact of the action itself.

Notes

1. Ironically, Lenin used a secret newspaper for this dual purpose as well, though his ideology was completely different from our anti-authoritarian collective. *Iskra*, or *Spark*, was the Bolshevik underground newspaper under the Tsar. Its purpose was to both disseminate the Bolshevik perspective while eluding censorship, and to help develop the Bolshevik movement through the practice of building a secret network of cells that would learn how to work together on a practical project.
2. We were also preparing other ideas in case of a lawsuit, such as creating a shadow organization to denounce ourselves in a farcically extreme manner, in order to deconstruct the arguments for censorship.
3. For lists of coverage of the fake *Times*, see http://visitsteve.com/made/the-ny-times-special-edition/ and http://theyesmen.org/hijinks/newyorktimes.
4. The *International Herald Tribune* was the *New York Times'* international newspaper, and has since been renamed the *International New York Times*.
5. At the end of a very long day, riding on the subway with a few fake *Posts* in my lap, a stranger looked at them and said slyly, "Those are fake, you know." I agreed with him.
6. As we acknowledged in the *IHT* press release, there have been quite a few of these fake newspapers, and it continues to be an option for creative action

to this day, though a labor-intensive one. A hoax *USA Today* featured the US presidential election result: "Capitalism wins at the polls: Anarchy brewing in the streets" ("Fake Papers," 2008). Also, a spoof edition of Germany's *Zeit* newspaper was issued, triumphantly announcing the end of "casino capitalism" and the abolition of poor-country debt ("Anti-globalization Group," 2009). The rash of fakes is likely to continue. "People are going to keep finding ways to get the word out about common-sense solutions those in power say are impossible," said Kelli Anderson, one of the designers of the fake *IHT*. "We already know what we need to do about climate change," said Agnes de Rooij of Greenpeace International. "It's a no-brainer. Reduce carbon emissions, or put the survival of billions of people at risk. If the political will isn't there now, it's our duty to inspire it" (Bogad & Servin, 2009).

References

"Anti-globalization Group Prints Fake German Paper." (2009) Reuters, 23 March 2009. http://in.reuters.com/article/2009/03/23/us-germany-newspaper-spoof-idINTRE52M5C820090323 (accessed 28 Oct 2015).

Bercovici, Jeff (2009) "Activists Behind NY Post Parody Detained by Police." *Daily Finance*, 21 Sept 2009. www.dailyfinance.com/2009/09/21/activists-behind-ny-post-parody-detained-by-police/ (accessed 28 Oct 2015).

Bogad, L.M.; Servin, J. (2009) Yes Men Press Release. http://theyesmen.org/blog/beyondtalknet (accessed 28 Oct 2015).

Del Signore, John (2009a) "Cops Detain Activists Giving Out Fake Post Outside News Corp." *Gothamist*, 21 Sept 2009. http://gothamist.com/2009/09/21/cops_arrest_volunteers_handing_out.php (accessed 3 Nov 2015).

Del Signore, John (2009b) "Yes Man Arrested, NY Post 'Flattered' by Hoax." *Gothamist*, 22 Sept 2009. http://gothamist.com/2009/09/22/yes_man_arrested_ny_post_flattered.php#photo-1 (accessed 28 Oct 2015).

"Fake Papers: Capitalism wins." (2008) *Charlotte Observer*, 6 Nov 2008. www.charlotteobserver.com/news/local/article9022037.html (accessed 28 Oct 2015).

Gittens, Hasani (2009) Fake *New York Post* Turns Red Paper Green. *NBC News New York*. 21 Sept 2009. www.nbcnewyork.com/news/local/Fake-New-York-Post-Turns-Red-Paper-Green-59989472.html

Jahn, M.; Ünsal, M. (2011) "The Baked Apple: On the *New York Post* special edition: An interview with Andy Bichlbaum, L.M. Bogad, and Andrew Boyd." In *Byproducts*. Toronto: YYZ Books: p. 146–51.

Letchford, Jessica (2009) "Greenpeace Spoofs International Herald Tribune." *Huffington Post*, 19 July 2009. www.huffingtonpost.com/2009/06/18/greenpeace-spoofs-interna_n_217663.html (accessed 28 Oct 2015).

Millman, Jennifer (2009) Cops Arrest "Yes Men" Co-Founder in Latest Prank. *NBC News New York*. 23 Sept 2009. www.nbcnewyork.com/news/local/Fake-Post-Guys-Pull-Another-One-Yes-Man-Arrested-60700217.html (accessed 28 Oct 2015).

Noor, Jaisal (2009) "A Closer Look at The Yes Men's 'We're Screwed' New York Post." *The Indypendent*, 24 Sept 2009. https://indypendent.org/2009/09/24/closer-look-yes-mens-were-screwed-new-york-post (accessed 30 Dec 2014).

Special Edition of the *International Herald Tribune*. From the author's personal archive.

Part IV

Serious but not solemn

Chapter 7

Crisis in Califorlornia

Creative protest at the University of California

I bring it home in this final discussion. The university is not an ivory tower, sheltered and separate from the world of exploitation and dissent. Academia is as implicated as any other workplace in conflicts between labor and capital, resistance and hegemony. When budget cuts, tuition hikes, and police brutality came to the University of California (UC), my own students, and many other intrepid students and graduate students throughout the system, experimented with creative and performative tactics to resist those changes, build a movement, and express dissent to the greater public.

A lovely stream flows through the campus at UC Davis. While the stream is widely believed to be tainted with agrochemical runoff, it offers an idyllic place for students, staff, and faculty to stroll or sunbathe. One day toward the end of the Spring Quarter of 2010, a young man named Robert Nuñez stood in that water, protected by hip-high waders. He wore a cowboy hat and overalls and looked like a character from the 1849 Gold Rush. With a pan in his hands, he called out to passersby to watch as he demonstrated his solution to widespread student financial problems. A sign planted in the ground near him said: "GOLD: THE TUITION SOLUTION." He cried out to passersby, "It's an old California tradition, and it's the only way I can pay for school!" He had several gold-painted rocks to prove that one could still strike it rich, and he offered them to spectators. As a small crowd gathered around to observe this Swiftian "modest proposal," he made his point about the desperate financial situation many students face at UC.[1]

As with many American public universities during the current economic crisis, UC found itself in dire times. Confronted with a disastrous shortfall in income, university President Mark G. Yudof decided to raise student tuition fees by 32% in 2009, and then by another 8% in 2011. A decision was also made to lay off and furlough staff and faculty, and reduce class offerings. Critics complained that Yudof's decisions showed misguided priorities and that he was not doing enough to cut the bloated upper-administrative sector of the university, which had increased greatly both in number of positions and salaries since 2000. Some wondered why new billion-dollar construction projects were continuing as planned while the university was drastically cutting back on basic services and lower- and mid-level staff salaries.

This culminated in a swell of protest in 2009 and 2010 that involved staff, students, graduate students, and faculty (Duke, 2009). The administrative building of UC Davis, Mrak Hall, was occupied, and campus police arrested 53 demonstrators. Similar occupations occurred at UC Berkeley and on most of the other campuses throughout the state. Protestors engaged in demonstrations, marches, street theatre, and walkouts. Many students were arrested, beaten, and pepper-sprayed in confrontations with university and municipal police on the various campuses of the UC system.

The protests and the use of police force attracted national attention. Stephen Colbert covered the beating of student protestors on the Berkeley campus on his popular television show, *The Colbert Report*, and aired a video clip of the police swinging batons at the heads and bodies of students who were standing peacefully with linked arms. He pointed out, while pausing the video, that the police had made sure to club a "small Asian woman," showing UC's "admirable commitment to diversity" ("Occupy U.C. Berkeley," 2011). As cutting as that humor was, it drew a strong reaction as the live audience, and many watching over national television, gasped and laughed bitterly at the dark absurdity apparent in the brutalization of protesting students on the same campus where the Free Speech Movement was born in the 1960s.

On my campus there were several occupations of Mrak Hall, and one incident where students were pepper-sprayed and beaten as they tried to block Federal Highway 80, the major traffic artery in northern California. However, the event that drew global attention and went viral on the internet was the pepper-spraying of students sitting in the middle of the Quad, refusing to stand up when ordered to do so by heavily armed and armored riot police. On 18 November 2011, as students peacefully sat on the grass with arms linked—blocking nothing—one officer calmly walked up and down the line, shooting orange pepper-spray directly into their faces. This was videoed from several angles and became an internet sensation (*UC Davis Protestors*, 2011).

The next day, Chancellor Katehi was giving a press conference in a campus building while a mass of students outside protested her policies and the brutality of the pepper-spray incident. Katehi told the media that she was concerned about leaving the building because she feared for her own safety. A negotiation with the students ensued, and the protestors agreed to move to one side of the concrete path, and made assurances that they were nonviolent. As Katehi stepped out of the building, escorted by staff and a few videographers, the entire mass of students sat in total silence. Not one of them made a sound as they watched the Chancellor walk by. The only sound to be heard was the clacking of her shoes on the path. The discipline of this protest was astonishing. Not one individual broke this deeply eloquent silence. Katehi appeared moved, and when a reporter quietly asked her "Do you still feel threatened by these students?" she answered that she did not. This video also went viral on YouTube and received a great deal of attention and comments. It showed how an elegant display of discipline can surprise, impress, and debunk stereotypes of dissenters—in this case, the stereotype of the students as wild and violent ("UC Davis Chancellor," YouTube).

A later investigation of the pepper-spray incident revealed that Chancellor Katehi had ordered campus police to clear the students and the few Occupy-style tents from the Quad before their tent village became as entrenched as the one on the Berkeley campus (Reynoso Task Force, 2012). After the incident, with a brutality scandal blooming, the tent village was allowed to remain. It doubled in size and stayed in place for several months until winter frost struck. At one point, the village included a large geodesic dome where political meetings and workshops were conducted, including those led by faculty members on Tactical Performance and Organizing.

The gratuitous use of chemical weapons drew the ire, and the creative response, of people around the world. The "Pepper Spraying Cop" became a popular internet meme, in which artists inserted this image into many famous works of art (*Pepper Spraying Cop*, n.d.). Soon the Pepper Spraying Cop could be seen spraying Jesus at the Last Supper, Pokemon, the Tank Man at Tiananmen Square, Alice in Wonderland, the dying villagers in Picasso's *Guernica*, the Founding Fathers as they signed the Constitution, E.T. as he rode his bicycle into the sky, and many others.[2] This use of simple cut-and-paste graphic design encouraged global participation in the protest, kept awareness of the incident alive, and gave protesters some grim anti-authoritarian humor to laugh at. Nevertheless, dark humor could not disguise the stark reality of ongoing repression and escalating tuition fees.

In referring to these tuition hikes, budget cuts, and ongoing protests, Yudof joked infamously in a 2009 *New York Times* article that being president of the UC system was "like being the manager of a cemetery: there are many people under you, but no one is listening" (Solomon, 2009). The interview was full of similar quips. When the article was published, several colleagues called me and asked if I had somehow impersonated Yudof and tricked the *Times* into publishing a satirical interview. I could only say: "No, he's writing his own material." This was the setup for a very strange incident that occurred eight months later.

Mark Yudof's *Thriller*

On 1 June 2010, Mark Yudof could be seen enjoying a luscious picnic lunch in the grounds in front of the student union on the UC Davis campus. Sitting comfortably on a red blanket, he poured himself wine and noshed on what looked like caviar on crackers. A young reporter came up with a microphone and began to ask him questions. He answered with the same glibness that he had displayed in the *New York Times* interview (Solomon, 2009).

As the interview continued, half a dozen students began slowly creeping up on him from behind. They wore white makeup and horror movie-style gore on their faces and hands. The eerie opening to Michael Jackson's song *Thriller* began to play from a sound system nearby. These undead students were just about to pounce on the President from behind when he repeated the infamous line about managing a cemetery. At that moment, the noon bell tolled ominously, and Yudof threw on a red leather jacket like the one Jackson wore in the music video for *Thriller*.

Before the gathering lunchtime student crowd knew what was happening, the Yudof lookalike was leading the zombie-students in a humorous formation dance that mixed familiar moves from the Michael Jackson video with mischievous new choreography that expressed a playful, but harsh critique of Yudof's policies. A servile student shines Yudof's shoe; he kicks her away in perfect rhythm. The students form a human staircase and Yudof steps on them all the way to the top; once there, he rubs a wad of cash on his crotch and gyrates his hips happily. Then he jumps off and kicks them over; the students collapse like undead dominoes. Yudof laughs, or rather laugh-syncs to Vincent Price's spooky laugh at the end of the song. He then sits down and resumes his sumptuous meal.

The lyrics to "Mark Yudof's *Thriller*," written and sung by UC Davis student Christina Noble, who was creator and choreographer of the project, are as follows (SOTA, 2010):

> **Start of the quarter, and something evil's lurking in the dark**
>
> **Inside your inbox, your billing statement almost stops your heart**
>
> **You try to scream, but you're not loud enough to reach the Board of Regents**
>
> **You start to freeze, McDonald's isn't hiring right now**
>
> **You're marginalized**
>
> **'Cause this is Yudof! Mark Yudof**
>
> **He'll stand up for his students, as long as it pays off**
>
> **You know it's Yudof! Mark Yudof**
>
> **You're fighting for your rights while your fees go up, go up, go UP!**
>
> **You hear the protests and realize that he simply doesn't care**
>
> **$600,000 a year just isn't quite enough to share**
>
> **You close your eyes and hope that this is just imagination**
>
> **But all the while he's lying out by the pool on your dime**
>
> **It's bamboozling time**
>
> **'Cause this is Yudof! Mark Yudof**
>
> **Goes to all the Regent meetings, and he stays awake for some**
>
> **You know it's Yudof! Mark Yudof**
>
> **He's not fighting for your rights as your fees go up, go up, go UP!**

What change can this kind of action bring? Noble reflected on this question:

> I am under no false pretenses—Mark Yudof's *Thriller* is not likely to change philosophies among the policy-makers of the University of California, lower our tuition, or put professors back in the classroom full-time. Rather, through the performance, I hoped to create a fun, creative, and safe outlet for dissent, and I hoped to achieve elevated morale among a community in dire need of change. While we're all suffering the burdens of a University in crisis, we can still find satisfaction in challenging and criticizing power dynamics—at least, in the case of Mark Yudof's *Thriller*, for three and a half mischievous minutes.
>
> (SOTA, 2010)

Silly string vs. pepper spray? A clownish re-enactment

The Gold Rush Tuition Solution and Yudof's *Thriller* did not affect the day-to-day operations of the university, nor did these actions target university staff as a primary audience. However, a third example provides a contrast. In the spring of 2012, a recruitment campus tour was taking place, in which high-school students and their parents were shown the facilities and dorms, and given a positive sense of the advantages of the university. These tours take place regularly on every college in the country, and are an important aspect of student recruitment. They are, therefore, a potential pressure point on the body politic of the university. On this particular tour, the students, parents, and the tour guides noticed silent clowns standing off to the side at key points along their path. The clowns held signs that said "⅓ OF DAVIS STUDENTS SKIP MEALS DUE TO TUITION COSTS" and "STUDENT DEBT > CREDIT CARD DEBT."[3] They smiled and quietly gestured to their signs; in the background, a clown in a top hat chased and leapt at a dollar bill hanging from the end of a stick held high by another clown running in front of him.

The campus tour guides were rattled at first, but the clown-students had already decided on their rules of engagement. They had determined that they just wanted to present another side of the story of recent events on campus. They did not want to harass their fellow students guiding the tour or stop the tour from continuing. The tour guide improvised a few jokes about what was happening and continued her description of the university.

When the tour approached the center of the Quad, where the infamous pepper-spray incident had occurred, the clowns came out from behind a large tree and sat in a line, linking arms, exactly where the students had sat on that day. In fact, some of the clowns were actually students who had been pepper-sprayed there. Would they block the tour's path? There was a short moment of tension as the tour approached the sitting line. Then a pair of clown-police appeared, and shot silly string into the faces of the sitting clowns, who immediately fell away from the path, writhing and giggling absurdly. The tour walked right through this chaos, unhindered. One parent said to his son: "You know about that pepper-spray thing? That happened here? That was unnecessary." The tour guide paused, recovered, smiled, and assured the visitors that there was nothing wrong with her eyes, and that Davis students were not pepper-sprayed routinely as part of their studies. Later, the clowns appeared one last time with a sign that said "JOIN THE STUDENT MOVEMENT." Their motivation was not to frighten prospective students away, but to have them enroll and join the movement for student rights (*UC Davis Students Welcome*, 2012).

These examples of student action refer to ideas discussed in the Introduction, such as *rules of engagement*, *chosen audience* for actions, *direct versus indirect action* (and hybrids of these categories), and effective *pressure points*. The Gold Rush Tuition Solution was an indirect action, designed to attract attention, break up the routine of the student day, express frustration shared by many struggling students, and stimulate conversation through irony. It was a modest, but effective piece. Yudof's *Thriller* was also an indirect action—not directly disrupting or affecting its target, but attempting to reach both a live, and later an online, audience by supplying a creative expression of dissent and a satire of the powerful for the enjoyment of the larger student movement. The clowns' engagement with the student tour is more of a direct/indirect action hybrid—indirect in that it was a performance for both online and immediate viewers, but it also had a direct element in that it did partially impact the normal workings of the university at a tender pressure point: the recruitment tour. One can imagine that if these "counter-tours" occurred regularly and on multiple campuses, the campus administration would be motivated to come up with a countermeasure—often a good indicator that a tactic has been effective.

As for rules of engagement, these were worked out in advance and are worthy of further comment. The gold miner stayed in character throughout his interactions with students—and let them figure out that he was joking in order to make the "Aha!" moment more poignant.

The *Thriller* performers were onstage in a more traditional sense—they performed, finished, and moved on. It was the more complicated hybrid action of the clown pepper-spray re-enactors that called for a real ethical discussion—how will the protestors treat the tour guides and the people on the tour? As detailed above, the protestors decided to provide a counter-narrative through silent signage and clowning, but not disrupt or overly distract from the tour. This decision fit in with the protestors' ethics and comfort zone, and made them more sympathetic to viewers who might have been alienated if the protest had ruined the tour. (Some students and parents had traveled a great distance for the tour.) Such conversations and decision-making must be part of action-planning, and protestors must always ask: "Is this a direct or indirect action?" "What are the rules of engagement?"

A spirit of justice haunts the campus

Inequity manifests itself not only in moments of police brutality or tuition hikes; there are more ongoing structural inequalities that haunt the university. Indeed, in the Spring of 2008, the ghost of Mary McCleod Bethune, heroine of African–American education from the first half of the twentieth century, was seen wandering the UC Davis campus crying out: "Where are all the African–American students?! I worked so hard all my life! Where are they? What went wrong?!" When she found black students, she would approach them joyously and then ask them about what went wrong in America. Behind her people handed out flyers that asked: "WHY HAS MARY McCLEOD BETHUNE COME BACK FROM THE DEAD?" The flyer explained succinctly who Bethune was, and then provided an analysis of the structural racism within the UC system that kept the percentage of African–American students so low.[4] Bethune, in period costume and realistic "ghost" makeup made her way to Mrak Hall. As administrative staff entered and exited the building, she asked them the same difficult question, with the gravitas of a heroine of American history and the poise of a graduating senior. This was the work of the irrepressible Shelley Grayson, then a student majoring in Theatre and Dance. Her own experience as a working class African–American student compelled her to confront the entire campus, to make the unmarked and rarely discussed scarcity of African–American students a condition that is suddenly strange, disturbing, and wrong in the finest Brechtian fashion.

The gold miner, the *Thriller* writer–singer–choreographer, the clown pepper-spray re-enactors and the ghost of Mary McLeod Bethune

Figure 7.1 "Mary McCleod Bethune" waits patiently at the Information Desk on campus, so she can ask where all the black students are. Photo by L.M. Bogad.

Figure 7.2 "Mary McCleod Bethune" stands vigil outside the administration building on campus, asking all who enter to tell her where all the missing black students are. Photo by L.M. Bogad.

had all been my Tactical Performance students. Quite a few students that I knew were beaten and arrested on several UC campuses. This encroachment of the budget crises and conflict into my own pedagogy compelled me to write this chapter, in which I analyze the challenges involved in performing with and for a diverse coalition about an issue as complex as the crisis in the UC system.

A complex campaign

Building an effective progressive movement to contest UC budget cuts and austerity measures offered unique challenges. Creating an effective movement made up of multiple constituencies is always difficult. Faculty, staff, graduate students, and undergrads all have varying interests and agendas, and different relationships with the administration and state government. However, during the recent crisis, all four stakeholder groups were hurt by decisions the administration and the state had made, and activists among the faculty, staff, and students formed a tentative and partial coalition.

The additional challenge was that the target was often amorphous, shifting, and slippery. Who is to blame for the crisis and the cuts? Who should we put pressure on, embarrass, lobby, or ally with? Are cuts the fault of the state legislature? Or the governor? Or the Regents or the President of the university? One thing was for certain: all of these power nodes have their own strengths and pressure points, and all were happy to pass the blame to others in a manner that can and has sent protesters spinning around fruitlessly. Saul Alinsky argued that because those in power constantly try to pass the buck in a never-ending cycle, social movements must choose the most promising target, fixate on it, and dramatize the situation in a radically compelling, urgent, and mobilizing narrative. This is what social-movement theorists refer to as creating a "collective action frame" (Alinsky, 1989; Tarrow, 1998: p. 109)

It is also difficult to convince the greater audience of California taxpayers of the importance of world-class public higher education in a time of crisis and neoliberal–neoconservative hegemonologue—by which I mean the relentless hegemonic monologue of the inevitability of crisis capitalism, in which there is no money for affordable higher education, but endless funds for war, tax breaks for the rich, and bailouts for Wall Street, and in which resistance is pathologized or criminalized. The hegemonologue drones on and drowns out dissent. In hard times, it places the necessity of investing in the future of civil society (maintaining and improving public education from kindergarten to doctoral programs) into competition with the immediate fiscal needs of low- and middle-income taxpayers. Interrupting that hegemonologue requires a canny and consistently creative application of sociodrama and tactical performance to show taxpayers that public education must be preserved for their own long-term good and that of their children.

The complex nature of the issues challenges the coalition's longevity and efficacy.[5] What amount of tuition is fair for students? What amount of financial aid is fair? How many work–study opportunities are needed? What is fair treatment for staff and faculty regarding pensions, salaries, and job security? Who is to blame for the current crisis, and what can fix it? Finally, what are the role and the relative importance of public education in a functioning and democratic civil society? Should education be a priority, or should it be allowed to wither? Should the public K-12 schools, community colleges, California State University, and the University of California be set in competition with each other for a shrinking education budget, or can they work together to pressure the government for more funding for all? If Proposition 13 were eliminated for corporate landholdings (as opposed to individual homes), would that be a just way of balancing the budget and restoring excellence to California's public-education system?[6]

Effective political performance is needed to express a convincing, compelling, progressive position on these difficult and intricate issues to the general taxpaying audience. This is what we as theatre and performance theorists and practitioners can offer to the movement—a sense of the dramatic and an ability to create sociodramas and "dilemma demonstrations," in which creative nonviolence is used to put one's institutional opponents in a no-win situation even though they have law, force, and legitimacy on their side (Lewis & D'Orso, 1999: p. 86; Duhamel & Pearson, 2004).

In this conflict, I propose that opening space is as important as occupying it. Several impressive occupations of administrative buildings have taken place.[7] Of those, the most inspiring actions involved opening up those public buildings and resources for creative reuse, and enacting what a better, different world might look like. Combining the act of occupying a space with opening that space for a new use seems to be key; opening space within the imagination by reworking traditional forms of action—picket lines, rallies, and so forth—is necessary in these dark times when protest is all too easily marginalized, preempted, shouted down, or ignored. These forms are not necessarily contradictory—in fact they can work in solidarity with each other, including in the same action.

To reiterate values laid out in the Introduction of this book: activists need to think dramaturgically (in terms of the chosen audience, timing, sightlines, tension, and suspense), create irresistible images, generate surprise as opposed to shock, and anticipate and incorporate the opponent's reaction. We need to keep in mind the qualities of established symbolism and rituals, and look for opportunities to coopt or disrupt them with performance. Protests need to be more surprising and engaging to be effective; a rally with predictable signs and chants may be hobbled by its own cliché.

For example, for a mass rally at the UC Berkeley campus, organizers contacted me because they were concerned with how to make the event more compelling. Some organizers were concerned that their rally, while large, would be boring and hackneyed. The demonstration was to take place at Sproul Plaza, the birthplace of the famous Free Speech Movement of the 1960s. While this is a logical and symbolically evocative location for a demonstration, it is also the constant site of protests and therefore a predictable choice. This was the advice I gave the organizers of the 24 September 2009 walkout demonstration:

1 Design a dramatic beginning of the demonstration. Many demonstrations seem to start without any dramatic intention or consideration. People mill around and gradually accumulate, and eventually someone gets up to the microphone on the platform and starts speaking. This is a missed opportunity. With a little organizing, you can build up dramatic tension and make the beginning of the demo something exciting. Have one group arrive from the east, banging drums and cheering. Five minutes later, with a joyous roar and banners flaring, another group arrives from the north! A few minutes after that, another group marches up from the south! This is fun, and before the speeches even begin there is a sense of an event that is important, and packed with social magnitude, momentum, and perhaps even *promise* because it is well organized.
2 Plan an exciting ending, and epilogue, for the end of the demonstration. Rather than allowing the demonstration to just peter out, as so often happens, the group could end on a high, energetic note. When possible and appropriate, allow this massing of people to lead directly to a tangible action: an occupation, a blockade, a radical costume ball, or a mass-participatory art creation (e.g. a mural, graffiti).

This is not to give short shrift to the speeches made or the music played during the actual rally itself, but theatre practitioners may have something to contribute to the success of these elements with our understanding of the importance of framing, timing, and dramatic tension. It's no small feat to get all of those people to show up, so why not provide them with a galvanizing, dynamic, and multifaceted experience?

University of California Movement for Efficient Privatization (UCMeP)

That same rally included a group of besuited activists called the University of California Movement for Efficient Privatization, or UCMeP. This group, in the tradition of Billionaires for Bush and other ironic moguls of radical performance, claimed that they not only supported the marketization and privatization of the UC system, but also felt that the University Regents were not moving this process forward quickly or ruthlessly enough. At first glance, this group seemed to be at odds with the other activists. In fact, they were not. UC Berkeley graduate student Shane Boyle stated that the group's "guiding logic . . . was to take the logic of the UC administration to its extremes in an effort to ridicule the authoritative discourse used by administrators to legitimate everything from furloughs to the criminalization of dissent" (Boyle, 2010).

For this first big demonstration, I suggested to the UCMeP innovators and organizers (Boyle and Brandon Woolf) that they "auction off" buildings on the Berkeley campus—after all, that's some great hillside real estate that would be better used in private hands. Boyle and Woolf radically improved on this idea during what they called the "buy-in" auction segment of the rally, when they auctioned off valuable commodities such as the rights to free assembly and free speech. UCMeP amused the crowds while making their critique. They went on to be a headline-grabbing magnet for media attention for the movement, creating many comedic, bitterly ironic events, manifestos, press releases, and YouTube videos to spread their message (Asimov, 2010; Gallagher, 2010; Kingston, 2010; "Using Humor," 2010; Rees, 2010). In fact, Woolf can be seen in close-up during the first few minutes of Robert Reich's movie, *Inequality For All*, declaring in suit and in character:

> **Come and join the one percent. It's a lovely percent.**

As Woolf put it:

> The kinds of critiques we hoped to perform at each action aimed to use—as best we could—the specifics of the particular issue at hand as a kind of internal logic governing our own dramaturgy. The September 24th "buy in," [the first big demonstration described above] for example, was an outright and broad-based call-to-arms against the rhetoric of efficiency, operational excellence, privatization, and future-oriented profits. The auction was designed to be highly legible to a large group—nearly 5,000—who had gathered for a rally in support of public education.
> (Woolf, 2010)

Other satirical proposals created by UCMeP included: Help Mark Yudof Buy A Plane, mocking the large salaries and benefits received by top administrators,[8] and Adopt-A-Regent, designed to inform the students of the identities and jobs, personal economic interests, and ideological positions of the UC Regents. They even ran a satirical slate of candidates for student government in the tradition of electoral guerrilla theatre (Bogad, 2016), and made a fake version of the website of the *Daily Californian*, the campus student newspaper, to promote their radical critique.

UCMeP presented Dan Mogulof, the official spokesperson for the Berkeley campus, the T.O.O.L. (Top Outstanding Oratorical Leader) Award, with an enormous golden hammer, for his excellence in making statements that criminalized student protesters. UCMeP had been upset by Mogulof's statements intimating that the student protesters were criminals—a grave accusation with real consequences for student safety in a context where campus police were beating students at demonstrations. They felt that if the students were successfully criminalized it could lead to more beatings with fewer public-relations or legal repercussions for the administration.

To their surprise, when they invited Dan Mogulof to this event, he accepted. Mogulof was a very capable and savvy spokesperson, and he chose to enter into a satirical space with the hope of showing a sense of humor, gaining sympathy, and opening a dialogue with the students. What followed was a very interesting chess game between angry satirical graduate students hoping to make additional points for their UCMeP campaign, and a major administration official trying to defuse some of that bitterness and express his side of the story.[9] Mogulof made two stipulations for his participation in this ironic "award" ceremony:

he would not actually hold the T.O.O.L. Award (because he did not want such a photo of him in circulation); and a senior Theatre professor, Catherine Cole, would read his speech for him while he stood next to her following along on paper. This second stipulation was interesting. Cole agreed to do this, and showed up in an ironic pro-privatization character. Mogulof read along quietly, occasionally moving his lips and looking up at the audience for responses. Perhaps he felt a trained theatre professional would do a better job of reading his speech—a largely good-natured and equally ironic "acceptance" that simultaneously told his side of the story.[10] At the end of this strange and tensive ceremony, he took questions from students that were at times sympathetic and at other times denunciatory.

The whole interaction was bizarre and fascinating to any scholar of satire, but hard to evaluate. Of the events, Boyle stated:

> I found the TOOL award to be very successful because it drew attention to what was becoming a very big problem at UC Berkeley at the end of the fall semester last year, particularly the UC administration's and California state government's discourse

Figure 7.3 The University of California Movement for Efficient Privatization members present the T.O.O.L. award to Dan Mogulof, executive director of the University's Office of Public Affairs. Photo by Benjamin Kiesewetter.

> that the activists at Berkeley "were criminals, not activists" as Chancellor Birgeneau declared in December 2009. The leading voice of this discourse was UC Berkeley spokesperson Dan Mogulof who throughout the fall semester of 2009 repeatedly gave out false information to the media about actions on campus, which painted student activists in a misleading light. By the time UCMeP wrote Mogulof's TOOL award letter that December, there was tremendous anger among activists towards him. But considering the fact that he was the official spokesperson of UC Berkeley and had a literal monopoly over what was passed on to and reported in the *SF Chronicle*, the *New York Times*, the *LA Times*, etc., many people—even sympathetic faculty and alumni—took what he said to be true. Judging from all the responses we got from the TOOL award from the media, website visits, emails, etc., I think our intervention pierced a hole in the authority of the discourse.
>
> (Boyle, 2010)

This was a reasoned evaluation. Such a ceremony was never meant to change the policies of Mogulof or the university, although that would have been a wonderful byproduct. The intention was to use irony (and a golden hammer) to articulate, both to a statewide audience and to the members of the student movement, a defiant, detailed, and humorously engaging account of the wrongful claims of the administration.

A red carpet on the picket line: from a habituated hate-place to a shaming sham-space

The protests and arrests continued throughout the spring term of 2010. A UC system-wide strike and walkout was planned for 4 March 2010 on all ten campuses. One of the problems that all strikes face is how to handle the picket line. What are the rules of engagement with "scabs," or people who cross the picket line?[11] Yelling and screaming? Chanting and sign-waving? Silently glaring? Engaging in cheerful conversation?

It is exactly in this kind of typical, habituated site of conflict—the picket line, the boycott line, demonstration vs. counter-demonstration—that all sides can descend into the familiar habits and clichés of interaction ("This is where we shout at you, and you throw rocks at us," etc.). Cliché or habit can lead to violence on the one hand—unexamined, automatic behaviors mutually escalating into fruitless battery—or just boringly familiar and easily ignored or dismissed events—another broken bank window, another burning trash bin, another hopeless punch up with the police—and the actual issue at stake is lost to the public imagination.

UCMeP decided that, true to its ironic tone, it would applaud and encourage people who crossed the picket line, taking their pictures and giving them celebrity treatment. For this action, UCMeP would form an elite anti-walkout unit called SCAB, or the Strategic Counter-Activism Brigade.[12] They made online spoof videos teaching students how to be a SCAB. As UCMeP organizer and showman Woolf explained:

> The Student Counter-Activism Brigade (SCAB) educational videos were meant to circulate virally and to encourage those students who might be hesitant to participate in a March 4th day of action to come out for a different kind of event: one which asked them to think about the importance of picket lines and the gravity of a decision to cross one.
>
> (Woolf, 2010)

I brought a glitzy red carpet to add to the spectacle. We offered people who were crossing the picket line the opportunity to walk down the red carpet as heroes of privatization and supporters of UCMeP's agenda to sell off the UC system to the highest bidders. In this way, the red carpet (actually, a long roll of sparkly red vinyl that read well on camera or from a distance) could serve as a playful shaming device.

The UCMeP organizers had devised a SCAB "Hall Pass" for people who wanted to cross the picket line. With their patient indulgence, I made a few changes at the last minute to make the little slips of paper interactive: in order to receive the pass and walk on the red carpet, people would have to tick a box and read what it said into our megaphone, either "YES! I am compliant! Please raise my tuition, cut my classes, lay off staff and faculty, and privatize my university!" or "No. I'm joining the walkout and rally! Public Education must be saved!" With the help of the great puppeteer–activist Amy Trompetter, we created a huge clay puppet head of movie star and then-California Governor Arnold Schwarzenegger. If people agreed to check "YES!" on the SCAB pass, they would be escorted down the sparkly red carpet, have rice flung at them, be cheered and photographed, and would even have the opportunity to kiss the "Governator" at the end of their stroll, as thanks for their complicity.

The result: unexpected rain on the day of the protest threatened to dissolve our Schwarzenegger puppet, so we substituted it for a cardboard version. Before setting up, we spoke to the "serious" picketers to make sure we weren't upstaging them: they thanked us and gave us a reasonable time limit for our absurd activities (such communication between ironic and earnest wings of the movement is crucial). We introduced the ideas in character with megaphones as we set up.

Unsurprisingly, nobody who really wanted to scab or break the strike took us up on our offer: the shaming device was clear enough that people steered clear and found another way onto campus. However, the UCMeP installation became an ironic play space for the protestors; the mass of people got the joke, and some decided to play along.[13] Folks were given an opportunity to speak into the microphone to sarcastically declare why they were complying with the neoliberal agenda or selling out their socioeconomic class, or whatever they wanted to say; they then goose-stepped or marched down the carpet, kowtowed to the image of the Governator, and generally embodied their ideological opponents as creatively as they could. One fellow even did an elaborate and painful-looking stage dive onto the red carpet. There was a spontaneous slow-motion race down the red carpet between Max Alper, a labor organizer for university staff, and Brandon Woolf.

Figure 7.4 Student Counter-Activism Brigade (SCAB) members beg people to cross the picket line and break the walkout/strike on the UC Berkeley campus. (Bogad with megaphone; Boyle with sign on right.) Photo by Benjamin Kiesewetter.

Figure 7.5 SCAB members find an ironically willing strikebreaker/collaborator in Professor Catherine Cole and escort her regally down the red carpet across the picket line while the Governator puppet watches approvingly. (From left: Woolf, Cole, and Bogad.) Photo by Benjamin Kiesewetter.

Figure 7.6 Woolf and Bogad escort another ironic collaborator (hidden between them) down the red carpet, megaphones in hand. Photo by Benjamin Kiesewetter.

In perfect slow motion, Woolf tripped and fell while the organizer laughed and pumped his fist in the air victoriously (UCMeP, 2010). We had created a moment where irony was more than a cool, detached cultural mode; the admittedly heavy-handed in-joke provided a creative outlet for participants, and a spectacle for passersby that was more engaging and interesting than the usual chanting and circular marching—and more empowering than our prepared Hall Pass device. The Red Carpet Shaming Device is an innovation that I hope will catch on more broadly. It has already been borrowed from my garage and used on several picket lines in the Bay Area. Experiment and riff on this idea in your neighborhood.

Another interesting side effect of this kind of ironic installation: when we got to the picket line, there was a solitary right-wing extremist marching around in front of the picket line with a sign that showed Obama with a Hitler mustache. He was enjoying upstaging the hundred or more people on the picket line and blocking the sightlines of some of the media cameras, etc. When we showed up, he tried to continue upstaging us, announcing that he thought the red carpet was great and he should march down it. Naturally, we agreed and said, "You're just the sort of fellow we need to support our cause!" He marched down the carpet with his sign, we applauded and he had nowhere to go from there once he realized he was adding to our dramaturgy rather than distracting from or sabotaging it. He walked away. This may be a useful lesson for similar situations in the future: create a scene that anticipates and incorporates your opponents as part of the story you wish to tell.

Saint Francis on the picket line

The picket line is a classic and key scene of confrontation. There are many ways to try to de-cliché it and convert it into a serious space for play and story—to tell the narrative your movement wants to tell, compellingly and charismatically. In the summer of 2005, UNITE-HERE hotel workers were locked out of ten hotels in San Francisco in an attempt to break the union. One of those hotels was the Saint Francis. Working with the local union, and with their permission, I wrote a press release declaring: "SAINT FRANCIS DESCENDS FROM HEAVEN; Protests at Saint Francis Hotel."

In the press release, Francis, the patron saint of the poor, the oppressed, and small animals, explains that he couldn't sit by while a hotel uses his name as it oppresses its workers:

> "I don't want to raise a fuss, but these guys are using my name," explained the holy one as he laid hands on a wounded hummingbird and it took flight, completely healed. "If they're going to exploit their workers with hardball tactics and another lockout, why can't they just change it to the Moloch Hotel or Chez Baal or something? Leave me out of it. I'm joining the boycott." Saint Francis said he would be joined by performers, theatre scholars, hotel workers, and other "saints and sinners" at the rally outside the hotel at 6pm this Thursday.
>
> (Bogad, 2005)

On the announced day, I joined the picket line dressed in a robe with a sign that read: "THE REAL SAINT FRANCIS WOULD NOT APPROVE." More importantly, Father Louie Vitale, a Franciscan priest and radical activist, showed up and spoke sincerely about how he appreciated the satire because, in fact, the real Saint Francis would not approve of the mistreatment of the workers. Andrew Boyd happened to be in town, and participated in character as Saint Francis's acolyte. Theatre activists William McCandless and Steve Mufson played a duo of manic Billionaires. The atmosphere was festive. At the end, I led a non-denominational ritual to exorcise the demons of greed from the hotel, as workers sprinkled "holy" tap-water onto its walls.

We planned for future actions, such as sightings of the Saint floating on the walls of the hotel (a guerrilla slide projection aimed at the hotel from the square across the street). Workers in the union began to brainstorm more ideas on this theme, always an encouraging sign. Another one of the locked-out hotels was the Hilton; they were preparing to have a drag queen appear as Paris Hilton to protest that hotel in a festive way. Before the next wave of creative actions happened, the conglomerate of hotels caved in and agreed to a union contract. Perhaps due to radical divine intervention, the Saint Francis was the first of the ten hotels to capitulate.

The worst of the crisis may be over, but that is not certain—there have been more tuition hikes since, and more waves of protest. The perennial questions persist: Could the Regents more equitably divide the resources they have? Or is it the state legislature and governor who might be pressured into reversing the drastic cuts in education, and making California's corporate tax structure fairer? How can a movement convince the hard-pressed, taxpaying public to appreciate the role of the public university in our social contract and our society? Besides the university's economic contribution to the state, such as the development of the wine and high-tech industries, is there not a social necessity for the critically thinking and educated public that universities could train? How can we express these values through tactical performance?

As an added challenge, the UC system now faces the chilling effect of the administration's threats to discipline, detenure, or fire lecturers and professors who take issue with the system in creative, disruptive ways. Ricardo Dominguez of UC Santa Cruz faced the threat of detenuring as a result of his own electronic civil disobedience "sit-in" of the UC Office of the President website. The threat to detenure was apparently also motivated by the controversy surrounding his Transborder Immigrant Tool, a mobile phone application that could be used to help migrants illegally crossing the US border find water in the deserts of southern California. Ken Ehrlich faced threats of investigation and discipline after he created a satirical website mocking President Yudof ("UC San Diego Professor," 2010; Ehrlich, 2010).

As budgets are slashed, we can run for cover and hope we are spared, or enter into complex, difficult, tensive, and tenuous solidarity with others who are also threatened by this neoliberal readjustment of the role of the public university. This means working with striking staff to make their picket lines more dynamic, colorful, and embarrassing to cross. It means working with students to develop disruptive performances that articulate our common critique of policy, and increases the political costs of those policies for policymakers. It means working with each other across disciplines, not just to write an article or a book, but to create hybrids of direct action and sociodramatic spectacles that expose and disrupt the processes of privatization and gentrification of the public university.

Professors are not above this fray; we are in the middle of it. We need to act that way. Professors of performance are uniquely positioned to contribute skills, aesthetics, and analysis to help make greater "ethical spectacles" (Boyd & Duncombe, 2004) that capture the imagination of the public, galvanize counterpublics, change the narrative, and interrupt the hegemonologue. Freedom is a "use it or lose it" proposition.

We must choose an underpinning philosophy of engagement for the system we inhabit. It is a system that, in a complex antagonistic–agonistic interaction, we hope to radically improve as well as to preserve from total corporatization. In this, we are confronted by the difference in philosophy typified by the contrast between the contemporary Critical Art Ensemble and the Dutch Kabouters of the late 1960s. Critical Art Ensemble has put forward the compelling proposition that revolution is futile—this system is here to stay and that the role of radical artists is inventively to monkey-wrench, resist, and sabotage it and "slow the velocity of capitalism" (Critical Art Ensemble, 2001: p. 14 & 15). The Kabouters preferred what they called the "two-handed strategy"—with one hand they would tear down the old corrupt society; with the other, they would build a new and better one "[growing] like a toadstool on a rotting tree trunk" (Bogad, 2016: p. 43 & 66). I propose that these two philosophies of action confront each other in the social movement to preserve public education.

Suggestions: to be tested in practice

1. Creative action designers must decide which audiences they hope to reach, especially in a conflict with many potential audiences and opponents; and what the succinct symbolic score should be.
2. Rules of engagement with passersby, media, opponents, hecklers, protesters, the state, and allies should be well worked-out in advance—including planning with allies so as not to distract from their efforts.
3. Activate and freshen habituated sites of conflict such as the picket line—don't lose the plot or surrender these sites, but try to convert them into serious play spaces that tell your story visually and compellingly.

Notes

1. In Jonathan Swift's *A Modest Proposal*, he ironically suggests that the starving Irish, victims of British imperialism, should eat their own children to survive (Swift, 1729).
2. The actual officer who did the spraying, Lieutenant John Pike, was put on paid administrative leave for 10 months, after which his employment was terminated. He recently received a $38,000 settlement from the university, for mental trauma relating to the negative attention and threats he and his family received after the incident.

3 Indeed, according to a recent study in the US, student debt has outstripped credit-card debt and automobile-loan debt (de Vise, 2012).
4 The student population is currently 3% African–American. See: http://ucdavis.edu/about/facts/uc_davis_profile.pdf
5 Graduations take away many of the most experienced activists every year. This is another perennial challenge for organizing students. Thus, university activists must constantly mentor younger students to sustain the movement.
6 Proposition 13 was a referendum passed in 1978 that froze county property taxes at 1%, with small adjustments for inflation. Property is not reassessed until it is sold. This means that many companies have extensive landholdings that have not been reassessed to their true value in decades, costing the state billions of dollars in revenue.
7 For examples, see: "Student Occupation at UC Santa Cruz Ends" (CNN, 2009); "Student Occupation of Berkeley's Wheeler Hall is Fifth in Two Days at UC" (Johnston, 2009); "UC Berkeley Students End Occupation" (Asimov & Berton et al., 2009); and "As UC Berkeley Investigates Police Brutality Against Students Protesting Fee Hikes, a report from inside the takeover of Wheeler Hall" (Goodman, 2009).
8 In that infamous *New York Times* interview (Solomon, 2009), Yudof was asked if he would be willing to slash his salary from $600,000 to the $400,000 annual income of the US President. He said he'd consider it if they made Air Force One part of the deal.
9 In an attempt to flatter protesters, defuse tension, and talk up UC Berkeley, Mogulof said:

> I think [UCMeP] is emblematic of Berkeley students at their best; passionate, intelligent, idealistic, committed, clever, and innovative. I don't necessarily agree with all their points or positions, but they certainly found an effective way to get their message out and it's one that you can't just walk away from.
>
> (Rees, 2010)

10 It is always important to have a Plan B for creative actions, and the author was that Plan B. In case Mogulof did not show up I was to stand up from the audience and speak for the spokesperson. I had prepared a brief speech, which, fortunately, did not need to be read:

> I am deeply moved to receive this TOOL award.
> What defines us as humans, what separates us from the lower orders of animals, is our use of tools.
> From the first rudimentary flint chips, to the most app-loaded iPhone, tools make us human.
> Tools played such a crucial part of our own evolution that they even affected our own biology. We evolved alongside of our ever-evolving toolkit.
> Tools are part of us.
> Where does tool end and human begin?
> Yes, tools make us human, but making humans into tools makes us MORE human.

It was that key moment, when we BEGAN TO USE OTHER HUMANS AS OUR TOOLS, that we really took off on our journey towards development, research, and civilization. Everything in our current social system follows from that.
I am proud to be a tool of those who make tools of others.
Until you know what it means to be held by a handle, to be spoken through as a mouthpiece, you will not know true fulfillment, that of a human tool.
Thank you.

11 As most readers may know, "scab" is slang for a worker who crosses a picket line, but it is also applied to consumers or students who cross picket lines, thus harming the effectiveness of a boycott.
12 Brainstorming resulted in other ideas for the acronym: Supporting Clean and Accessible Buildings; Supporting Clear Avenues and Buildings; and Schtupping Cooperative Approaches to Being.
13 For more on the use of play in activism, see Ben Shepard's *Queer Political Performance and Protest* (2009) and *Play, Creativity, and Social Movements* (2011).

References

Alinsky, Saul (1989) *Rules for Radicals: A pragmatic primer for realistic radicals.* New York: Vintage.

Asimov, Nanette (2010) "Students Sharpen Attack on UC Costs with Satire." *San Francisco Chronicle*, 10 Feb 2010. www.sfgate.com/cgi-bin/article.cgi?f1/4/c/a/2010/02/15/ BA6A1BUGLU.DTL (accessed 11 Nov 2010).

Asimov, Nanette; Berton, Justin; Garofoli, Joe (2009) "UC Berkeley Students End Occupation." *San Francisco Chronicle*, 21 Nov 2009. http://articles.sfgate.com/2009-11-21/news/17181267_1_trespassing-charges-campus-police-protesters (accessed 16 Nov 2010).

Bogad, L.M. (2005) Unite-Here Action Press Release. Author's personal archive.

Bogad, L.M. (2016) *Electoral Guerrilla Theatre: Radical ridicule and social movements*, 2nd edition. New York and London: Routledge.

Boyd, Andrew; Duncombe, Stephen (2004) "Manufacturing Dissent: What the Left can learn from Las Vegas." *Journal of Aesthetics and Protest* [online]. www.joaap.org/new3/duncombeboyd.html (accessed 28 Oct 2015).

Boyle, Shane (2010) Email to the author. 9 Dec 2010.

Critical Art Ensemble (2001) *Digital Resistance: Explorations in tactical media.* Brooklyn, NY: Autonomedia.

Duhamel, Philippe; Pearson, Nancy (eds.) (2004) *The Dilemma Demonstration: Using nonviolent civil disobedience to put the government between a rock and a hard place.* Minneapolis: Center for Victims of Torture. www.newtactics.org/en/TheDilemmaDemonstration (accessed 5 Feb 2011).

Duke, Alan (2009) "University of California Students Protest 32 Percent Tuition

Increase." *CNN.com*. 20 Nov 2009. www.cnn.com/2009/US/11/19/california.tuition.protests/index.html?iref=24hour (accessed 28 Oct 2015).

Ehrlich, Ken (2010) Academic Freedom Under Attack at UC – A public statement by UCR Lecturer Ken Ehrlich. *UCAFT*. 8 April 2010. http://ucaft.org/academic-freedom-under-attack-uc (accessed 6 Feb 2011).

Gallagher, Conor (2010) "UCs Look for Solutions to Solve Increases." *Golden Gate Xpress*, 9 March 2010. http://xpress.sfsu.edu/archives/arts/014605.html (accessed 11 Nov 2010).

Goodman, Amy (2009) "As UC Berkeley Investigates Police Brutality Against Students Protesting Fee Hikes, a report from inside the takeover of Wheeler Hall." *Democracy Now!*, 24 Nov 2009. www.democracynow.org/2009/11/24/as_uc_berkeley_investigates_police_brutality (accessed 16 Nov 2010).

Johnston, Angus (2009) "Student Occupation of Berkeley's Wheeler Hall is Fifth in Two Days at UC." *Studentactivism.net*. 20 Nov 2009. http://studentactivism.net/2009/11/20/wheeler-hall/ (accessed 16 Nov 2010).

Kingston, Gwen (2010) "UCMeP Plays with Humor and Art to Draw Attention to UC System's Issues." *Daily Californian* (UC Berkeley), 1 March 2010. www.dailycal.org/article/108467/ucmep_plays_with_humor_and_art_ to_draw_attention_t (accessed 11 Nov 2010).

Lewis, John; D'Orso, Michael (1999) *Walking with the Wind: A memoir of the movement*, 13th edition. New York: Mariner Books.

"Occupy U.C. Berkeley" (2011) [Digital video clip] *The Colbert Report*. Comedy Central. 11 Nov 2011. http://thecolbertreport.cc.com/videos/g1tcu5/occupy-u-c--berkeley (accessed 20 Dec 2014).

Pepper Spraying Cop. (n.d.) [Digital photos] *Tumblr* photo gallery. http://peppersprayingcop.tumblr.com/ (accessed 28 Oct 2015).

Rees, Kelley (2010) "Group Shines Spotlight on UC Administrative Actions Through Use of Satire and Irony." *The California Aggie* (UC Davis), 24 Feb 2010: p. 5. http://theaggie.org/article/2010/02/24/group-shines-spotlight-on-uc-administrative-actions-through-use-of-satire-and-irony (accessed 11 Nov 2010).

Reynoso Task Force, UC Davis. "Pepper Spray Incident" Task Force Report. 18 Nov 2011. http://reynosoreport.ucdavis.edu/reynoso-report.pdf (accessed 20 Dec 2014).

Shepard, Ben (2009) *Queer Political Performance and Protest: Play, pleasure and social movement*. New York: Routledge.

Shepard, Ben (2011) *Play, Creativity, and Social Movements: If I can't dance, it's not my revolution*. New York: Routledge.

Solomon, Debra (2009) "Big Man on Campus." *New York Times*, 24 Sept 2009. www.nytimes.com/2009/09/27/magazine/27fob-q4-t.html?scp1⁄41&sq1⁄4mark%20yudof% 20manager%20of%20a%20cemetary&st1⁄4cse (accessed 14 Dec 2010).

SOTA (2010) "Mark Yudof's *Thriller*: A performative protest." SOTA Blog. 27 July 2010. https://ucsota.wordpress.com/2010/07/27/mark-yudof's-thriller

(accessed 14 Dec 2010). (At the time of writing, video of this protest could not be viewed on YouTube.)

Student Occupation at UC Santa Cruz Ends. *CNN.com*. 22 Nov 2009. http://articles.cnn.com/2009-11-22/us/california.student.protest_1_student-protesters-angry-students-police?_s1⁄4PM:US (accessed 16 Nov 2010).

"Students Sharpen Attack on UC Costs with Satire." *San Francisco Chronicle*, 16 Feb 2010.

Swift, Jonathan (1729) *A Modest Proposal for Preventing the Children of the Poor from being a Burthen to Their Parents or Country*. Dublin: Printed for S. Harding.

Tarrow, Sidney (1998) *Power in Movement: Social movements and contentious politics*, 2nd edition. Cambridge: Cambridge University Press.

UC Davis Chancellor Katehi Walks to Car Amidst Protestors. [Digital video] YouTube. 20 Nov 2011. www.youtube.com/watch?v=nmfluKelOt4 (accessed 20 Dec 2014).

UC Davis Protestors Pepper Sprayed. [Digital video] YouTube. 18 Nov 2011. www.youtube.com/watch?v=6AdDLhPwpp4 (accessed 28 Oct 2015).

UC Davis Students Welcome "New Customers." [Digital video] YouTube. 3 June 2012. www.youtube.com/watch?v=aMSd6nLueEE (accessed 28 Oct 2015).

"UC San Diego Professor who Studies Disobedience Gains Followers – and investigators." *LA Times*, 7 May 2010. http://articles.latimes.com/2010/may/07/local/ la-me-ucsd-professor-20100507-53 (accessed 6 Feb 2011).

UCMeP (2010) "UCMeP Rolls Out the Red Carpet for Scabs . . ." [Digital video clip] UCMeP Blog. 13 March 2010. https://ucmep.wordpress.com/2010/03/13/rolling-out-the-red-carpet-for-scabs/ (accessed 21 Jan 2011).

"Using Humor to Criticize U. of California Leaders." *Inside Higher Ed.*, 17 Feb 2010. www.insidehighered.com/news/2010/02/17/qt#220439/ (accessed 11 Nov 2010).

de Vise, Daniel (2012) "Student Loans Surpass Auto, Credit Card Debt." *The Washington Post*, 6 March 2012. www.washingtonpost.com/blogs/college-inc/post/student-loans-surpass-auto-credit-card-debt/2012/03/06/gIQARFQnuR_blog.html (accessed 15 Dec 2014).

Woolf, Brandon (2010) Email to the author. 10 Dec 2010.

Conclusion

Earning moments for the movement

> Could I hold back the sea with my hands?
>
> —Napoleon Bonaparte, facing overwhelming enemy forces in 1814 (Hibbert, 2003: p. 66)

> Let your way be as the way of water, running deep and full of peace
> Do not struggle or compete. Go with the flow and be serene.
>
> —Tao Te Ching #8

Sometimes power seems permanent and solid, while resistance seems fleeting—fleeting and fleeing, running pell mell down the road, hotly pursued. But resistance can flow like water—inexorably eroding, corroding, and carving. As tactical players, when faced with seemingly hopeless situations, we do not try to hold back the sea with our hands, nor do we accept the flow of things without resistance—but, outnumbered and outgunned, we find ways to channel and divert some eddies of that tide, to fill the pools and valleys we have scouted in the terrain, to dodge the expected waves and nimbly stay one step ahead. As Brecht said, we tack our sails, using the cultural winds to maneuver at an angle, rather than trying fruitlessly to sail against them.[1]

Tactical performance can serve as a force multiplier or a voice amplifier for social movements. It can stimulate the imaginations of fellow activists and the public. It can help movements achieve nonviolent tactical surprise in public confrontations. It can trigger a temporary creative disruption of the articulation of power, or synaptic disruption in the minds of passersby as clichés are broken up through playful and surprising action. Its more whimsical forms can raise the political cost of state repression. It can push Marcusian "repressive tolerance" to its limits and perhaps create a decision dilemma for authorities. It can provide a prefigurative vision of the world we want to see, and thus help to make that other, better world possible. It can call new attention to inequalities or injustices that have been accepted as "normal," and dispel social amnesia, whether by performing the censored image, interrupting the hegemonologue, or just clowning around in the face of power. Tactical performance can dispel fear in the ranks, disrupt defeatism, and channel anger into productive, creative suffering and sociodrama.

Tactical performance can also fall flat and fail. That is part of the game, too. The idea is to accept that risk and learn from praxis—our own and that of our opponents—to improve our game for the next action.

Tactical performance also has applications that are internal to movements. Taking part in these actions, with all the silliness, close calls, and absurd situations they create, forms bonds and deeper networks between activists. They are the source of personal stories that sustain a subculture for the long haul. It makes for a sustainable movement that recognizes, embraces, and harnesses the pleasure principle. It can jam the culture, but it can also sustain us when defeats plunge us from denial to despair. Rather than a here-and-gone form of carnival, it can serve as a generator for sustained resistance. Barbara Ehrenreich recognized the value of carnivalesque and pleasurable protest (2007); while the carnivalesque is only one complicated form of tactical performance, other forms of serious play can serve these purposes as well.

In Cairo's Tahrir Square in 2011, hundreds of thousands of Egyptian people massed together to bring down the dictatorship of President Hosni Mubarak. They faced deadly violence from the state and its paramilitaries, but engaged in sustained occupation that resulted in the resignation of the President. One important aspect of this victory was the use of humor and acts of symbolic solidarity. The regime that has replaced Mubarak is a repressive one, but there are still positive lessons to be learned from the brave example of the Egyptian movement. Egyptians often define themselves through their distinctive sense of humor in the face of adversity, and this struggle provided many examples. An old man held up a sign for days that said "MUBARAK: RESIGN ALREADY. MY ARMS ARE TIRED." When the regime's media made the bizarre claim that the protesters were all mercenaries being paid by foreign agents and fed free fast food by KFC, hundreds of thousands of bemused occupiers began to chant together, "Where is my Kentucky Fried Chicken?" This is pointed absurdity, and it is sustaining. When Wisconsin unions and their allies drew inspiration from Egyptian protestors and occupied the State Capitol in protest of a law that would disempower organized labor, Egyptian activists placed an international call and ordered them pizzas. Far beyond the calories provided, this humorous symbolic act excited the Wisconsinites and inspired them to fight on. They had been recognized as comrades in a global movement for human dignity and justice.

Of course, these symbolically savvy actions were only one element of the Egyptian movement; street-smart tactical organization was key—for example, organizers launched the marches on Tahrir Square from numerous far-flung points in narrow alleys. In this way, even if only a few people showed up, the small alleys were still filled and it looked like something hopeful was happening. This emboldened more people to join. As these rivulets of people then moved into wider streets, they were able to fill those streets as more people joined in—and again, the sense of momentum drew more out into the streets to join them. Tahrir Square is such a huge plaza, and the idea of filling it with peaceful protesters by calling a rally there during martial law in a police state was truly daunting. The Egyptian organizers addressed this problem with ingenuity and an understanding of the dynamics of perception and momentum. Many rivulets pooled together into streams, and finally several great rivers of people filled the square from all directions (Saleh, 2013).

Due to media monopolies, political party duopolies, and the corruption of the very idea of what a republic should be, there is a dearth of legitimate dialogue in the public sphere of many global states. Tactical performance can supplement this dialogue, providing new ways for counterpublics to make incursions into and revive exchanges of ideas in these finance-corroded and coopted spaces. The society of the spectacle has achieved levels of alienation and contemplation[2] even beyond Debord's original analysis, creating a vacuum in our experience of our own lives (Debord, 1995).

But power abhors a vacuum, and creative collective acts of defiance and disruption can fill that vacuum and help communities to reclaim their existence for something besides obedient production and consumption. In Spain, the conservative ruling party, reeling from years of mass protest by the *indignante* movement, has passed an Orwellian "Citizen's Safety Law" that imposes massive fines on people for "insulting Spain," videoing or photographing police behavior at protests, and wearing masks. Spaniards protested the bill while it was being drafted,[3] and, when enacted into law months afterwards, another massive wave of defiant protests followed. Members of the innovative Enmedio

Figure C.1 In defiance of the Orwellian "Citizen's Safety Law," demonstrators in Barcelona carry images of smiling faces during a protest. Photo by Collective (CC) Oriana Eliçabe/enmedio.info.

Figure C.2 Holograms for Freedom, part of the We Are Not Crime movement, protesting the "Citizen's Safety Law" in front of the Parliament in Madrid, Spain, 10 April 2015. They hold ghostly signs that say "No to the Gag Law," and "Freedom of Expression." Photo by Marcos del Mazo / Demotix / Demotix/Press Association Images.

Collective in Barcelona printed enormous signs with photos of open mouths shouting and smiling, and held them up as a symbol for what was at stake—freedom of speech and thought. This added elegant and eloquent imagery to the masses of bodies in the streets. On 12 April 2015, the group Holograms for Freedom created a "march" of thousands of spectral hologram figures in front of the Spanish Parliament in Madrid. The law also punishes unpermitted mass protests near government buildings, so this protest beautifully, ironically, and hauntingly made the argument that this law, which controls bodies so closely, will only leave the right to free assembly in the ghostly hands of the virtual (Boren, 2015).

To pie or not to pie: a political pastry parable

When it comes to action design and action logic, it helps to think about choosing the right tool for the right job. We can learn from failures and missteps as much or more as from successes. For example, why literally throw pies at people in power? The Biotic Baking Brigade (BBB), who have pied a plethora of powerful public personae, might argue that the intention is to call attention to an unexamined or ignored issue. The rudeness, the transgression of pieing someone like Bill Gates is so outrageous it draws public attention and begs the question: "Why did that fool hit that famous person in the face with a pie?" At times, this has given the activist and supporters the chance to expound upon the malfeasance of the corporate head. I should add that the rudeness of this act is mitigated by its playful allusion to old-school slapstick, and to a smaller degree by the ethical stance of the BBB, in that they only use vegan homemade pies made from locally grown, organic ingredients. We must live our values, after all.

In July 2011, a pie-throwing incident occurred that was an example of the wrong tool for the wrong job. Rupert Murdoch was being questioned by the British Parliament for a "phone-hacking" scandal involving the wrongdoing of journalists from one of his papers, who were accused of searching the mobile phones of dead people for their contacts and other data. Comedian Jonnie Marbles jumped up from the crowd and tried to pie Murdoch. Murdoch's wife blocked, and the pie missed, but more importantly, the stunt missed the point of what pieing is for. Murdoch was, at that very moment, being internationally televised and raked over the coals for wrongdoing. Rather than calling attention to an unpublicized wrongdoing, this pieing incident drew attention away from a publicized one. The coverage was deflected to the pieing, and what fast reflexes Murdoch's wife possessed, etc. Murdoch, rather than being a billionaire mogul on his back foot, looked like an elderly victim of cruelty. This seems a useful example of a bad idea, poorly executed, and a tactic misused and backfiring (Kennedy, 2011). To be fair, Marbles wrote a thoughtful defense of his action, arguing that the hearing was a farce and attention needed to be called to that. In response to charges of senior discrimination, he also asserted that he did not hate octogenarians (Marbles, 2011).

Greenpeace made a surprising mistake in 2014. Over the objection of some of its leaders, a group of its activists trespassed onto a Peruvian hillside, a precious and protected landmark, and placed words that could be photographed from the sky to send an environmental message. The letters were made of felt, and were environmentally harmless. However, the activists left footprints that damaged the ground of this very sacred site. Greenpeace is making amends, but obviously this was a setback, and a lesson to be learned by all. Mistakes are inevitable; the point is to learn from them and, most importantly, to avoid them through careful planning before each action. It makes little difference whether the planning entails horizontalist dialogue, workshops, or Boalian Forum Theatre sessions. Forethought is the key. The idea of the irresistible image works in reverse; it helps to imagine damaging, distracting, or disastrous images and to try to avoid creating them.

Moving forward: micro and macro innovation

On a micro level—the level of prop and costume design—we can continue to experiment with innovations. The thought-bubble sign is one example. In the 1980s, a clown and peace activist in Philadelphia found a spot on the highway congested with bumper-to-bumper traffic for part of the day. He took to standing by a prominent bend in the road, holding a thought-bubble sign to his infant child's head that read: "What's a bomb for, Daddy?" Thousands of people every day saw this sign and it was just open enough in its rhetoric to jar some clichéd thinking loose. In this kind of action, the impact may not be visible immediately, but works on a poetically molecular level—a sort of *dissensmosis*. Persistent actions can inspire positive change in unpredictable ways.[4]

Costumes can provide protection while communicating a message. The Wombles wore thick armor made of tires and other material, rendering them impervious to police clubs. They looked like radical Michelin Tire Men, but they were able to stay in the streets and withstand police assault. Since then groups have innovated further on this idea, making costumes that both protect and communicate. Protesters have taken to wearing thick cardboard armor—thus providing some protection from rubber bullets. Student protesters have arrived at protests with shields for personal protection—and those shields are painted to look like the covers of great works of philosophy or literature—protecting themselves from attack with the ideas that inspire them. I discussed the use of functional, but festively decorated gas masks in Chapter 4.

On the macro level, we can draw inspiration and find points of solidarity with the examples of new movements. The Black Lives Matter movement in the US was sparked by a series of police killings of unarmed black men in 2014 and 2015, many of them documented on smartphone video cameras by onlookers. As the surveillance state becomes more and more pervasive, citizens in turn use mobile phones and digital cameras to provide their own surveillance of the state, at least on a tactical level. Every example of police brutality captured on a passerby's phone is an example of this.

Black Lives Matter argued that recent killings were only the latest, publicized examples of thousands of such incidents throughout US history. In this movement, which has gained momentum in cities all over the country, a conversation about white privilege developed in tandem with the movement's larger frame of contention. The slogan "White Silence Is Violence" echoes throughout demonstrations and is visible on signs held by white demonstrators. At the same time, the idea has spread that the movement's white activists should "stand up and step back"—in other words, show up in the streets in solidarity, but follow the leadership and initiative of people of color.

Recently, in Oakland, California, an affinity group of African-American activists locked down in the West Oakland Bay Area Rapid Transit (BART) train station as part of a protest supporting this movement. Using metal cylinder tubes to link their arms, a tool long employed in direct action, they chained themselves to each other and to the train platform. When the BART trains arrived from either direction, they stepped inside and linked themselves to the trains. This act of civil disobedience was risky—if the trains moved they would be torn apart. Singing songs from the civil rights movement of the 1950s and 1960s, they shut down the transit system from their base in the historically black and working class neighborhood of West Oakland. This action won attention for the cause of a militant and creative movement led by the nation's most oppressed. This was only one of an array of creative actions during this period.

We have seen gestures such as "hands up don't shoot"—a tensive act that inverts a common gesture of surrender into one of mass defiance.[5]

Also a wave of artistic contributions: protest signs that form street-wide, haunting reproductions of the eyes of a black man, a collective creation that reminds everyone of the value of one individual's face and the windows to his soul; guerrilla sculptures; graffiti; street theatre; and of course, nonviolent civil disobedience including the blockading of the Oakland Police Department Headquarters (Bloch, 2015). It is in spaces of protest created by social movements that everyday people can express their own stories to each other, and show that we are not only consumers of culture. We are producers of culture too, and we form a collective frame of contention for sustained action.

The 2011 Occupy movement, inspired by the Arab Spring and the Iberian *indignado* movement, and to a lesser extent by the 2009 University of California student movement, had an impact beyond the creation of tent communities in the public squares of cities around the world. In the US, Occupy brought the issues of economic inequality and oligarchy back into public dialogue more than any other single recent movement. The larger context of the banking crisis of 2007, and

Figure C.3 In New York City, marchers of the Black Lives Matter movement march with signs that combine to show the eyes of a black man. Photo by Lisa Merrill.

the massive bank bailout, which cost more than the entire New Deal of the 1930s, fueled the fire for this movement. Occupy also drew inspiration from the other rebellions abroad, and showed great creativity.

The tent cities were a visible evocation of the Hoovervilles of the Great Depression, and were impossible to ignore due to their prominent locations in cities and towns, and in their unique, horizontalist, and prefigurative method of self-organizing. The movement called for greater economic and participatory democracy, and performed an admittedly *ad hoc* and imperfect demonstration of how that could work. In the end, the tent cities were dispersed forcibly, but the movement did not disappear. Its energy shifted into other forms, such as local Occupy neighborhood groups that have successfully prevented banks from evicting people from their homes through human blockades, embarrassing banks into calling off foreclosures and renegotiating mortgage loans for neighbors. These are all tangible accomplishments, if less spectacular or mediagenic than erecting a tent city near Wall Street.

Veterans of the Occupy movement have gone on to contribute to others, such as the anti-fracking cause, voting rights movement, and most recently, Black Lives Matter. Yes, the tent cities were dispersed. But in half the cities in the country they might have been shut down anyway a month later when it got too cold. And the tent cities themselves were not the change that the movement sought. They were simply part of the creative disruption that the movement devised in order to change the conversation around class in America.

Game theory

The theory and practice of serious play leads us to game theory, and the use of serious games in the training of activists. In game terms, the state and corporations "level up" more reliably than social movements—they have a greater institutional memory. They learn more consistently from their mistakes and successes, and have a more complex and well-resourced playbook to draw on. This is why, for social movements, the recording of history and constant tactical innovation are both so crucial. On the other hand, states are often solely reactive in their game play, and savvy social movements can innovate more wildly as their multitudes swarm and play tactically (Negri & Hardt, 2000 & 2009).

There is a long tradition of activists channeling and harnessing the pleasurable energy of sports, board games, and other forms of play into social-movement organizing, campaigning, and collective action. The Haymarket-era labor movement in the US knew that bowling and beer should be part of any good workers' gathering on a Sunday, along with speeches. This need for play and pleasure as an integral part of struggle is revealed in the old "Bread and Roses" slogan.[6] But games and play can also help us to brainstorm and hone our skills in a safe space. As Boal stated, games allow us to rehearse for reality (Boal, 1979).

In my Tactical Performance workshops, one segment is always devoted to role-playing. An affinity group meets to brainstorm a creative action for a given scenario. Participants learn the methods of consensus communication and facilitation, used in many horizontalist movements. They even use the hand signals that Stephen Colbert made fun of in an episode of his show at the height of the Occupy movement ("Colbert Super Pac," 2011). I also secretly ask one of the participants to play the role of an infiltrator or agent provocateur. That player should try to derail discussion, filibuster, or suggest ideas for action that will backfire against the group. At the end of the game, when the player reveals his hidden agenda to the group, their looks of betrayal speak volumes—it's just a game, but the revelation inspires real emotions. However, while students rarely guess that one of them is playing an agent during the game scenario, if the group remains true to its agreed ethics and values, and to the facilitation method, the provocateur usually fails to derail or sabotage the process. On the other hand, when the group is lax, and abandons the process and their core values, mayhem ensues. As noted in previous chapters, even groups such as Reclaim the Streets, Billionaires for Bush, and the Clown Army have been infiltrated. It is a common practice worldwide. The affinity group model helps to minimize the impact of this tactic, but as soon as a group becomes a mass, open movement, it is best to assume that infiltrators and provocateurs are present, and to prepare an ethical and playful solution for defusing this problem.

Another critical part of these workshops is to "Imagine Winning." Activists should envision, in the case of a particular campaign, what winning would look like. Having imagined that, they must think backwards from that point, and describe or illustrate or role-play the paths they took to get there. This is, of course, an imperfect exercise—it uses game theory and applies it to complex social conflict. Participants are aware that it is only a sketch. However, using the idea of "winning" does stimulate the imagination, and breaks up old habits of defeatism and uninspired incrementalism.

In the late 1970s and early 1980s, Marxist professor Bertell Ollman created and produced a board game called *Class Struggle*. Players play Capitalists or Workers. They move around the board, trying to defeat each other in a series of escalating confrontations. If there are more than two people playing, the others can be Minor Classes—Students, Small Shopkeepers, Professionals, and Farmers. The text on the board and playing cards reveals a particular ideological positionality—but then, so do those of *Monopoly*, *Pay Day*, or *The Game of Life*. *Class Struggle* is reasonably fun to play, at least for the arguments and conversations it sparks. The game is now a collector's item, translated into several other languages, and its battered boxes reside in the closets of many radicals. Ollman even wrote a book about the process of becoming, temporarily, an (unsuccessful) small businessman so he could produce his Marxist game (Ollman, 2002).

Naturally, there is an ideological bias in every game's rulebook and structure, just as the rules we live under in reality reflect powerful and important biases. Minor tweaks in a point structure, chance cards, or incentives, change the political argument of any game. Playing a game at a meta-level, analyzing and critiquing the rule structure even as you play, is good practice for activism.

Stephen Duncombe's book, *Dream,* includes an entire chapter about the popular video game *Grand Theft Auto* and the lessons such games have for progressive artist–activists (2007). There is something about the game, as offensive as it is for so many, that is compelling, and lessons can be learned from it, argues Duncombe. The game is driven by open-ended possibilities, freedom of movement, and choices. For example, you can fulfill a mission, or you can simply drive to a random city, pull over en route and sit by a lake for a while. Hence, *Grand Theft Auto* offers options and agency that many feel they do not have in reality. If you could extract the misogyny, hyperviolence, and general sociopathy from the game, could you use some of these elements as ingredients in a compelling radical game of mobilization?

The activist video game *A Force More Powerful* might benefit from some of the admittedly expensive and high-tech flourishes of *Grand Theft Auto*. *A Force More Powerful* is essentially a training game on how to build a nonviolent movement for social change while living under repression. You learn a lot when playing it, but it is a dry experience compared to games with more exciting effects. Better video and audio effects, and more visual dynamism and decision-making might make the game more effective politically, attracting more players—to the game and perhaps then to the streets.

Paolo Pedercini is an important member of the larger movement that uses gaming to explore social and political issues from a radical, critical perspective. His games are enjoyable to play and beautifully troubling.

Oiligarchy looks at climate change and the role of the oil industry in frustrating attempts to make policy changes to address our current crisis. The player plays the mega-CEO of the US oil industry, possessing the power to sink wells all over the world, dominate domestic politics, and spark military intervention to open up new oil reserves abroad. What players cannot control is the inevitable peak and decline of oil supply, the resistance of local populations, and the eventual destruction of the ecosystem—it is only through playing the game that you realize the points—or dollars—that you have been avidly amassing are not actually a valid marker of success if the biosphere has been destroyed.

Pedercini has other powerful games on his website, Molleindustria.[7] In one, the player is the CEO of McDonald's and must maintain the flow of burgers to the customers by cutting down rainforests to make room for cows, feeding cows to other cows in the feedlot, firing disgruntled employees, and creating ever more mind-bending marketing schemes. One problem with this game is that, while players realize its political point, they may get lured into the game and the goal of amassing as many dollars/points as possible. They quickly become exploitive fast-food capitalists. Is this a problem? Are players being corrupted? Try the game for yourself and decide.

Some of Pedercini's projects question the underlying structures of conventional video games. In *Unmanned*, you play an American drone operator, looking in the mirror and shaving in the morning. You choose which thoughts you are having from a list of options, while trying not to cut yourself shaving. It is poetic, strange, personal, and a very different form of critical experience. At the end of the workday, having blown up a few people, flirted with colleagues, and talked to your estranged wife during a smoke break, you are playing a video game with your son while trying to have a conversation with him. It is actually difficult to do—your attention is divided between a first-person shooter game and a conversation game. The artful reproduction of the feelings of distraction and split-attention makes for poignant post-game reflection.

Unmanned harks back to an earlier Molleindustria offering where you play an assembly line worker. The point is to push the right buttons to assemble objects in the right order as the objects come past you on the line. And that's it. You just keep doing it until you realize how miserable and redundant this work is. Having worked on a real assembly line, the author can say that this game was amusing, aggravating, and highly reminiscent. Paolo and his Molleindustria project point the way towards a radical, critical, and inventive usage of play and games, revealing the potential power of this form.

Since games are such a huge part of contemporary culture, how can this form be harnessed to bring the struggle of social movements into the homes of everyday people, adding a new form of click to the "clicks and bricks" struggle in our culture? For several years, I have been experimenting with a performance hybrid that fuses interactive live theatre with role-playing games, such as *Dungeons & Dragons*, which I call *Possible Pasts*. Role-playing games became massively popular in the 1970s with the creation of *Dungeons & Dragons* and its many genre spin-offs. In these games, players create and inhabit characters in imaginary worlds crafted by a player known as the Game Master. Sessions are fun and spark group imagination, but sometimes reflect the acquisitive and anti-social trends found in many popular video games. What if the joy of play, teamwork, and collective imagination fostered by these games were channeled into fascinating and troubling historical scenarios? *Possible Pasts* attempts to do this. It provides a structured and dramatic framework for performers and audiences to explore and rethink moments in history. Audience volunteers become role-playing participants. They make difficult decisions under pressure—as citizens trying to survive a coup, a natural disaster, or any number of scenarios. The performer guides them in a rigorous, structured, and fluid dialogical scenario of co-creation.

I envisaged *Possible Pasts* as a *jouissance*-inducing exercise, incorporating Barthes' ideas of an active "writerly text" (Barthes, 1975). Performer and audience co-write the story together, with a thoughtful and structured set of "given assumptions," but with genuine openness to the consequences of their decisions. I am attempting to answer Brecht's call for an experience that does not provide an emotional catharsis, but rather challenges the participants' critical-thinking skills. The game demonstrates that it is not fate, but the decisions we make in our given circumstances that determine the society we create together. The game always starts in the same way, but ends differently every time. Participants exercise their power of empathy and "what if?" capabilities to explore the oppressions of others across borders of epoch, identity, and ideology. In this way, players, audiences, and performers gain a deeper understanding of history, agency, and social change. To harness the fun and energy of game theory and play for activism, not only in the street but in the global culture of gaming, is one attempt to tack with the winds of the culture instead of trying to row against it.

More broadly, the idea of tactical creative action follows a form of general game theory—anticipating your opponent's moves, incorporating their moves into your game plan, and thinking several moves ahead. As a tactical player, you are not to be bogged down in a premature concentration of forces, or a toe-to-toe slugfest with the strategic power; rather, like any artful boxer, you stick and move, stick and move. When your moves become predictable, you must mix it up. Team morale and energy, and a sense of momentum and proactive initiative are key elements of any campaign. In December 2015, activists created the Climate Games, using the fun of gaming to encourage and excite more original and inventive participation in mass protest at the United Nations Climate Change Conference in Paris (www.climategames.net).

A beautiful tactical performance can impress organizers who have treated artistic activism as mere decoration or a fringe aspect of protest. Take, for example, the massive People's Climate March in New York City in September 2014. With about 400,000 participants, it was the largest climate-change demonstration on record, and serves as an example of an event that demonstrated the movement's strength and proved the value of activist creativity. The march was a pageant that told a story, with sections of the miles-long parade of protestors organized in blocs that communicated a narrative to those watching. Each section had its own banners, according to chosen aesthetics and membership. Front-line communities and indigenous people, the people most impacted by climate change, led the march. Next came a bloc called, "We Can Build The Future," which was composed of a cross-section: laborers, families, students, and the elderly. The next bloc, "We Have Solutions," included groups working to organize a just transition to renewable energy, and others fighting for food and water justice. "We Know Who Is Responsible" called out the political and corporate villains responsible for the destruction of our biosphere. "The Debate Is Over" included scientists and religious leaders who acknowledge the global peer review process that has confirmed the reality of climate change. Finally, "To Change Everything, We Need Everyone!" was the last bloc, which included groups from communities across America, all part of the coalition for climate justice. With floats and costumes and festive parade trappings, this march showed strength, commitment, and creative energy while making its political argument to the world, step by marching step.

Matt Leonard, organizer for the group 350.org, explained that this nod to culture was significant for the movement's future. He noted that the climate justice movement includes artists, but it does not have a cultural wing with the same deep history and tradition as older movements in the areas of labor, feminism, and peace. Its organizers haven't always considered the cultural aspect as crucial. However, the climate justice movement needs tactical performance because of the communication challenges it faces. For example, the relationship between oil drilling in Nigeria and flooding around the world is real, but complicated to explain. Performance can overcome the gap of abstraction. In the case of the 2014 march, non-governmental organizations (NGOs) and grassroots movements were able to negotiate their differences in style without tension. Stereotypically, NGOs tend to be bureaucratic and controlling, whereas movements are more democratic and freewheeling. This has led to conflict at times in the past. However, this time NGOs contributed resources from offices in midtown Manhattan without imposing creative control, and movement artists in a warehouse in Brooklyn made the most of those resources, brainstorming wildly and building stunningly mediagenic visuals for the movement (Leonard, 2015).[8]

Tactical performance is an integral aspect of mass movements for social change. It is no replacement for the core work of organizing, but it is a key to better campaigns, both during and between cycles of contention. Tactical performance can spur momentum or sustain a movement during darker times. Mock-billionaires, militant clowns, imaginary agents of pretend power, and poetically earnest actors—whether they be veterans, seniors, or scientists—are all performers. All of these activists think theatrically and flexibly in order to act in coordination with social movements. Even when we satirize our opponents, we need to take them seriously enough to learn from them.

There is no binary between "theatrical" actions and "nontheatrical." Even the most direct, clear, *sans*-shtick, earnest action—a blockade, a tree-sit, a boycott—should be designed and framed to tell a compelling story. It is still a performance of collective commitment and coalition, defiance and solidarity—and that solidarity, that commitment, that coalition, is constituted in part by the performance itself. Whether dour or playful, we must design *charismatic action*—by which I mean action that attracts and mobilizes more and more people. In this way movements can begin to revise the script of power. We may begin our authorship in the margins. However, with forethought, training, creativity, and discipline, we can rise up rebelliously from the footnotes, and leave our mark on the front pages of history.

Notes

1 Brecht, 1977: p. 6–8; see also Duncombe, 2002: p. 183–85.
2 I use the term "contemplation" here in the same negative sense as Debord. He argues that we have become passive spectators of our own lives.

I would add that we are now compulsive digital confessors, documenters, and informants on our lives.

3 In December 2013, in support of this Orwellian bill, The Ministry of Dreams, Hopes, and Fears set up shop outdoors in George Orwell Square in Barcelona. This was an administrative "office" complete with desk, carpet, plant, and lamp. Citizens who got the joke or were just curious lined up to fill out forms with their most personal dreams, hopes, or fears, which were processed by a silent bureaucratic character in absurd ways—redacted, doodled upon, rolled into cigarettes and smoked, snipped to pieces, stamped, folded into monstrous origami shapes, etc. (See https://vimeo.com/123059067.)

4 Thought-bubble signs come in handy; for example, at a labor protest outside a Wal-Mart, in the well-manicured hands of "Sam Walton." Holding a thought-bubble sign saying "It's ALL MINE!" the author, as Sam, pleaded to the crowd that if only they could read his mind, they would know he had their best interests at heart. This Wal-Mart action in Richmond, CA, was part of a national strike and day of action (Black Friday, the day after Thanksgiving, 2014), to protest the retailer's poor labor and environmental practices. At the end of the skit, Sam is forced to work in his own store . . . all too aware of the terrible conditions he will face, he joins the union.

I had proposed a "Wail-Mart" action, in which hundreds of people would go into the Wal-Mart, spread out, and begin to weep. If asked why, each would continue to cry and have their own relevant reason for wailing: "There used to be small stores in this town!" or "The child labor!" etc. In communication with the workers and organizers, it was decided that this would be too invasive and place the jobs of the striking workers at risk, so we stayed with the picket line and street theatre. It is essential to brainstorm strange ideas, and it would be interesting if this Wail-Mart idea was enacted one day. However, it is more important to respect the different levels of privilege and costs of participation in any coalition.

5 "Irresistible Images," interview of the author by Michael Shane Boyle, *Contemporary Theatre Review* online, 31 July 2015. www.contemporarytheatrereview.org/2015/irresistible-images/

6 The slogan is derived from a speech by US labor leader Rose Schneiderman, in which she states: "The worker must have bread; but she must have roses too."

7 See www.molleindustria.org

8 These wonderful constructions included: a parade float in the shape of a huge dinosaur built from car parts and oil cans, representing the menace of fossil fuels; a swarm of whimsical swordfish on bicycles (swordfish are considered environmental activists of nature because they regularly puncture undersea pipelines); and a tandem bicycle converted into an SUV, driven by caricatures of two oil executives (the author and the irrepressible Ben Shepard). We rode alongside the marchers, to entertain those who had waited for hours and marched for many hours more: "This is the climate march isn't it? We're big boosters! I'm all about climate change! In fact, I'm causing climate change RIGHT NOW!"; and "Peer review, shmear review! Embrace the mystery of climate change!" The body needs to both laugh and cry in order to thrive: this is also true of the body politic (Haugerud, 2014).

References

Barthes, Roland (1975) *S/Z: An essay*. New York: Hill and Wang.

Bloch, Nadine (2015) "The Art of #BlackLivesMatter," *Waging Nonviolence: People-powered news & analysis*. 8 Jan 2015. http://wagingnonviolence.org/feature/art-blacklivesmatter/ (accessed 24 Oct 2015).

Boal, Augusto (1979) *Theatre of the Oppressed*. Trans. Charles A. and Maria-Odilia Leal McBride. London: Pluto Press.

Boren, Zachary Davies (2015) "Spain's Hologram Protest: Thousands join virtual march in Madrid against new gag law." *The Independent*, 15 April 2015. www.independent.co.uk/news/world/europe/spains-hologram-protest-thousands-join-virtual-march-in-madrid-against-new-gag-law-10170650.html (accessed 28 Oct 2015).

Brecht, B. (1977) *Brecht on Theatre: The development of an aesthetic*. In S. Giles and M. Silberman (eds.) and Trans. J. Willett. New York: Hill and Wang. (Original work published 1964.)

"Colbert Super Pac – Stephen Colbert Occupies Occupy Wall Street Pt. 1" (2011) [Digital video clip] *The Colbert Report*. Comedy Central. 31 Oct 2011. www.cc.com/video-clips/d4hmi3/the-colbert-report-colbert-super-pac---stephen-colbert-occupies-occupy-wall-street-pt--1 (accessed 28 Oct 2015).

Debord, G. (1995) *The Society of the Spectacle*. Trans. D. Nicholson-Smith. New York: Zone Books. (Original work published 1967.)

Duncombe, Stephen (ed.) (2002) *Cultural Resistance Reader*. New York: Verso.

Duncombe, Stephen (2007) *Dream: Re-imagining progressive politics in an age of fantasy*. New York: The New Press.

Ehrenreich, Barbara (2007) *Dancing In the Streets: A history of collective joy*. New York: Metropolitan Books.

Haugerud, Angelique (2014) "Satire and Solemnity in the People's Climate March," *Stanford University Press blog*. 22 Oct 2014. http://stanfordpress.typepad.com/blog/2014/10/satire-and-solemnity-in-the-peoples-climate-march-.html (accessed 10 Jan 2015).

Hibbert, Christopher (2003) *Waterloo: Napoleon's last campaign*. New York: Cooper Square Press.

Kennedy, Helen (2011) "Rupert Murdoch Attacked With Shaving-cream Pie Over Hacking Scandal." *Daily News*. 19 July 2011. www.nydailynews.com/news/world/rupert-murdoch-attacked-shaving-cream-pie-hacking-scandal-rebekah-brooks-testifies-article-1.157233 (accessed 28 Oct 2015).

Leonard, Matt (2015) Interview with the author. 4 Jan 2015.

Marbles, Jonnie (2011) "Why I Foam-pied Rupert Murdoch." *The Guardian*. 20 July 2011. www.theguardian.com/commentisfree/2011/jul/20/why-i-foam-pied-rupert-murdoch (accessed 28 Oct 2015).

Negri, A.; Hardt, M. (2000) *Empire*. Boston: Harvard University Press.

Negri, A.; Hardt, M. (2009) *Multitude: War and democracy in the age of empire*. New York: Penguin Books.

Ollman, Bertell (2002) *Ball Buster? True confessions of a Marxist businessman.* Brooklyn: Soft Skull Press.
Saleh, Ahmed (2013) Lecture in Oakland, California. 2 March 2013.

Index

Note: Page numbers followed by "f" refer to figures, and followed by "n" refer to notes.